50 RELICS

of the

RESTORATION

50 RELICS
of the
RESTORATION

CASEY PAUL GRIFFITHS *and* MARY JANE WOODGER

CFI • AN IMPRINT OF CEDAR FORT, INC. • SPRINGVILLE, UT

For my parents, who have always supported me.
—Casey

For Chris: In the relics of my life,
those worth saving will all include you!
—Mary Jane

ISBN 13: 978-1-4621-3816-6

Published by CFI, an imprint of Cedar Fort, Inc.
2373 W. 700 S., Springville, UT 84663
Distributed by Cedar Fort, Inc., www.cedarfort.com

Library of Congress Control Number: 2020946477

Cover design and interior layout/design by Shawnda T. Craig
Cover design © 2020 Cedar Fort, Inc.

Printed in the United States

10 9 8 7 6 5 4 3 2 1

Printed on acid-free paper

— *Acknowledgments* —

This book would not have been possible without the gracious cooperation of hundreds of people who assisted us. We are particularly grateful to the staff of the museums and repositories who allowed us access to photograph and examine the objects found in this book. Carrie Snow and Alan Morrell at the Church History Museum were invaluable in helping us find many unique and beautiful objects and steered us toward those important in the international history of the Church. Among our friends at Community of Christ we want to express our deep gratitude to Rachel Killebrew, Lack Mackay, Andrew Bolton, and Matthew Frizzell, who assisted with access to their amazing collection. Several prominent private collectors, led by Brent Ashworth and Reid Moon, allowed us to handle and photograph their collections, and we are deeply grateful for the assistance. We are also grateful to historians working at the Church History Library and Church Pacific History Center who offered expertise and suggestions, including Rangi and Vic Parker, Lisa Olsen Tait, and Jenny Reeder. We would also like to thank our colleagues at Brigham Young University, including Alex Baugh, Ken Alford, Craig Manscil, Craig Ostler, Michael Mackay, Scott Esplin, Devan Jensen, Barbara Morgan Gardner, Linda Godfrey, J.B. Haws, and Robert Freeman, who offered their assistance and suggestions. We also wish to thank our wonderful photographers, Cordale Ottley and Joshua Lynch. Finally, we are particularly grateful to several student research assistants, writers, and editors: Hannah Murdoch, Brooke Anderson, Kiersten Robertson, Sydney Busse, Alayna Een, Petra Javadi-Evans, Kaika Cole, McKenna Park, and Hunter Markus for sharing their scholastic talents.

Last, and most important of all, we offer our thanks for our family and loved ones who patiently offered support during the long hours, late nights, and extensive travel required for this project.

Contents

"WE ARE *witnesses* TO A PROCESS OF *restoration.* IF YOU THINK THE CHURCH HAS BEEN FULLY RESTORED, YOU'RE JUST SEEING THE BEGINNING.

THERE IS *much more to come.*"

—RUSSELL M. NELSON

PREFACE

———◆———

Are the gold plates in this book?

That is the most common question we have been asked during the course of this project. Unfortunately, the answer is no, but the question itself reveals much about the historical perspective of The Church of Jesus Christ of Latter-day Saints. Materiality is infused in the religion of the restored church, and spirituality is often linked to physical experience. When the Book of Mormon was published in 1830, within its pages was a testimony from eight witnesses concerning the physicality of the plates of gold. Their collective statement declared they were shown the gold plates and "we did handle with our hands; and we also saw the engravings thereon, all of which has the appearance of curious workmanship."[1] While spirituality was important, from the beginning the restored gospel was also a physical experience. For those witnesses, the witness of the work of God was something they could examine, heft, and feel for themselves. Materiality is reality, and a large part of the restoration of The Church of Jesus Christ is seeing and knowing for yourself. Material history is found in thousands of museums around the world where precious pieces of history reside, but also in homes where family heirlooms are passed from one generation to the next. In some ways it is the most literal and participative form of history: a person doesn't even have to be able to read to participate. If you have held a grandparent's jewelry, looked in a musty journal from years past, or even snuggled in a quilt stitched by an ancestor, you have participated in material history.

So, why aren't the gold plates in the book then? In embarking on this project, we followed a strict set of rules for the object chosen. First, we wanted to be able to take a photograph of every object in the book. We traveled around the world to see and handle these sacred treasures of the Restoration and wanted the reader to have the experience of seeing them for themselves in all of their glory and flaws. Since the gold plates now reside with the angel who oversaw the translation, they are not on our list. When the plates return we will undoubtedly need to produce a revised and updated version of this text!

Second, we eliminated any object without a clear origin. For some it is extremely difficult to eliminate all doubt about the genuine nature of an object, especially the further back in time we travel. At the same time every effort was made to work with scholars, collectors, and archivists to ensure the objects in this book are really what they claim. Where provenance is impossible to settle entirely we have tried to explain the controversy, rather than avoiding it.

Third, we wanted the objects in this book to span the entire history of the Church. The colorful early history of the Church certainly seems to fire

---

1   "Book of Mormon, 1830," p. [590], *The Joseph Smith Papers*, accessed October 8, 2018, http://www.josephsmithpapers.org/paper-summary/book-of-mormon-1830/596.

the interest of the Latter-day Saints, but miracles exist in all eras of Church history as do heroes and role models. We wanted the objects in this book to represent both the distant past and the remarkable future and present history of the Church.

Finally, we wanted the objects we selected to represent as many different groups within The Church of Jesus Christ of Latter-day Saints as possible. Special attention was paid to objects linked to the history of women in the Church. We also traveled as widely as possible to view objects related to the global reach of the restored Church. With only fifty objects it was impossible to represent every country where the Saints live, but we wanted to cast a healthy spotlight on countries where the first chapter of Church history is being written. As we reflect back on places such as Palmyra, Kirtland, and Nauvoo, we didn't want to forget the new stories being created in Phnom Penh, Cambodia, Lagos, Nigeria, Salvador, Brazil, and thousands of other places around the world.

Even though The Church of Jesus Christ of Latter-day Saints is approaching its 200th birthday, it is still relatively young among Christian religions. Just as early Christians sought out pieces of the cross or searched for the location of Noah's Ark, it is natural for Latter-day Saints to seek to interact with their history. The objects of this book constitute a glimpse at the richness of our history. One of the most intriguing aspects of our history is that it is still being discovered. Material history allows us to see, heft, and handle the same objects our forbearers did, giving us a tangible way to interact with the story, and even become a part of it.

Casey Paul Griffiths

Mary Jane Woodger

Brigham Young University, 2019

"If there is anything *virtuous, lovely,* or of good report or *praiseworthy* we seek after these things.

(Article of Faith 1:13)

"Behold
THERE SHALL BE
A *record kept*
AMONG YOU.

(D&C 21:1)

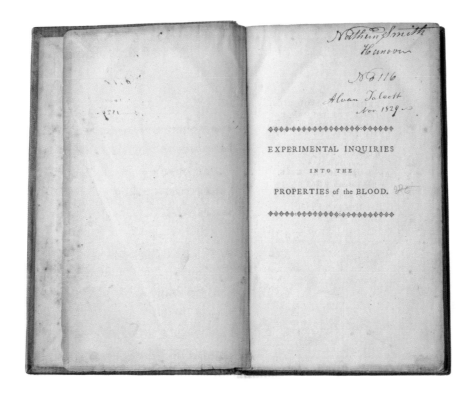

1. Experimental Inquiries into the Properties of the Blood

— Private Collector —

Prior to the First Vision, the most well-known story about the Prophet Joseph Smith's childhood concerns a harrowing operation he underwent in 1813. Related by Joseph's mother, Lucy Mack Smith, in her history recorded in 1844–45, the operation was the first dramatic event in the life of the young prophet. The event is often used as an example of the fortitude of Joseph at a young age, but it also illuminates the family dynamics of the Smith family. Lucy Mack Smith, passionate and fiery, confronted the doctors when they suggested that Joseph's leg be amputated. Joseph Smith Sr., more tender-hearted, burst into tears at the prospect of one of his sons losing a limb. Hyrum Smith, the dutiful elder brother, stayed by Joseph's side during his illness, even massaging his young brother's legs to alleviate the intense pain. But the reason this object was selected is that it illustrates the role of divine providence in bringing one of the finest medical professionals in New England to the bedside of the young boy destined to lay the foundation of the kingdom of God in the latter days.

Nathan Smith (no relation to the Joseph and Lucy Mack Smith family) was one of the most important innovators in the field of medicine in early nineteenth-century America. He founded the Dartmouth Medical School and participated in the founding of the Yale and Bowdoin Medical

Schools. He published numerous works, including *Practical Essay on Typhous Fever* and *Observation on the Pathology and Treatment of Necrosis*, both seminal texts in the American medical understanding of the specific ailments affecting Joseph Smith Jr. In his time, he was one of the premiere medical educators in New England. He was also, in the estimation of one historian, "the only physician in the United States at the time who had the vision, knowledge, and necessary surgical experience to deal successfully with Joseph Smith's medical problems."[1]

Experimental Inquiries into the Properties of the Blood is a 1772 medical text by Dr. William Hewson, a prominent British medical researcher.[2] It was part of Nathan Smith's library and contains one of the only known signatures from Smith on its title page. The book itself plays no role in the story of Joseph Smith's leg operation, but it does illustrate Nathan Smith's thirst for knowledge and the way he obtained his expertise. In an era when almost all medical professionals were self-taught, Smith worked to gain and spread knowledge of the best medical research and techniques. The lack of opportunity did not deter Smith from gaining all the training possible. At age thirty-five, with no college degree and no training except a seven-month course of study at Harvard Medical School and a year of study in England, Smith established the fourth medical school in the United States. He eventually received an MD from Dartmouth in 1801 and another from Harvard in 1811. When he arrived at the Smith home in 1813, he was president of the New Hampshire Medical Society.[3] With such a distinguished background, the question must be asked: What brought this outstanding physician to the home of an obscure family of country farmers?

Before his arrival at the home of Joseph Smith Jr., Nathan Smith was already coping with an epidemic of typhoid fever sweeping through the local countryside. Four of Dr. Smith's own children fell ill with the disease; none died. In March 1813 Dr. Smith wrote to a colleague, "We hear of new cases every day, and almost every day bring [sic] me an account of the death of some friend or acquaintance."[4] The typhoid epidemic ravaged the Smith home, where all of the children felt the grip of the deadly disease. Joseph's sister Sophronia was ill for ninety days when an attending doctor told her mother she would die. Father and Mother Smith "clasped [their] hands together upon [their] knees by the bed side and poured out grief and supplications," begging God for the recovery of their daughter. Sophronia eventually recovered, as did all the Smith children, though young Joseph immediately began exhibiting complications from the disease. Lucy Mack Smith records, "Joseph, who had so far recovered that he sat up when one day [he] suddenly screamed out with a severe pain in his shoulder." A few days later doctors discovered a fever sore on Joseph's chest so large that when it was lanced, it discharged "a full quart of matter." Almost immediately the boy felt a sharp pain in "the marrow of his leg" and the limb began swelling.[5]

Modern-day physicians have diagnosed the pain in Joseph's leg as the result of osteomyelitis, a bacterial infection in the interior of the bone. The infection causes the death of segments of the bone and can lead to serious complications or death of the patient.[6] During Joseph's suffering, his mother carried him in her arms "continually soothing him," and she noted that his brother Hyrum "sat beside him almost incessantly day and night grasping the most painful part of the affected leg between his hands" and gently massaging to alleviate the pain of his brother.[7] The infection continued to worsen, so the Smiths called in a consulting surgeon who alleviated the boy's suffering by making an eight-inch incision, almost from knee to ankle. When the incision began to heal, the intense pain began again, and the surgeon treated it by reopening the wound, this time cutting all the way to the bone. Once this wound was healed, the swelling and pain again returned, so a council of surgeons, including Nathan Smith, arrived at the Smith home to discuss how to help the young patient.[8]

According to Joseph's mother, the council of surgeons "decided that there was no remedy but amputation."[9] This is curious given that Dr. Smith knew a better way. The first surgery to relieve osteomyelitis took place in England in 1786, and Dr. Smith himself began to independently and aggressively operate to repair the condition as early as 1798. Notes from a lecture he gave the year prior at Dartmouth also indicate that he knew the best treatment for the disease.[10] Historian Richard Bushman has speculated that Dr. Smith and the council may have suggested amputation to prepare Joseph's parents for a difficult alternative to amputation.[11] Lucy Mack Smith may have also remembered the incident incorrectly, because in her recollection she was the one who suggested cutting out the infected part of the bone in order to save the leg. The procedure involved drilling into the bone, then sawing or breaking off the infected portions. When Joseph's father heard about the procedure "he burst into a flood of tears, and sobbed like a child."[12]

The team of surgeons brought cords to bind the boy and liquor to dull the pain, but Joseph refused both. He did, however, have two requests. First, he asked his father to hold him during the procedure and his mother to leave the room. According to Lucy, her son told her, "I know that you cannot endure to see me suffer so. Father can bear it." Lucy agreed and left the room as she saw the surgeons bring out a set of drills and pincers to break off the infected parts of the bone. Lucy remembered walking about a hundred yards from the house when the first scream pierced the air. Overcome with concern she ran back and burst into the room, prompting Joseph to cry, "Oh Mother go back!" She later recorded, "What a spectacle for a mother's eye—the wound tore open to view my boy . . . he was pale as a corpse and big drops of sweat were rolling down his face, every feature of which depicted agony that cannot be described."[13] Lucy was taken from the room and did not witness the end of the operation. The operation was a success, and though Joseph endured a long period of convalescence, he eventually recovered and retained the use of his leg, though he walked with crutches for over a year afterward and retained a slight limp throughout the rest of his life. In his manuscript history written in 1838, Joseph Smith mentioned that "fourteen additional pieces of bone afterwards worked out before my leg healed."[14]

We do not know if Nathan Smith performed the operation personally or only supervised. We do know that Dr. Smith's practices were not standardized until more than one hundred years later, making him the only surgeon in the United States at the time with the experience necessary to prevent amputation. In his history, Joseph mentions eleven doctors who came from Dartmouth medical college and mentions his care under the hands of "Drs. Smith, Stone & Perkins."[15] Nathan Smith, already a distinguished educator before he met Joseph Smith, continued to enjoy a career as one of the eminent medical professionals of his time. Oddly enough, Nathan Smith's official biography only briefly mentions the surgery. But Smith's biographer does ask an interesting question: "Whether Nathan Smith can be credited with having saved Joseph Smith's life, certainly he saved the boy's leg. Who knows whether religious history might have turned out quite differently if Joseph Smith had been an amputee from early childhood?"[16] That the future prophet was living only a few miles away from one of the great healers of his time, and one who was more qualified than any other person to help, is a remarkable sign of the tender mercies of God in the life of Joseph Smith.

2. THE BROWN SEER STONE

– The Church of Jesus Christ of Latter-day Saints –

The most tangible evidence of divine restoration of the gospel is the Book of Mormon. The book, just over 530 pages in English, was produced in an astonishingly brief period of time. It has a depth and complexity which defy claims that any nineteenth century mind could have produced no matter how brilliant. That it came from an uneducated farm boy in rural upstate New York is equally astounding. From the first edition, published in 1830, to the present, every copy of the Book of Mormon has included a claim from Joseph Smith that he "translated [the text of the book] by the gift and power of God."[17] Since that time, the term "translation" has been widely utilized as a catch-all description of how the book was produced, though the process was very different from any traditional form of translation. The translation of the Book of Mormon was miraculous and involved the use of instruments utilized by human hands beyond any mortal understanding of traditional processes. Those who witnessed the translation of the Book of Mormon sought to emphasize the supernatural nature of the translation process. Many of the sacred objects present during the translation—the Nephite interpreters, the Liahona, the sword of Laban, and most notably the plates themselves—are no longer in the hands of mortals. But one instrument likely used in the translation, the brown seer stone, is still found on earth.[18]

The brown seer stone in possession of The Church of Jesus Christ of Latter-day Saints matches some descriptions of a seer stone used by Joseph Smith during the translation process. One contemporary observer described the seer stone as an "oval-shaped, chocolate-colored stone, about the size of an egg, only more flat."[19] The stone is about 5.5 by 3.5 by about 4 centimeters in size. It has resided in Church custody since the nineteenth century. According to David Whitmer, one of the Three Witnesses of the Book of Mormon, the stone was given to Oliver Cowdery after the translation was completed. When Cowdery died in 1850, Phineas Young, brother to Brigham Young, acquired the stone from Oliver's widow, Elizabeth Whitmer Cowdery. The first photographs of the brown seer stone were published in 2015 as part of *The Joseph Smith Papers* project, and it is pictured here alongside a small leather pouch, apparently made by Emma Smith, in which the stone was stored for safekeeping.[20]

Though the first images of the brown seer stone became available only recently, the use of the stone was widely spoken of among the individuals involved in the translation process. Historical descriptions of the translation process are also limited by the fact that the two people most involved in the translation process, Joseph Smith and Oliver Cowdery, provided little information about their work. Both also died relatively young, Joseph in 1844 and Oliver in 1850, while most witnesses of the translation process recorded their experiences in the later phases of their lives. Nevertheless, among those interviewed most extensively about the process, the use of divine instruments remains a prominent part of their recollections.

The stone was one of several instruments used in the translation. Joseph Smith and his associates often spoke of "interpreters" buried alongside the plates as one of the tools used to receive the text. In the Book of Mormon, the prophet Moroni spoke of having "sealed up the interpreters, according to the commandment of the Lord" (Ether 4:5). Martin Harris described the interpreters as "two stones set in a bow of silver . . . about two inches in diameter, perfectly round." He continued, "The stones were white, like polished marble, with a few gray

streaks." Lucy Mack Smith gave a similar account, describing the interpreters as "2 smooth 3 cornered diamonds set in glass and the glass was set in silver bows connected with each other in the same way that old fashioned spectacles are made."[21]

Both the Nephite interpreters and the seer stone were used in the translation. In her recollections, Emma Smith explained that Joseph began translating "by use of Urim and Thummim, and that portion of the translation was the part that Martin Harris lost. *After that he used a small stone,* not exactly black, but was rather a dark color."[22] Sources from the time indicate that Joseph Smith owned more than one seer stone, though evidence generally points to the brown seer stone as the instrument used in translation. It can be difficult to determine which instruments were used during the translation process, since both are referred to as *interpreters* or described through the use of the biblical term *Urim and Thummim* by participants in the translation process.[23]

The use of seer stones may seem strange to readers today, but such instruments existed as a familiar part of the culture Joseph Smith grew up in. Both Joseph Smith and his father attested to the use of a seer stone in private ventures before Joseph received the plates.[24] "Folk magic," as some scholars have identified it, was a part of the cosmology Joseph Smith grew up in as a young man on the American frontier. In a review of contemporary records scholars identified that several residents from the Palmyra/Manchester region Joseph grew up in possessed seer stones used in a number of different endeavors.[25] According to some accounts, Joseph may have found the brown stone while digging a well on the property of Willard Chase, another Palmyra resident who used seer stones. Wilford Woodruff stated that Joseph Smith obtained the stone "by digging under the pretense of excavating for a well."[26] Throughout his life, Joseph was open about his past in these treasure-seeking endeavors. In 1838, Joseph was asked, "Was not Joe Smith a money digger?" He replied, "Yes, but it was never very profitable job to him, as he only got fourteen dollars a month for it."[27]

When it comes to the use of the brown stone in translation, several participants described how the stone was used. Emma Smith, who served as scribe while she and Joseph were living in Harmony, Pennsylvania, said that she "frequently wrote day after day" and described Joseph "sitting with his face buried in his hat, with the stone in it, and dictating hour after hour with nothing between us." When Emma was asked to share her testimony of the translation process near the end of her life, she said, "The Book of Mormon is of divine authenticity—I have not the slightest doubt of it. I am satisfied that no man could have dictated the writing of the manuscripts unless he was inspired; for, when acting as his scribe, your father would dictate to me for hour after hour; and when returning after meals, or after interruptions, he would at once begin where he left off, without either seeing the manuscript or having any portion of it read to him."[28]

We may never know all of the exact details of the translation process of the Book of Mormon, but it is important to keep in mind that translation was a supernatural process, aided by the power of God. The use of seer stone or other divine instruments in another example of the miracle of ancient days returning to bring about the "marvelous work and a wonder" prophesied for the latter days. In ancient times prophets used physical objects like the rod of Aaron (Exodus 7:12), a brass serpent (Numbers 21:8), or sacred arks (Joshua 3:15) to mediate divine power. In our time sacred anointing oil, common bread, and water are used for the same purposes. In Joseph Smith's time, seer stones and divine interpreters played a vital role in allowing the Prophet and his associates to translate "by the gift and power of God."[29]

3. Hyrum Smith's Box for the Gold Plates

– Church History Museum –

Seventeen-year-old Joseph Smith was pouring out his heart in prayer on the night of September 21, 1823, asking for forgiveness. He later recalled, "I betook myself to prayer and supplication to Almighty God for forgiveness of all my sins and follies, and also for a manifestation to me that I might know of my state and standing before him" (JS—H 1:29). The Angel Moroni appeared and told him about an ancient record buried in a hill close to his home.[30] The angelic appearance and message repeated itself three times that night. The next morning as Joseph stood "on the west side of the hill" toward its north end, "not far from the top," he saw the plates for the first time.[31] The next day he shared some instructions he had received from the Angel Moroni with his family, explaining, "We must be careful not to proclaim these things or to mention them abroad For we do not any of us know the wickedness of the world which is so sinful that when we get the plates they will want to kill us for the sake of the gold."[32]

Though the Smith family took the angel's warning to heart, word of the gold plates found its way outside of the family circle, "and even before Joseph received them four years later, various people were plotting how they might obtain them."[33] The Smith family did share knowledge of the plates with trusted friends. For instance, Joseph Knight Sr. and Joseph Knight Jr. said that Joseph told them that sometime during 1827 he would obtain the plates.[34] Whatever the source of the information, several unseemly people knew about the plates and that Joseph would soon obtain them; therefore, Joseph took precautions to protect the record. As Church historian Andrew H. Hedges informs, "Keeping the sacred record out of harm's way required his constant surveillance."[35]

Four years after the Angel Moroni had first appeared to him, around midnight on September 21, 1827, Joseph Smith went to his mother, Lucy Mack Smith, asking if she had a chest with a lock and key. It would seem that Joseph's request was last-minute, since the Angel Moroni had told him much earlier than the night before he was to obtain the plates to find "a chest or trunk having a good lock and key," where he could keep the plates once he obtained them. It is also reasonable to assume that Lucy knew why Joseph wanted a trunk, though Joseph did not inform her of how he was going to use the chest. When Lucy told her son that she had no such container, Joseph reassured her that all would be well, and he and Emma left the house in Joseph Knight's horse-drawn wagon, telling no one of their destination.[36]

Early in the morning on September 22, 1827, Joseph Smith set out for the hill near his home, the location where the ancient record was buried; it was a site he had visited annually on the same day for the previous four years. Each year, Joseph had received instruction preparing him for the future work of translating the plates. However, in 1827, the Angel Moroni "delivered" the plates with a warning that he "should be responsible for them," adding that "if [he] would let them go carelessly, or through any neglect . . . [he] should be cut off; but that if [he] would use all [his] endeavors to preserve them . . . they should be protected" (JS—H 1:59). Lucy recorded Moroni's warning with more detail: "Now you have got the record into your own hands and you are but a man therefore you will have to be watchful and faithful to your trust or you will be overpowered by wicked men for they will lay every plan and scheme that is possible to get them away from you and if you do not take heed continually they will succeed while they were in my hands I could keep them and no man had power to take them away but now I give them up to you beware and look well to your ways— and you shall have power to retain them until the time for them to be translated."[37]

Rumors had circled around Palmyra about the gold plates, and Joseph feared that someone might try to steal them the very morning he received them. After getting the plates at the hill, with Emma waiting below, "finding an old birch log much decayed, excepting the bark, which was in a measure sound, Joseph took his pocket knife and cut the bark; then turned it back and made a hole of sufficient size to receive the plates; and laying them in the cavity thus formed, he replaced the bark, after which he laid old stuff across the log in several places, that happened to lay near, in order to conceal, as much as possible, the place in which they were deposited."[38] Though he did not bring the plates home that morning, he did bring the Urim and Thummim wrapped in a silk handkerchief and let his mother hold them the next day. Lucy then instructed Joseph to hire a cabinetmaker to make a chest to hide the plates in. To pay the cabinetmaker Joseph went to work for a widow living in Macedon, who hired him to build a wall around her well. While Joseph built the wall, the plates remained in the hollow log. Although Joseph's hope was that the excitement about the plates would die down, it never did. Several days later, when he heard that men had hired conjurers to find the plates, he returned to Palmyra.[39]

Shortly before leaving his home to retrieve the plates from the hollowed-out log, Joseph asked his brother Hyrum to have a chest with a good lock "ready by the time [he got] home" to securely hold the plates. Whether this was the same chest the cabinetmaker had been commissioned to construct is unclear; however, it is clear that after arranging for the chest Joseph immediately went to get the plates from the log, and it must have been "well after noon" by the time he arrived at the plates' hiding place.[40] Once he took them out of the log, Joseph wrapped the plates in his linen (tow) frock, which was something he wore every day, not necessarily something he brought specifically to wrap the plates in.[41]

On his way back home, Joseph was assaulted multiple times. Originally, he went by way of the Canandaigua Road, but then fearing for his safety, he soon changed his route and traveled through the woods. He was first attacked in a large windfall where several trees had fallen. His mother recounted that while Joseph was jumping over a log, a man sprang up from behind and gave him a heavy blow with a gun. Whirling around, Joseph was able to knock the man to the ground and then flee as fast as he could. A short distance later, he was attacked again, this time by a different man but in the same way as the first. He was also able to bring down this man and continue running. Joseph was not yet home when he was attacked a third time. This time he suffered another hard hit from the butt of a gun, but he counterattacked with such force that Joseph dislocated his own thumb. Continuing to run, Joseph was closely pursued until he drew very near to his own home. The attackers, for fear of being caught, stopped their chase, and Joseph, completely out of breath, paused for a moment and leaned against a fence to recover his strength to some degree.[42] Upon his return, his mother, Lucy, and his sister Catherine nursed his bruises and injuries. Meanwhile, he asked for his father and Josiah Stowell to go after the assailants and sent his eleven-year-old brother, Don Carlos, to remind their brother Hyrum of their previous arrangement to get a box for the plates.[43]

Hyrum had located a box but unfortunately had forgotten to empty it and take it to Joseph. When Don Carlos came to report that Joseph had returned with the plates, Hyrum and his wife, Mary, were hosting her sisters. Upon hearing the news, Hyrum immediately leapt up from his seat, dropping a cup of tea in the process, and then grabbed the box and emptied its contents on the floor. He threw the box over his shoulder and left the house in a hurry.[44] Hyrum's guests thought he was "positively crazy," but Mary reassured her sisters that he had merely "thought of something that he [had] neglected and it's just like him to fly off in a tangent when he thinks of anything that way."[45] Hyrum's chest had originally belonged to Alvin Smith, who used it both for storing small tools and as a lap desk. Its dimensions were fourteen inches wide, sixteen inches long, and six and a quarter inches deep in the back, and it sloped to about four inches in the front. The wood was three-quarters of an inch thick, with a top and bottom made of walnut and sides made of boxwood.[46]

According to the Eight Witnesses, the gold plates that would be kept in Hyrum's chest were about six to seven inches wide by eight inches long, and four to six inches thick. The thickness of each plate was reported as being between the thickness of parchment paper and common tin, and they were bound together by three large rings.[47] Although the plates themselves had the appearance of gold, they were not made of pure gold. Professional genealogist Read H. Putnam's study estimates that a block of pure gold that size would weigh more than two hundred pounds, but several of the Eight Witnesses put the weight of the plates at around sixty pounds, and it has to be considered that Joseph both ran from and fended off attackers while maintaining possession of the plates. There is also the possibility that because the individual plates were handcrafted they would not be perfectly flat, thus the air space between them would cause them to weigh less.[48] Nonetheless, it is highly likely that the plates were made of an alloy, with the "appearance of gold," and many witnesses were careful to word it as such.[49] Putnam suggests that the plates may be *tumbaga*, an alloy created from both gold and copper. Tumbaga is known to last a substantially long time, and some of the earliest artifacts created from this material date back to the same century in which Moroni hid the plates.[50]

Hyrum's chest, which held the gold plates that were translated into the Book of Mormon, was handed down through his family as a sacred object. The last Smith descendant to possess the chest was Eldred G. Smith who served the Presiding Patriarch of the Church from 1947 to 1979. After Patriarch Smith received emeritus status in 1979, he often spoke at firesides where he displayed artifacts from the lives of Joseph and Hyrum Smith, including the chest. In 2013, when Eldred Smith died at the age of 106, the chest was donated to the Church History Museum. This box serves as a reminder of the plates that Joseph Smith struggled to preserve until he could translate them into the Book of Mormon.

4. The "Caractors" Document
– Community of Christ Library –

Martin Harris served as the first scribe of the translation of the Book of Mormon. Considerably older and more established than Joseph Smith, Harris provided many of the resources necessary to start the translation process and ensure the publication of the Book of Mormon. The translation also took part largely in Harmony, Pennsylvania, a long distance from Martin's home and interests in Palmyra, New York. Martin believed in Joseph Smith's work but also wanted assurances that the plates and the translation were genuine. To that end, he asked Joseph Smith if he could take some of the characters from the plates to several well-known scholars to receive assurance of the reality of the work.

Joseph Smith's history of the events reads as follows: "Martin Harris came to our place, got the characters which I had drawn off of the plates and started with them to the City of New York." Martin's account of the event continues: "I went to the City of New York and presented the Characters which had been translated, with the translation thereof, to Professor Anthony [Charles Anthon] a gentleman celebrated for his literary attainments. Professor Anthony stated that the translation was correct, more so than any he had before seen translated from Egyptian." According to Martin Harris, Anthon gave him a certificate declaring the translation to be genuine. When Anthon asked about where the plates with the characters came from, Harris responded by telling him an angel of God had revealed them. Upon hearing this news, Anthon tore up the certificate, declaring there was no such thing as angels, and asked for Harris to bring the record to him. Harris responded that the plates were sealed, to which Anthon replied, "I cannot read a sealed book," fulfilling a prophecy found in Isaiah 29. Harris concluded his account by writing, "I left him and went to Dr. Mitch [Samuel Mitchell] who sanctioned what Professor Anthony had said respecting both the characters and the translation."[51]

The episode has long been dissected by defenders and debunkers of Joseph Smith's work. The plates themselves are not available for examination, but is there a document with the characters on the plates available for examination?

Housed in the Community of Christ archives in Independence, Missouri, is a document many have believed is the paper that Martin Harris took to visit the scholars in New York City. The paper was sold in 1902 to the Community of Christ (previously called the Reorganized Church of Jesus Christ of Latter-day Saints) as part of a collection of documents related to the family of David Whitmer, one of the Book of Mormon witnesses. Early provenance surrounding the document is difficult to ascertain, but there is evidence suggesting that David Whitmer possessed several transcripts of characters from the Book of Mormon plates. For example, when a man named E. C. Brand visited Whitmer in 1875, he recorded seeing "a facsimile of the characters of the plates."[52] In 1884 George Q. Cannon, a member of the First Presidency, visited Richmond, Missouri, to interview David Whitmer, the last survivor of the Three Witnesses of the Book of Mormon. President Cannon described seeing a "paper which I thought of surpassing interest. It was the characters drawn by Joseph himself for Martin Harris to show to professors Mitchell and Anthon." Cannon later reflected in his journal, "Here was the very paper which Isaiah saw in vision years before and which he called 'the words of a book.'"[53]

While the document is likely linked to participants in the Book of Mormon translation, it is likely not the actual document Martin Harris showed to Charles Anthon and other scholars. In the *Comprehensive History of the Church*, B. H. Roberts argued that the "Caractors" document, which contains only seven horizontal lines, is at best a fragment of what Anthon and Mitchell saw, and not the complete document. Martin Harris wrote that Anthon certified both the characters and their translation as genuine, but the "Caractors" document contains no translation. Further, Charles Anthon's recollection of the document Harris brought him does not match the description of the manuscript he was shown. Anthon recalled a document with "perpendicular columns" in the "Chinese mode of writing," pointing toward vertical, not horizontal columns. He also noted that "the whole ended in a rude representation of the Mexican zodiac." None of these characteristics are found in the "Caractors" document. Anthon disputed other aspects of Harris's account of their meeting, but there is no reason to dispute these details of his recollection.[54]

Given this evidence, it is likely that the "Caractors" document is not the manuscript Martin Harris took to New York, as it has long been assumed. However, evidence exists that, even if the document is not the Martin Harris transcript, it may still be a real representation of what the characters on the Book of Mormon plates actually looked like. Recent analysis of the handwriting of the "Caractors" document by historians working for *The Joseph Smith Papers* project has led to the conclusion that the document was written by John Whitmer, the first Church Historian (see D&C 47). "Caractors" was likely copied from a number of documents created by Joseph Smith in the winter of 1827 and 1828. None of these documents precisely match the description given by Charles Anthon, but evidence suggests that during this time Joseph Smith employed Emma Smith, and possibly her brother Reuben Hale, to create copies of the characters on the plates.[55]

Part of the reason "Caractors" was long assumed to be the document Martin Harris took with him to New York was that the characters matched the earliest known published copy of any characters from the gold plates. The characters, found in *The Prophet,* the Church-affiliated newspaper in New York, were published in 1844. The editors of *The Prophet* asserted, "We have published a very neat specimen of the original characters or hieroglyphics that were copied from the plates which the Book of Mormon was translated from." [56] It is very unlikely that the editors of *The Prophet* had the "Caractors" document in their possession because the Whitmer family left the Church in 1838, six years before the characters were published. At the same time, the characters shown in *The Prophet* and the characters on the "Caractors" document match each other almost exactly, suggesting that both documents came from the early manuscripts produced by Joseph Smith in the Book of Mormon translation. [57]

While the "Caractors" document has a more complicated history than was originally assumed and is likely not the manuscript Martin Harris took with him, it is most likely a genuine representation of the characters found on the gold plates. The unlikely witness of this simple piece of paper lines up with other documents from the period to create another tantalizing look into the miraculous coming forth of the Book of Mormon.

5. LUCY MACK SMITH'S 1830 BOOK OF MORMON

– Community of Christ Library –

There is no greater chronicler of the early days of the Restoration than Joseph Smith's mother, Lucy Mack Smith. The history of Mother Smith, recorded in 1844–45 after the Prophet's death, provides more vivid detail to the formative events of Joseph Smith's life than any other source. It paints a portrait of a caring mother caught up in extraordinary events surrounding her family and eventually affecting the course of religious history. She is also one of the most important witnesses of the coming forth of the Book of Mormon. Lucy's history provides invaluable accounts of the story of the lost manuscript, descriptions of the instruments of translation, and information on Joseph's transformation from itinerant farm boy to the leader of a new religion.

In the home of Lucy and Joseph Smith Sr., religion was a frequent topic of conversation. The first visit of the Angel Moroni, sparked by Joseph Smith Jr.'s desire to know his standing before God, was in turn inspired by a conversation the Smiths held on the subject of religion: "One evening we were sitting till quite late conversing upon the subject of the diversity of churches that had risen up in the world," Lucy recorded in her history. Joseph "never said many words upon any subject but always seemed to reflect more deeply than common persons of his age upon everything of a religious nature. . . .

After we ceased conversation he went to bed and was pondering in his mind which of the churches were the true one. . . . He had not laid there long till he saw a bright light entered the room where he lay he looked up and saw an angel of the Lord stood standing by him."[58]

Later, as Joseph began his years-long apprentice-ship under the tutelage of the angel, he involved his family in the course of study, sharing recitals with them of what he learned about the ancient culture of the Nephites. Wandle Mace, a Church member who visited with Lucy in her later years, recalled Lucy saying, "During the day our sons would endeavor to get through their work as early as possible, and say, Mother, 'have supper early, so we can have a long evening listen to Joseph.' Some times Joseph would describe the appearance of the Nephites, their mode of dress and warfare, their implements of husband-ry, etc., and many things, he had seen in vision." Lucy looked back fondly on these times, with the felicitous family life of the Smiths only broken by the persecution of religious leaders perturbed by Joseph's visions. "Truly ours was a happy family," she told Mace, "although persecuted by preachers who declared, 'There was no more vision, the canon of scripture was full, and no more revelation was needed.' But Joseph had seen a vision, and must de-clare it."[59]

Once Joseph obtained the plates, his enemies made several attempts to steal them. Lucy felt a great deal of anxiety over the safety of the record. On one occasion, Joseph attempted to soothe her fears by demonstrating to her how he kept the plates safe. "Mother, do not be uneasy," he told Lucy. "All is right. See here, I have got a key." Lucy continues, "I knew not what he meant but took the article in my hands and upon after examining it with no cov-ering but a silk handkerchief found that it consisted of 2 smooth 3 cornered diamonds set in glass and the glass was set in silver bows connected with each

other in the same way that old fashioned spectacles are made. He took them again and left me but did not tell me anything of the record."[60] On another occa-sion, Joseph also showed his mother the breastplate he was given along with the plates, and she provid-ed a detailed description of it. "It was wrapped in a thin muslin handkerchief; so thin that I could see the glistening metal, and feel its proportions without any difficulty," she wrote. "It was concave on one side and convex on the other; and extended from the neck downwards as far as the centre of the stom-ach of a man of extraordinary size. It had four straps of the same material for the purpose of fastening it to the breast: two of which ran back to go over the shoulders, and the other two were designed to fasten to the hips. These straps were just the width of two of my fingers; (for I measured them); and they had holes in the end of them for convenience in fasten-ing. The whole plate was worth at least 500 dol-lars. . . . Joseph placed the Urim and Thummim in the chest after I examined it."[61] Though she was not chosen as one of the witnesses of the plates, Lucy gave the most detailed description of the artifacts accompanying the plates (see D&C 17).[62]

The most vivid episode described by Lucy sur-rounds Martin Harris and the lost manuscript of the Book of Mormon. The tension is palpable in the nar-rative as she describes the slow and reluctant walk of Martin Harris as he approaches the Smith house-hold. "We saw him walking with a slow and mea-sured tread toward the house, his eyes fixed thought-fully upon the ground when he came," she recalled.[63] Lucy had prepared a meal for Martin, but when he entered he picked up his knife and fork and then suddenly dropped them. Lucy then recalled, "Martin pressed his hands upon his temples and cried out in a tone of anguish, 'Oh! I have lost my soul, I have lost my soul.' Joseph, who had smothered his fears till now sprang from the table exclaiming, 'Oh! Martin have you lost that manuscript! Have you broken your oath and brought down condemnation upon my head as well as your own?' 'Yes,' replied Martin, 'It is gone and I know not where.'"[64] Joseph was beside himself with guilt, and his mother moved to comfort him. "I besought him not to mourn so—that, perhaps the Lord world forgive him after a short season of humiliation and repentance," she remembered. "But what could I say to comfort him, when he saw all of the family in the same situation of mind of himself: sobs and groans, and the most bitter lamentation filled the house; but Joseph was more distressed than the rest, for he better understood the consequences of disobedience. [Joseph] continued walking back and forth, meanwhile weeping and grieving, until about sunset; when, by much persuasion he took a little nourishment."[65]

Though the loss of the manuscript was devastating for Lucy and her family, her straightforward account and genuine grief over the lost manuscript greatly enhances the authenticity of the miraculous coming forth of the Book of Mormon. Elder Jeffrey R. Holland commented on Lucy's account, "My goodness, that's an elaborate little side story—which makes absolutely no sense at all unless, of course, there really were plates, and there really was a translation process going on, and there really had been a solemn covenant made with the Lord, and there really was an enemy who did not want that book to 'come forth in this generation' (D&C 10:33). Talk about literary flair and a gift for fiction! Lucy Mack Smith gets an 'A,' right along with her son, if this is all an imaginary venture, to say nothing of the terrific performances by Mr. and Mrs. Harris and the entire first generation of the Church."[66]

A few months later, Lucy was relieved when during a visit to Joseph's home in Harmony, Pennsylvania, Joseph "attracted my attention was a red morocco trunk, that set on Emma's bureau; which trunk Joseph shortly informed me, contained the Urim and Thummim and the plates."[67] She also shared in Joseph's elation at the end of the summer

of 1829, when Joseph was at last allowed to select three witnesses, among them a repentant Martin Harris, who received the privilege of beholding the plates and the angel. Lucy recalled waiting in the Whitmer home with her husband and Mary Whitmer when "Joseph came in he threw himself down beside me." "'Father!—Mother!'—said he, you do not know how happy I am. The Lord has caused the plates to be shown to three more besides me who have also seen an angel and will have to testify to the truth of what I have said for they know for themselves that I do not go about to deceive the people." Joseph told his mother he felt "as though I was relieved of a dreadful burden which was almost too much for me to endure, but they will now have to bear a part and it does rejoice my soul that I am not any longer to be entirely alone in the world."[68]

Throughout the translation and printing process of the Book of Mormon, Lucy played a vital role in encouraging her son and protecting the work. On one occasion Oliver Cowdery became aware of a plot to steal the manuscript of the book, and Lucy offered to personally guard the manuscript overnight. She placed it in a chest under her bed and went to sleep. During the night Lucy "fell into a train of reflections" about her past life and all the events leading to the current moment. She reflected on the teaching given by her father and mother and almost seemed to hear the voice of her brother, Jason, and her sister Lovina in their religious yearnings. She felt transported in time to the deathbed of her sister Lovina repeating the words of a favorite hymn before she passed into the next life. When the morning came, Lucy reflected, "Thus I spent the night surrounded by enemies and yet in an ecstasy of happiness and truly I can say that 'my soul did magnify and my spirit rejoiced in God my Savior.'"[69]

Several days later, a delegation from Lucy's former church approached the house with a request to see the "gold bible." Lucy refused to show them the manuscript but "proceeded to give them the substance of what is contained in the Book of Mormon, particularly the principles of religion which it contains."[70] When a deacon from the delegation asked to cease her proclamations about the Book of Mormon, Lucy replied, "Even [if] you should stick my body full of faggots and burn me at the stake I would declare that Jose[p]h has that record and that I know it to be true as long as God gave me breath."[71]

When the Book of Mormon was published in 1830, Lucy received a copy and studied it diligently. At several points in her history, she records exchanges with inquirers who noticed her reading the book in public.[72] This copy, tattered and worn with pages falling out but bearing the signature of Mother Smith, was handed down through the Smith family until it passed into possession of Community of Christ archivists. Her copy is one of five thousand copies printed in 1830 and sent out into world as another testament of Jesus Christ. Though Lucy's name is not included in the list of witnesses given in the book, she is undoubtedly one of the most courageous witnesses of the Book of Mormon.

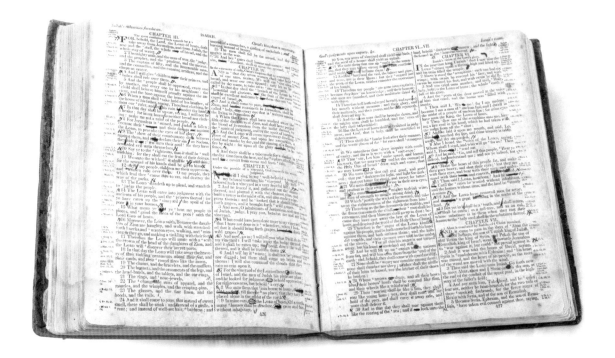

6. Joseph Smith's Marked Bible
– Community of Christ Library –

Joseph Smith loved the Bible. A letter written by Joseph and other Church leaders to priesthood holders declared, "He that can mark the power of Omnipotence, inscribed upon the heavens, can also see God's own handwriting in the sacred volume [the Bible]: and he who reads it oftenest will like it best."[73] While revering the sacred scripture, Joseph Smith also held no illusions about the perfection of the Bible having learned from the Book of Mormon that "there are many plain and precious things taken away from the book, which is the book of the Lamb of God" (1 Nephi 13:28). On one occasion, the Prophet summarized his feelings toward the Bible, stating, "I believe the bible as it read when it came from the pen of the original writers; ignorant translators, careless transcribers, or designing and corrupt priests have committed many errors."[74]

Even while the Book of Mormon was being printed, Joseph Smith and his associates began plans to complete a translation of the Bible, intended to correct many of the errors that had crept into the text and place back many of the plan and precious truths lost. On October 8, 1829, Oliver Cowdery purchased a large King James Bible from the Grandin Press, the printer of the Book of Mormon. This Bible, which is currently in the custody of the Community of Christ, is one of the most important objects in understanding the nature of the Joseph Smith Translation. The Bible is a large, pulpit-style edition containing the Old and New Testaments along with the Apocrypha. It is nine inches wide, eleven inches long, about two and a half inches thick, and weighs just under five pounds. On the inside cover in the large handwriting of Joseph Smith is the inscription, "The Book of the Jews and the property of Joseph Smith Junior and Oliver Cowdery, bought October 3, 1829 at Egbert B Grandin's Book Store, Palmyra, Wayne County, New York. Price $3.75. Holiness to the Lord."[75] It is believed that this Bible served as the primary study text for Joseph Smith's New Translation of the Bible.

The "New Translation," as it was referred to by the Lord in the Doctrine and Covenants (D&C 124:89), was not a translation in the traditional sense. One scholar described the translation as "recasting the text into a new form by means of inspiration from the Holy Spirit."[76] The Prophet's translation did not consist of taking ancient Hebrew or Greek texts and rendering them into modern English. Instead, the translation consisted of an intensive study of the Bible with changes implemented to restore the original intent of the writers and to make it more understandable to modern readers. Kent Jackson, a historian who made an intensive study of the Joseph Smith Translation (JST), placed the changes made to the biblical text into five categories. First, in some cases the translation was a restoration of the original text. For instance, the entirety of Moses 1, found in the Pearl of Great Price, is missing from the text of the book of Genesis. The restoration of Moses 1 to the scriptural canon brings back critical truths about the nature of God, mankind, and Satan in their respective roles within the plan of salvation.

Second, at the time, the JST served to restore what was once said or done but which was never in the Bible. The JST of Genesis 14:25–40 contains an engaging description of the ministry of Melchizedek, the king of Salem. We do not know if this appears in the original Genesis text, but it appears in the Book of Mormon in Alma 13 and serves as important backstory to the role Melchizedek plays in the narrative about Abraham in Genesis. The added narrative helps us understand why Melchizedek was such a dynamic leader that his name became for-

ever associated with the "Holy Priesthood, after the Order of the Son of God" (D&C 107:3).

Third, the JST at times consisted of editing to make the Bible more understandable to modern readers. Language in the JST was at times modernized. For example, in many instances the archaic KJV word *wot* was changed to *know*, as in Exodus 32:1 where "we *wot* not what is become of him" was changed to "we *know* not what has become of him." In other places *saith* was changed to *said*, *that* and *which* was changed to *who*, and *ye* and *thee* were changed to *you*, though these changes are not always consistent throughout the manuscript. In other places the JST replaced ambiguous pronouns with proper names, as in Genesis 14:20, where the KJV reads "and he gave" but is clarified in the JST to read "and Abram gave."

Fourth, alterations made in the JST serve to bring biblical wording into harmony with truths found in other parts of the Bible or in modern revelation. For instance, the KJV text of John 1:18 reads, "No man hath seen God at any time," a confusing teaching that contradicts a fair number of passages in the Old and New Testament, as well as the experiences of the Prophet in the First Vision and on other occasions (Gen. 32:30, Ex. 33:11, Deut. 34:10, Isa. 6:5). The inspired revision of this verse reads, "No man hath seen God at any time, except he hath born record of the Son; for except it is through him no man can be saved" (JST, John 1:19), emphasizing the divine role of God the Father in witnessing on behalf of the Son.

Finally, at times the JST includes changes not written by the original authors that are helpful to modern readers. Elder Bruce R. McConkie, noting the differences between the early chapters of Genesis and the JST of the same material declared, "Both of them are true." He also stated his belief that John 1 in the Bible "is true" but that the JST of the same passage provides "an entirely different perspective," adding, "These are illustrations of the fact that there can be two translations of the same thing and both of them can be true."[77] A frequently cited example of this is found in Romans 13 where Paul writes concerning the Saints' obligation to submit to secular powers. The JST rewrites that passage to apply it toward cooperation with Church authorities. It is likely both passages are correct, and the JST revision is a revelation intended to instruct the modern Saints (see JST, Romans 13:6–7).[78]

Most of the important doctrinal changes found in the Prophet's work of translation are found in the JST manuscripts and not in the marked Bible. This particular Bible is valuable for two specific reasons. First, the inscriptions in the front of the Bible provide us with the basic timeframe for the work of the New Translation, giving us a basic start date of 1829. Second, the Bible is useful in illustrating *how* the New Translation was carried out. The actual text of the translation is not found on the pages of this Bible, but it does show the intensive study and search carried out by Joseph Smith and his associates in the New Translation.[79]

Casually leafing through the pages of the marked Bible, the dramatic, messy, and life-changing interaction of the Prophet and his scribes with the Bible comes to life. While there is evidence of a systematic study of the texts, there are also markings indicating a delighted engagement with the words in which the reader immersed himself again and again. In some places there are pencil markings and ink markings on the same page, indicating a return to favorite passages. There are no markings in Genesis 1–24 because those passages were written out entirely in the JST manuscripts. The same is true for the four gospels in the New Testament, which were written out, and only show two obscure ink marks in Luke 18. Some books, such as Exodus, Isaiah, Romans, and the book of Revelation are marked extensively. Other parts, such as the Song of Solomon and the Apocrypha, have no markings at all (see D&C 91:4-6).

Throughout the Bible many italicized words are crossed out, while others are not touched. The exploration and marking of the minor prophets in the Old Testament ends without explanation in Zechariah 8:7. Though the primary text of the JST is found in the manuscripts, the Bible itself illustrates the complex, messy, and thoroughly human way a mortal prophet interacted with a divine text.[80]

Though Joseph Smith initially completed the JST manuscripts in 1833,[81] he never entirely left the translation behind, and his intensive study of the scriptures remained a facet of his daily life until his death in 1844. After his death the marked Bible, along with other JST materials, remained with the Smith family. The Bible eventually came into the custody of Alexander H. Smith, Joseph and Emma's third surviving son, who presented the Bible to his daughter Vida as a wedding present in 1886. The Bible remained in her keeping until 1942, when she gave the Bible to Israel A. Smith, Joseph Smith's grandson and a counselor in the First Presidency of the Reorganized Church of Jesus Christ of Latter-day Saints (now called Community of Christ), headquartered in Independence, Missouri. Since that time to the present the marked Bible remained in the archives of the Community of Christ. It is available for public viewing upon request from Community of Christ archivists. A quick perusal through its pages allows the viewer to feel and see the love and esteem Joseph Smith held for the Bible, and its critical importance in his thought and faith. While Latter-day Saints reject the concept of a closed canon, they also hold to the established scriptural canon as the foundation of their faith. On one occasion Joseph Smith held aloft a Bible and stated, "I believe in this sacred volume. In it the 'Mormon' faith is to be found. We teach nothing but what the Bible teaches. We believe nothing, but what is to be found in this book."[82] The worn and marked pages of this Bible demonstrate the Prophet's intensive devotion to the Bible, its teachings, and its role as a conduit to the mind of God.

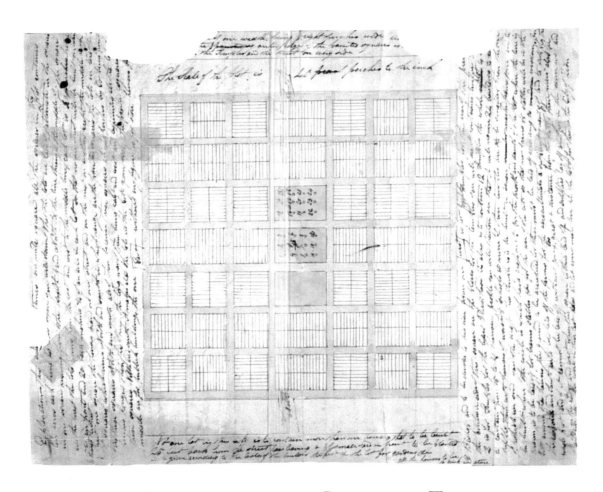

7. Plat of the City of Zion

– Church History Museum –

◆

No concept fired the imagination of the early Saints of this dispensation more than the construction of a holy city of God on the American continent. One survey found that in early Latter-day Saint literature the most quoted passage from the Book of Mormon was Ether 13:4–8, where the ancient prophet Moroni foretold "that a New Jerusalem should be built up upon this land, unto the remnant of the seed of Joseph" (Ether 13:6).[83] Interest in this New Jerusalem continued as Joseph Smith's translation of the Bible restored the knowledge of a city called Zion built by the antediluvian prophet Enoch, where the people "were of one heart and one mind and dwelt in righteousness" (Moses 7:18).[84] In fact, one of the most telling indications of the fascination the early Saints held with Zion is witnessed in one of the first serious challenges to Joseph Smith's role as revelator for the Church.

In September 1830, in the midst of Joseph Smith's work on the New Translation of the Bible, Hiram Page, one of the Eight Witnesses of the Book of Mormon, claimed to have received a series of revelations through a seer stone. Little is known about what Page's revelation contained, but one witness recounted that one of topics discussed in Page's revelation was the location of the City of Zion.[85] When Joseph inquired about the matter, he received a revelation from the Lord correcting Page, explaining that "those things which he hath written from that stone are not of me and that Satan deceiveth him" (D&C 28:11). At the same time, the Lord, perhaps seeing the anxiousness of His disciples in the matter, also provided the first substantial clue about the location of the New Jerusalem, stating, "No man knoweth where the city Zion shall be built, but it is given hereafter. Behold, I say unto you that it shall be on the borders by the Lamanites" (D&C 28:9). In the same revelation, Oliver Cowdery was given the task of leading a mission to the Lamanites (D&C 28:8), and he departed the following month in October 1830.[86]

The Lamanite mission was fruitful in several ways. First, the Lamanite missionaries taught and baptized Sidney Rigdon and many of his followers in the areas around Kirtland, Ohio. Second, after their successful sojourn in Ohio, Oliver Cowdery and his companions continued their travels until they arrived in one of the most prominent locations in Church history: Jackson County, Missouri. The Lamanite missionaries were frustrated in their efforts to teach the Native Americans on the Missouri frontier, but they persisted and established a permanent Latter-day Saint presence in Jackson County. A few months later, Joseph Smith was commanded to lead a group of elders to Jackson County and hold a Church conference there (see D&C 52:1–2).[87] When Joseph arrived in Missouri in July 1830, he received another revelation designating Independence, Missouri, as "the land of promise, and the place for the city of Zion" (D&C 57:2).[88] For the remainder of Joseph Smith's life and beyond, "Zion" became shorthand for Jackson County.

In the following years, the number of Latter-day Saints living in Jackson County grew steadily. The flood of members of this peculiar faith was alarming to some of the original settlers. Missouri was a slave state at the time, and Latter-day Saint converts for the most part came from the abolitionist Northern States. The Saints also held controversial views regarding the fate and destiny of the Native Americans and ambitions to remake the county after their own designs. While the Saints appear to have been aware of the growing tensions, they were also enamored of the dream of the holy city.

The Plat of the City of Zion, sent to Church leaders in Missouri early in the summer of 1833, illustrates the grand plans of the city but also the practical details of its creation. Created as a collaborative effort among the members of the First Presidency—Joseph Smith, Sidney Rigdon, and Frederick G. Williams—the plat is essentially the master plan for the city of God. Written around the edges of the plans are detailed notes about the nature of the city. The city was to be one square mile with a grid system outlining rectangular blocks with lots laid out for homes and gardens. In many ways the plat resembled urban land division patterns utilized throughout the United States in the 1830s. In other ways the plat was highly unusual.[89]

The place where the design of the city diverged from other American communities was found at the heart of the map, where two prominent rectangles sat with numbers from 1 to 24 inside of them. This was meant to designate a sacred place at the center of the city where a complex of twenty-four temples was to be built. Based on the plans, these temples were intended for a different function than later Latter-day Saint temples. Rather than concerning themselves primarily with ordinances for the living and the dead, these temples were intended to serve as administrative centers. In divisions of three temples each, they were assigned to various Church organizations to house their labors. For instance, temples 10, 11, and 12 were designated as "the house of the Lord for the presidency of the high and most holy priesthood." Other temple trios were identified by titles such as "the house of the Lord for the presidency of the high priesthood after the order of [Aaron]," "the house of the Lord for the teachers in Zion," "the house of the Lord for the Deacons in Zion," and so forth.[90]

Though the city in Independence was supposed to be the center place and the starting point for the kingdom of God on the earth, it was not intended to be the only city built after this pattern. In the explanatory notes, the First Presidency explains, "When this square is laid off and supplied lay off another in the same way and so fill up these last days and let every man live in the City for this is the City of Zion."[91] The early Saints held on to this utopian dream of filling the world with celestial cities to serve as places of refuge for the righteous, even after Joseph Smith's death in 1844. The year after the Prophet was martyred, Apostle Parley P. Pratt even wrote a piece of speculative fiction where he imagined the world a hundred years in the future, after the Savior had already returned to earth in triumphal glory. Pratt imagined "digging the foundation of our new Temple in the 124th city of Joseph, near where it is supposed the City of New York once stood."[92]

Over time, the Saints' conception of Zion underwent refinement. In the midst of severe persecution, the Lord explained to the Saints, "Let Zion rejoice, for this is Zion—the pure in heart (D&C 97:21).[93] Only a few months after the design for the city was sent to Missouri, severe persecutions erupted in Jackson County, and the Saints were forcibly ejected from their promised land. The dream of Zion persisted, however, and not just as an abstract concept. While the Lord designated Zion as the pure in heart, in the same revelation he also declared, "Zion cannot fall, neither be moved out of her place" (D&C 97:19),

and in another revelation He declared, "Zion shall not be moved out of her place, notwithstanding her children are scattered."[94]

Is the June 1833 plat the final design for the city the Saints will build before Christ returns to earth? It is unlikely that the design will be followed with complete exactness, if only because Joseph and his contemporaries continued to tinker with the design in their own lifetimes. In early August 1833, the First Presidency sent a more detailed and expanded design for the city to the Saints in Missouri.[95] In a letter accompanying the new plat, Oliver Cowdery explained, "Those patterns previously sent you . . . were incorrect in some respects, being drawn in great haste. They have therefore drawn these, which are correct."[96] The new plan was even more explicit about the heart of the city consisting of a temple complex, with small temples drawn in the center instead of numbers. It also appears that, though the general design of the city was given by inspiration, the details of the city became a product of mutual collaboration. For instance, in September 1833, Presiding Bishop Edward Partridge sent a proposed revision of the temple complex designed to create more equal spacing between the structures.[97] These changes suggest that when the City of Zion is eventually built it will be a collaborative effort among Church leaders. The composition of the temple complex in the city reflected the nature of Church organizations at the time. If the city was built today it would undoubtedly include a complex of temples for the Twelve Apostles, the Presidency of the Seventy, and perhaps even the Relief Society or other important administrative bodies within the Church. Church leaders might also take greater pains to cooperate with surrounding communities. The June 1833 plat of Zion assumed the new city would be built over the top of half of the existing city of Independence, while the August 1833 plan covered Independence entirely.[98]

Today, the lot at the heart of the City of Zion contains no Latter-day Saint temples, though a stately temple was dedicated in Clay County, just a few miles to the north, in 2012. A temple built by the Community of Christ was dedicated on the temple lot in 1993, and parts of the lot are currently owned by different groups, including the Church of Christ (Hedrickite), Community of Christ, and The Church of Jesus Christ of Latter-day Saints. Though the land is still treated as a sacred space by Latter-day Saints, the design of the city ultimately became more influential as the Saints expanded throughout the world. Traces of the city's design are found wherever Latter-day Saints have built cities or clustered around temples. Though Latter-day Saints fervently believe the city of God will yet be built, it must also first have a people fit to occupy it. As Elder Orson F. Whitney taught, "The conquest of Zion is more than the purchase or recovery of lands, the building of cities, or even the founding of nations. It is the conquest of the heart, the subjugation of the soul, the sanctifying of the flesh, the purifying and ennobling of the passions."[99]

8. PHOEBE WOODRUFF FAMILY LETTER

– *Private Collector* –

Although the life of Wilford Woodruff, fourth prophet of The Church of Jesus Christ of Latter-day Saints, is well known, relatively little is known about his first wife, Phoebe Carter Woodruff, and her equally remarkable journey of faith.[100] Phoebe's journey began in the year 1834 when, at the age of twenty-seven, she came into contact with Latter-day Saint missionaries and embraced the message of the restored gospel of Jesus Christ.[101] Like many converts of her generation, she felt compelled to leave her home in Maine and join with the gathering Saints in Kirtland. Her parents, still unconvinced of the truth of their daughter's newfound faith, were grieved at the thought of losing her to the Latter-day Saints. Her mother in particular, much opposed to Phoebe's conversion, told her that "she would rather see her buried than going thus alone into the heartless world," and was especially concerned about her leaving home to cast her lot among the Mormons. 'Phoebe,' she asked impressively, 'will you come back to me if you find Mormonism false?' To this Phoebe answered thrice, 'Yes mother I will.'"[102]

On the day of her departure, one year following her conversion, Phoebe "dared not trust herself to say farewells," so she wrote a goodbye to each member of the family, the many errors of spelling and punctuation a testament to her haste. Leaving the letters on the table, she rushed out the door and into a waiting carriage. "Thus I left my beloved home of childhood, . . . to link my life with the saints of God."[103]

Only recently have the letters Phoebe wrote that day come into circulation. A treasure trove of Church history, they highlight the faith and conviction of this new convert. "Mother," she writes, "I believe it is the will of God for me to go to the west and I have been convinced that it has been for a long time." Phoebe's parting words were characteristic of her emphatic faith and obedience, "I go because my Master calls." And at the close of the letter she leaves this counsel to her family: "You know not what the Lord can do for you until you give up to him and obey his command."[104] Having given up home and family, embarking on the 1,000-mile journey alone, Phoebe proved that she was indeed willing to obey.[105]

Shortly after her arrival in Kirtland, Phoebe found acquaintance with a young man by the name of Wilford Woodruff, and, after a "lengthy" courtship of two and a half months, they were married on April 13, 1837, at Kirtland, Ohio.[106] In May of the same year when Wilford was called on a mission to the Fox Islands, Phoebe returned home to Maine to be in the care of her family. On July 14, 1838, while residing at home, Phoebe gave birth to their first child, a little girl named Sarah Emma.[107] When Woodruff received communication that he was called to be one of the Twelve Apostles and was to leave for Missouri, Phoebe's parents "pled for her to stay with them for the sake of the child, but she went on to Nauvoo with her husband to be with the body of Saints."[108]

Three years prior, in 1835, in the letter that Phoebe had left for her family before first leaving for Kirtland, she had written, in apparent response to her mother's concern that should she leave she might die on the journey, "If it is for the best for me to go there and lay down this body I think I feel willing."[109] The test of that conviction came on a Tuesday evening in early December of 1838, while Phoebe and Wilford were traveling with their infant, Sarah, to join the body of Saints in Nauvoo.

On November 23, while she and Wilford were travelling, Phoebe was attacked with a severe headache which progressed into brain fever. At the same time, their child, Sarah, also became very ill. After a week on the trail, Wilford, seeing the worsening condition of his wife, took his family to an inn. On the evening of December 3, Phoebe called Wilford to her bedside and said "she felt as though a few moments more would end her existence in this life. She manifested great confidence in the cause she had embraced and exhorted [him] to have confidence in God and keep his commandments."[110]

"To all appearances," Wilford wrote, "she was dying. I laid hand upon her and prayed for her, and she soon revived." However, two days later, her condition again worsened, and it appears that her spirit did leave her body. Phoebe later recounted to Wilford that whilst he and the other sisters present were gathered around weeping, Phoebe had looked down on them, on her sick infant, Sarah, and on her own body lying on the bed. While thus gazing on the scene, she had conversed in spirit with two messengers that had entered the room. They told her that they had come for her body.

One of these messengers informed her that she could have her choice: she might go to rest in the spirit world, or, on one condition she could have the privilege of returning to her tabernacle and continuing her labors upon the earth. The condition was that she felt that she could stand by her husband, and with him pass through all the cares, trials, tribulation, and afflictions of life that he would be called to pass through for the gospel's sake unto the end. When she looked at the situation of her husband and child she said, "Yes, I will do it!"[111]

At the precise moment of Phoebe's declaration, Wilford felt the power of God rest upon him and, for the first time during Phoebe's sickness, faith filled his soul. Acting on a strong impression, Wilford Woodruff laid hands on his wife and blessed her that her spirit return to her body. Her spirit entered her tabernacle, and she saw the messengers exit the room.

It was a mere year and a half later when Phoebe was again faced with death. This time it came not to her but to her two-year-old daughter, Sarah Emma. When Phoebe wrote her mother to inform her of her daughter's death, she acknowledged her mother's fears that her daughter would die on the journey. In the letter, she expressed in touching verse both the death of her daughter and her unyielding faith: "My daughter first could sing away the cold, but when thin hands were still and laughter sighed, I gathered all that memory could hold. . . . I would return were this, my faith, not true, but neither child nor I can come to you."[112]

Despite continuing hardship, Phoebe held fast to the promise she had made at the time of her near-death, that she would stand by her husband through whatever trials he may be called to pass through. One of the greatest tests to her willingness to keep this promise came with the preaching and practice of plural marriage. Some time after her husband was made President of the Church, Phoebe was asked to address the women of the Church on this subject. "We are sealed to our husbands for time and eternity, that we may dwell with them and our children in the world to come; which guarantees unto us the greatest blessing for which we are created," Phoebe declared. And then she continued, "If the rulers of the nation will so far depart from the spirit and letter of our glorious constitution as to deprive our prophets, apostles and elders of citizenship, and imprison them for obeying this law, let them grant this, our last request, to make their prisons large enough to hold their wives, for where they go we will go also."[113]

Phoebe's faith was characteristic of many of the early Saints who left family and home to join with the Church. It was that faith, inscribed deeply in each word of her letter and lived valiantly in every ensuing act of her life, that enabled her to be true to her word, standing by her husband and her faith amidst every trial through which they were called to pass and every sacrifice they were called to make.

No doubt influenced by their daughter's faith, Phoebe's parents and siblings eventually joined the Church, eventually baptized by Wilford Woodruff. In his later years, President Woodruff would remark of his devoted wife, "Phoebe possessed too much firmness and faith and confidence in God to put her hand to the plough and then look back, or to give way to trials, however great."[114]

9. VILATE KIMBALL MISSION TAPESTRY

– Private Collector –

On July 23, 1837, Heber C. Kimball delivered a historic sermon in the Vauxhall Chapel in Preston, England. This address to a group of investigators, given only three days after Heber C. Kimball arrived in England with a group of missionaries, was the first sermon by a Latter-day Saint given in England. To commemorate this important event, Heber C. Kimball's wife, Vilate Kimball, made a 22-by-34-inch hook rug depicting the Vauxhall Chapel with the initials of her husband on one side and the year of the sermon on the other. This hook rug, which the Kimball family used as a tapestry in their home, is regarded as "one of the earliest surviving Mormon handicrafts."[115] Besides this fact, the rug/tapestry is meaningful because it also represents an important moment in the history of missionary work in The Church of Jesus Christ of Latter-day Saints and the growth of the early Church in England.

On June 4, 1837, a little less than a month before this historic event, Joseph Smith approached Heber C. Kimball in the Kirtland Temple and whispered, "Brother Heber, the Spirit of the Lord has whispered to me: 'Let my servant Heber go to England and proclaim my Gospel, and open the door of salvation to that nation.'"[116] Kimball was then set apart by the First Presidency "to preside over a mission to England, to be the first foreign mission of the Church of Christ in the last days."[117]

Elder Kimball, along with Orson Hyde, Willard Richards, Joseph Fielding, John Goodson, Isaac Russell, and John Snyder, immediately set sail for England. The missionaries arrived in Liverpool on July 20, 1837, and traveled to Preston, England, where Joseph Fielding's brother, James Fielding, taught as a reverend at the small Anglican church building known as the Vauxhall Chapel. Elder Kimball remembers that on Sunday, July 23, he and the other Elders sat in the chapel "praying to the Lord to open the way for us to preach."[118] To their surprise, the reverend then announced to the congregation that the missionaries would be speaking at three o'clock that day. Elder Kimball, summarizing the events of this historic day, wrote,

> I declared that an angel had visited the earth, and committed the everlasting Gospel to man; called their attention to the first principles of the Gospel; and gave them a brief history of the nature of the work which the Lord had commenced on the earth; after which Elder Hyde bore testimony to the same, which was received by many with whom I afterwards conversed; they cried, "glory to God," and rejoiced that the Lord had sent His servants unto them. Thus was the key turned and the Gospel dispensation opened on the first Sabbath after landing in England.[119]

Another meeting was held that same evening where Elder John Goodson spoke. Then on Wednesday night Elder Orson Hyde addressed the congregation. Of this, Reverend James Fielding famously remarked, "Kimball bored the holes, Goodson drove the nails, and Hyde clinched them."[120] Reverend Fielding, realizing that many members of his congregation planned to be baptized, subsequently banned the missionaries from preaching in the Vauxhall Chapel.

Only a week following the Vauxhall Chapel sermon, Elder Heber C. Kimball baptized the first members of The Church of Jesus Christ of Latter-day Saints in England in the River Ribble in Preston. He wrote that at nine o'clock in the morning on July 30, 1837, he baptized nine converts, "hailing them brethren and sisters in the kingdom of God." Kimball also wrote, "A circumstance took place which I cannot refrain from mentioning, for it will show the eagerness and anxiety of some in that land to obey the Gospel. Two of the male candidates, when they had changed their clothes at a distance of several rods from the place where I was standing in the water, were so anxious to obey the Gospel that they ran with all their might to the water, each wishing to be baptized first. The younger, George D. Watt, being quicker of foot than the elder, outran him, and came first into the water." These two men were the first "persons baptized into the Church in a foreign land."[121] It is estimated that there were more than six hundred convert baptisms that first year. Convert baptisms increased drastically over the following decades with an estimated thirty-four thousand in the 1840s and forty-three thousand in the 1850s. In this way, "the opening of the British Mission may properly be recognized as the beginning of the internationalization of the Church."[122]

Missionary work in England, which began in the Vauxhall Chapel, contributed greatly to the growth of the Church as a whole in these early years. As Brigham Young, Heber C. Kimball, Orson Pratt, and Parley P. Pratt wrote in a letter to the members of the Church, the first mission to England will certainly "stand on record, for the wondering gazes of succeeding ages."[123] The tapestry—now in the possession of collector Reid N. Moon, the descendant of Mathias and Hannah Moon who Elder Heber C. Kimball baptized while serving in Preston—commemorates the early missionary work in England and the thousands of faithful English converts who responded to Heber C. Kimball and other missionaries' call to be baptized.[124]

10. KIRTLAND SAFETY SOCIETY NOTES

– Community of Christ Library –

The pentecostal outpouring accompanying the dedication of the house of the Lord in Kirtland was a spiritual feast unlike any known in the history of the Church. It is somewhat ironic that this season of revelation and light was almost immediately followed by one of the worst apostasies in the history of the Church. The temple dedication took place in the spring of 1836. By January 1838, just over a year and half later, Joseph Smith and most of those still loyal to him left Kirtland in a forced exodus. What was the cause of such a dramatic reversal of fortune in Kirtland? Many historians tie the collapse of the Church in Ohio to the financial difficulties surrounding the Kirtland Safety Society, and with good reason. At the same time, finance was only one factor of many in the apostasy in Kirtland. The larger question under consideration was, what is the role of a prophet in the Church of Jesus Christ?[125]

By 1836, the Church was grappling with a number of difficulties linked to the influx of converts into the regions around Kirtland. The number of members in the Church had grown significantly in a relatively short period of time, and the new converts flooding into the region tended to be impoverished and in possession of little wealth. At the same time, the construction of the Kirtland Temple placed a considerable strain on Church resources. In Decem- ber 1836, Church leaders held a special conference to address the issue. The minutes of the conference demonstrated the desire to slow the growth in the area,[126] following the directives given to the Missouri Saints in an earlier revelation, which reads, "Now verily I saw unto you, let all the churches gather together all their moneys; let these things be done in their time, but not in haste; and observe to have all these things prepared before" (D&C 101:72).[127]

The situation was also exacerbated by the pressure Joseph Smith felt to provide for all of the poor in the Kirtland area. Joseph ran a store in Kirtland but felt compelled to give away much of his merchandise on credit to help the disadvantaged members in the area. During a sermon given in 1852, Brigham Young explained the Prophet's dilemma: "Joseph goes to New York and buys 20,000 dollar's worth of goods, comes into Kirtland and commences to trade. In comes one of the brethren, 'Brother Joseph, let me have a frock pattern for my wife.' What if Joseph says, 'No, I cannot without the money.' The consequence would be, 'He is no prophet,' says James. . . . After a while, in comes Bill and sister Susan. Says Bill, 'Brother Joseph, I want a shawl, I have not got the money, but I wish you to trust me a week or a fortnight.' Well, brother Joseph thinks the others have gone and apostatized, and he don't know but these goods will make the whole Church do the same, so he lets Bill have the shawl."[128]

In this case Brigham was trying to demonstrate the difficulties present in trying to provide for the people both temporally and spiritually. While the Kirtland Saints enjoyed some of the most profound spiritual manifestations of any era, their community collapsed when the Kirtland Safety Society ran into difficulty. In January 1837, Sidney Rigdon, Joseph Smith, and other officers of the Kirtland Safety Society met together to draw up a new set of rules to govern the operation of the society. Elder Orson Hyde was assigned in November 1836 to locate a politician to petition the Ohio state legislature for a bank charter. Hyde was unable to present his petition to the legislature until February 1837, so the society was officially named the Kirtland Safety Society Anti-Banking Company. The Ohio state legislature refused to grant any bank petitions that year, but the need for capital in the Kirtland area was so great that Joseph and his associates moved ahead with the Safety Society.[129]

Beginning in January 1837, the Safety Society began printing notes intended to function as currency. The notes, many of which are still in existence today, were printed through the use of printing plates likely ordered by Oliver Cowdery during a trip to New York City in October 1836. Because of the name change made to the society when its articles were drawn up in January 1837, the words "ANTI" and "ING CO" appear on many of the first notes. Most of the notes featured pastoral scenes of farm life, though the $100 dollar note was adorned with a picture of the American constitutional convention. Most of the notes carried the signatures of Joseph Smith and Sidney Rigdon, though some of the notes were signed by three interim officers of the society, Newell K. Whitney, Frederick G. Williams, and Horace Kingsbury.[130]

The Kirtland Safety Society began to experience difficulty almost immediately after it opened. By the summer of 1837, Joseph Smith and Sidney Rigdon had both resigned as officers of the institution. By August of that year, Joseph Smith publicly warned investors not to affiliate with the society or use its notes. By September of 1837, the Kirtland Safety Society was closed permanently, leaving in its wake a massive amount of debt and bringing financial ruin upon the Church in Kirtland.[131]

What caused the rapid and cataclysmic fall of the Kirtland Safety Society? Several factors were involved. First, a financial panic swept through the nation beginning in 1837. The Panic of 1837, as it came to be known, was caused in part by the anti-banking policies of President Andrew Jackson. It led to the closure of hundreds of banks throughout the United States.[132] Second, Grandison Newell, a merchant from the neighboring city of Painesville, organized a run on the banknotes issued by the society. Large amounts of the bills were collected and cashed in, with the bank unable to provide the specie promised by the notes.[133] Finally, internal dissensions among Church members contributed to the failure of the society. As the society spiraled into ruin, many Saints who invested heavily in its success became disaffected with the Church. For example, John Johnson, a wealthier member in the Kirtland area, purchased 3,000 shares in the society, pledging much of his property as collateral. When Johnson withdrew from the Church, he took his property with him, a move that threatened the solvency of the society. Though Johnson's actions violated the terms and conditions of the Safety Society, no legal action was ever taken against him. In the midst of these reversals, Joseph Smith and Sidney Rigdon left the society, leaving it in the hands of Warren Parrish and Frederick G. Williams, who were both disaffected from the Church. Though the society was on the brink of ruin, Parrish and Williams continued to make loans by issuing more banknotes. A review of the financial records indicates that Parrish in particular abused his position as president of the society until its closure.[134]

Joseph Smith and his family held more shares in the Kirtland Safety Society than any other group and in turn suffered the greatest losses.[135] The collapse of the society led to a crisis of confidence in Joseph Smith's prophetic leadership. Joseph never denied the role his revelations played in the creation of the Safety Society, though he did remind his critics that "he always said that unless the institution was conducted upon righteous principles it could not stand."[136] Wilford Woodruff likewise recorded in his journal that when the Prophet announced he had received the word of the Lord concerning the society, he also commented "that if we would give heed to the Commandments the Lord had given this morning all would be well."[137] Nevertheless, the faith of many of the Saints was shaken by Joseph's inability to prevent the collapse of the bank.

During the ensuing months, discontent and apostasy within the Church in Kirtland grew. Brigham

Young described these dark times in Kirtland: "This was a crisis when earth and hell seemed leagued to overthrow the Prophet and the Church of God. The knees of many of the strongest men in the Church faltered."[138] Several prominent Church leaders, including Martin Harris, became disaffected, while several Apostles became critical of Joseph Smith. Brigham Young attended one meeting where a group of embittered Saints proposed the removal of Joseph Smith in favor of David Whitmer. Remembering the meeting, Brigham later recalled, "I rose up, and in a plain and forcible manner told them that Joseph was a Prophet and I knew it, and that they might rail and slander him as much as they pleased, [but] they could not destroy the appointment of the Prophet of God; they could only destroy their own authority, cut the thread that bound them to the Prophet and to God, and sink themselves to hell. Many were highly enraged at my decided opposition to their measures."[139]

Opposition became so bitter that Joseph Smith and Sidney Rigdon, under threat of their lives, left Kirtland for good on January 12, 1838, just a few days past the year mark since the opening of the Kirtland Safety Society. They arrived a few weeks later in Far West, Missouri, establishing it as the new headquarters of the Church. Supporters of Joseph Smith remained in Kirtland, including Church agents such as Oliver Granger who were directed to sell Church properties to take care of debts (see D&C 118:12–16). In the following months, most of the ardent supporters of Joseph Smith left Kirtland behind, and the city failed to continue as a meaningful center for the Latter-day Saints. The Kirtland bank crisis and subsequent apostasy became one of the most trying times of Joseph Smith's prophetic leadership. Shortly thereafter, the Lord comforted Joseph in a revelation, stating, "I, the Lord, will build up Kirtland, but I, the Lord, have a scourge prepared for the inhabitants thereof" (D&C 124:83).

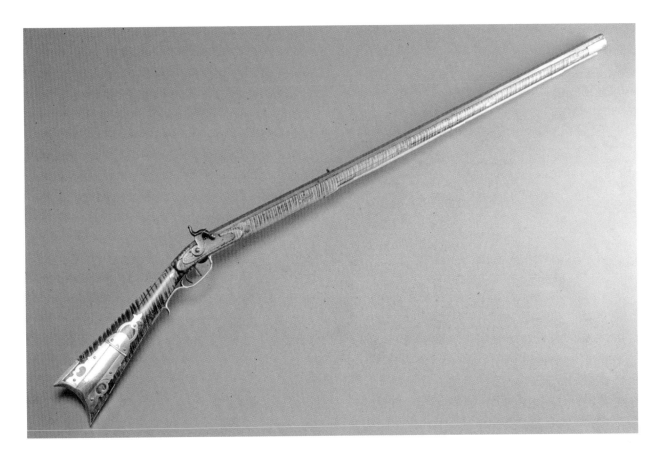

11. DAVID PATTEN'S RIFLE

– Church History Museum –

From the earliest days of the Restoration, the Saints contended with persecution and conflict in their quest to build up the kingdom of God on the earth. Church members saw their homes and livelihoods decimated as they were driven from place to place during the first two decades of the Restoration. Along the way they lost friends and family to mob violence. The most serious violence inflicted on Church members during the leadership of Joseph Smith occurred in the fall of 1838 in northern Missouri. By the end of the conflict, the Church lay in ruins, Joseph Smith and several of his close associates sat in a horrific prison, and the first apostolic martyr of this dispensation, David W. Patten, was laid to rest.

The conflict, known as the Mormon War of 1838, was the end result of a long chain of conflict beginning with the first Latter-day Saint missionaries to arrive in Missouri in 1830. Revelations given to Joseph Smith identified Jackson County, Missouri, as the place for the city of Zion in the latter days (see D&C 57:13).[140] The persecutions of 1833 in Jackson County led to the ejection of the Saints from the location of Zion. For several years following the persecutions, the Saints in Missouri struggled as religious refugees in

Clay County and the surrounding areas. Hope appeared again for the Saints in December 1836, when the Missouri legislature created Caldwell County in northern Missouri specifically for the settlement of the Latter-day Saints.[141]

As Church members gathered in the new county, tensions with their neighbors continued to rise. Joseph Smith himself relocated to the new Church headquarters of Far West in March 1838, following the collapse of the Church in Kirtland. Following in his path came several companies of Saints from Kirtland, some of whom stopped to rest at the settlement of Hawn's Mill in the southwest corner of Caldwell County. Hawn's Mill was a burgeoning settlement threatening to spill over into non–Latter-day Saint territory.[142]

Tensions continued to build throughout the summer of 1838. After Joseph Smith's arrival in Far West, several prominent Latter-day Saints, including Oliver Cowdery, were excommunicated. On June 17, 1839, Sidney Rigdon, Joseph's first counselor, preached a fiery sermon condemning the apostates as "salt that had lost its savor" and declaring them to be "good for nothing but to be cast out." At the same time several Church members formed a group known as the Danites, a quasi-militant organization intended to defend the Saints and "to cleanse the Church of very great evils."[143] All the while Saints continued to pour into Caldwell County, a development viewed with disdain by many of the original settlers. Tensions finally boiled over in Gallatin, Missouri, on August 6, 1838, when an angry crowd physically blocked a group of Latter-day Saints from entering voting booths for a local election. Tempers flared, and soon a full-fledged riot broke out.[144]

Over the next few weeks an escalating series of conflicts took place as both sides raided the other's settlements. Elder Patten led a targeted raid on Gallatin to disperse the opposition forces. Property was burned and families displaced, but no lives were

taken until the Battle of Crooked River. On October 24, 1838, Reverend Samuel Bogart led a contingent of Missouri state militia into a disputed tract of land on the southern end of Caldwell County. As the militia ranged about through the region, it harassed Latter-day Saints in their settlements and destroyed property along the way. During these actions the militia took three young Latter-day Saint men, Nathan Pinkham Jr., William Seely, and Addison Green, as hostages. The militia then withdrew to a carefully selected encampment on Crooked River. When word of the attack reached Far West, a militia unit led by Elder David Wyman Patten, an Apostle, was dispatched to rescue the hostages.[145]

David Wyman Patten was baptized into the Church by his brother, John Patten, on June 17, 1832.[146] One physical description of David reads, "He stood six feet and one inch in height, and weighed over two hundred pounds; but there seems to have been no room in his whole generous composition for a particle of doubt."[147] Patten soon proved himself to be a gifted missionary, noted for his faith in a number of remarkable healings. According to Abraham O. Smoot and Wilford Woodruff, contemporary missionaries with Patten, "neither knew an instance in which David's petition for the sick was not answered."[148]

One of Patten's most remarkable converts was a young student at Oberlin College in Ohio named Lorenzo Snow. The two fell into each other's company during a journey from Snow's home in Mantua, Ohio, to Kirtland. President Snow later recalled, "On the way our conversation fell upon religion and philosophy, and being young and having enjoyed some scholastic advantages, I was at first disposed to treat his opinions lightly . . . but as he proceeded in an earnest and humble way to open up before my mind the plan of salvation, I seemed unable to resist the knowledge that he was a man of God and that his testimony was true." President Snow added, "What impressed me most was his absolute sincerity, his earnestness and his spiritual power."[149]

In 1835, Patten was selected to serve as one of the original Apostles of this dispensation. Since all of the Apostles received their call around the same time, seniority in the quorum was determined by age. Thomas B. Marsh misremembered his date of birth (something not uncommon at the time) and was chosen to serve as president of the quorum. Research carried out by scholars in the twentieth century revealed that Patten was born on November 17, 1799, while Marsh was born on November 1, 1800. Marsh mistakenly believed his birthday was in 1799. The mistake was never discovered in Patten's lifetime, but if Church leaders had been in possession of all the facts at the time the Quorum of the Twelve was ordained, David W. Patten would have been ordained as the first president of the quorum in this dispensation.[150]

In November of 1835, Joseph Smith received a revelation chastising the Twelve for a lack of humility and unity. Elder Patten, along with Elders William Smith, Orson Hyde, and William E. McLellan, were specifically singled out in the revelation, though the entire quorum was rebuked because, in the Lord's words, "they have made themselves unequal and have not hearkened unto my voice."[151] Very little is known about the reasons for this rebuke, but unlike Elders Hyde and McLellan, who both challenged Joseph Smith over the revelation, Elder Patten accepted the rebuke and nothing was said further.[152]

Elder Patten apparently suffered one serious break with Joseph Smith during the financial crisis in Kirtland in 1837. Patten arrived in Kirtland when the crisis was at its height. The Apostles initially met with Brigham Young, who intended to explain the problem while absolving Joseph Smith of any guilt. Patten instead met with Warren Parrish, his brother-in-law and one of the primary leaders of the insurgency against Joseph Smith's leadership. David was also influenced negatively by Thomas B. Marsh and Parley P. Pratt, who were both disaffected at the time. After listening to Parrish and others, David confronted the Prophet. Years later, Wilford Woodruff related the incident as he had heard Brigham Young tell him: "He [Brigham Young] said that David Patten & T. B. Marsh came to Kirtland in the fall of 1837. He said as soon as I got Marsh to go to Joseph, but Patten would go to W. Parrish. He got his mind prejudiced & when he went to see Joseph David in[sult?]ed Joseph & Joseph slapped him in the face & kicked him out of the yard. This done David good."[153] Apparently, David and Joseph reconciled after this incident. There are no further mentions of Patten's apostasy from the time.

Following the collapse of the Church in Kirtland, Patten relocated to Missouri. Along with Thomas B. Marsh, he was appointed to serve as President pro tempore of the Church in Missouri when the previous presidency, consisting of W. W. Phelps, John Whitmer, and David Whitmer, were released for apostasy.[154] In April 1838, Joseph Smith received a revelation calling on Patten to "settle up his business as soon as he possibly can . . . that he may perform a mission unto me next spring."[155] One of Patten's biographers connected this revelation to a conversation reported by Wilford Woodruff: "David made known to the Prophet that he has asked the Lord to let him die the death of a martyr, at which the Prophet, greatly moved, expressed extreme sorrow, 'for,' he said to David, 'when a man of your faith asks the Lord for anything, he generally gets it.'"[156]

Several months after this episode Elder Patten led a contingent of militia to rescue the three hostages by the Missouri militia. Elder Patten's company discovered the encampment of the hostile militia, but came under fire from fortified positions. It is not known who fired first, but it quickly became clear that the Missourians held a strategic advantage in their positions of cover. Realizing his men were completely exposed to enemy fire, Patten ordered a charge directly into the enemy positions. The charge startled the Missourians, who fled in panic, but came at a steep cost. Patten led the charge, exposed to fire and an obvious target wearing a bright white coat. "He was brave to a fault," Ebenezer Robinson later wrote, "so much so, that he was styled and called, 'Captain Fearnaught.' He seemed reckless of his life, as though it was scarce worth preserving." Charles C. Rich was nearby when he saw Patten receive his fatal wound, later recalling, "Patten ordered us to charge—the enemy fired a few shots and fled, two lingered behind, brother Patten pursued one, and I the other; the man that he pursued wheeled and shot him."[157]

The hostages were rescued and the Missourians routed, but when the smoke cleared, one Missourian was dead. The Saints fared worse—a non–Latter-day Saint guide and two members of the militia were fatally wounded, including Elder Patten. With blood now spilt, Governor Lilburn L. Boggs, an old antagonist of the Saints from Jackson County, accused the Saints collectively of having "made war upon the people of this State." He then issued an order to the Missouri militia, which reads, "The Mormons must be treated as enemies and must be exterminated or driven from the state . . . their outrages are beyond all description."[158]

Suffering a serious wound in the lower abdomen, Patten and other wounded members of the company began the journey back to Far West, carried by their companions. According to one account, Patten was in so much distress that he asked to be left behind. As they traveled northward, they were met by a group led by Joseph Smith heading south to assist with the wounded. The group stopped at the home of Stephen Winchester to allow the wounded to recuperate. Heber C. Kimball remembered people offering Patten assistance but writing, "Yet his wound was such, that there was no hope entertained of his recovery; this he was perfectly aware of." On his deathbed, perhaps thinking of the recent apostasy of several Apostles, Patten reaffirmed his testimony of the gospel and his faith in eternal life. Speaking to his childless wife, Phoebe Ann, he said, "Whatever you do else, O, do not deny the faith!" A few minutes before his death, he prayed, "Father I ask thee, in the name of Jesus Christ, that thou wouldst release my spirit and receive it unto thyself." He then turned to the men surrounding his bed and said, "Brethren, you have held me by your faith, but do give me up and let me go I beseech you." David W. Patten died a few moments later.[159] At Patten's funeral held the following day, Joseph Smith remarked, "There lies a man that has done just as he said he would—he has laid down his life for his friends."[160]

The rifle David W. Patten carried with him on that fateful day at Crooked River, made of curly maple wood with silver inlays, now resides in the custody of the Church, along with a shot pouch and powder horn also used by Elder Patten at the battle.[161] It is not known if the rifle was fired in the battle. Most accounts indicate that Patten and his company charged into the murderous fire and scattered the Missourians with their swords drawn, not using their firearms.[162]

David W. Patten is not only unique for being the first apostolic martyr of this dispensation, but also in having the Lord specifically note the final destination of his soul. In a revelation given to Joseph Smith in 1840, the Lord declared, "David Patten I have taken unto myself" (D&C 124:130).

12. Liberty Jail Door

– Community of Christ Temple –

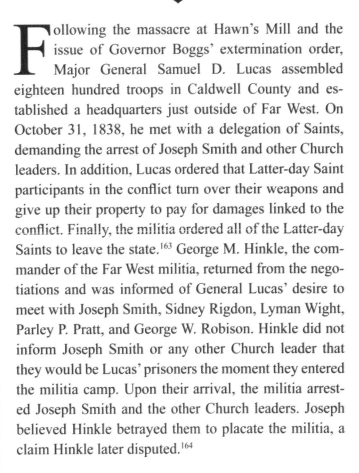

Following the massacre at Hawn's Mill and the issue of Governor Boggs' extermination order, Major General Samuel D. Lucas assembled eighteen hundred troops in Caldwell County and established a headquarters just outside of Far West. On October 31, 1838, he met with a delegation of Saints, demanding the arrest of Joseph Smith and other Church leaders. In addition, Lucas ordered that Latter-day Saint participants in the conflict turn over their weapons and give up their property to pay for damages linked to the conflict. Finally, the militia ordered all of the Latter-day Saints to leave the state.[163] George M. Hinkle, the commander of the Far West militia, returned from the negotiations and was informed of General Lucas' desire to meet with Joseph Smith, Sidney Rigdon, Lyman Wight, Parley P. Pratt, and George W. Robison. Hinkle did not inform Joseph Smith or any other Church leader that they would be Lucas' prisoners the moment they entered the militia camp. Upon their arrival, the militia arrested Joseph Smith and the other Church leaders. Joseph believed Hinkle betrayed them to placate the militia, a claim Hinkle later disputed.[164]

A trial was quickly held, and Lucas sentenced the prisoners to execution. He sent his official orders to Alexander W. Doniphan, which read, "Sir: you will take Joseph Smith and the other prisoners into the public square of Far West, and shoot them [at] 9 o'clock tomorrow morning." Doniphan was outraged at the order and wrote back to Lucas, "It is cold-blooded murder. I will not obey your order.

My brigade shall march for Liberty tomorrow morning, [at] 8 o'clock; and if you execute those men, I will hold you responsible before an earthly tribunal, so help me God!" Doniphan's bold stance caused Lucas to back down and postpone the execution.[165]

On November 1, Hinkle accepted the surrender terms of the militia. Latter-day Saint settlements in Far West, Adam-ondi-Ahman, and Hawn's Mill were looted over the next few days as the militia swept into the midst of the unprotected Saints. Apostate William E. McLellin, a former member of the Quorum of the Twelve, now cooperating with the militia, plundered Joseph Smith's home. He was followed by George Hinkle, the former owner of the home, who stole property from the residence and then ejected Emma Smith and her children from the house. During the chaos, members of the militia committed multiple acts of sexual violence, raping several Latter-day Saint women. Approximately forty Latter-day Saints lost their lives in the battles before and during the sack of the Latter-day Saint settlements in Northern Missouri.[166]

The militia paraded Joseph Smith and other prisoners in front of the Saints in Far West. Joseph later wrote, "We were taken to the town, into the public square; and before our departure from Far West, we, after much entreaties, were suffered to see our families, being attended all the while with a strong guard; I found my wife and children in tears, who expected we were shot by those who had sworn to take our lives, and that they should see me no more."[167] Lucy Mack Smith, the Prophet's mother, ran up to the wagon he was being taken away in and grasped his hand through the canvas cover before being torn away.[168]

Over the next few weeks, Joseph Smith and the other prisoners moved from confinement in various locations throughout Missouri, ranging from Independence to Richmond. While in Richmond, the Prophet and his associates were confined in chains and kept in a vacant log house near the courthouse. Parley P. Pratt, one of Joseph's companions, recalled a night in Richmond where the guards "boasted of defiling wives, daughters, and virgins, and of shooting or dashing out the brains of men, women, and children." Joseph became so enraged by the taunts of the guards that he jumped to his feet and "spoke in a voice of thunder" declaring, "SILENCE, ye fiends of the infernal pit. In the name of Jesus Christ I rebuke you, and command you to be still; I will not live another minute and bear such language. Cease such talk, or you or I die THIS INSTANT!" Joseph's rebuke left the guards quailing with shame and begging for Joseph's pardon. Pratt later remarked, "dignity and majesty have I seen but *once*, as it stood in chains, at midnight, in a dungeon in an obscure village of Missouri."[169]

During a trial held in November 1838, Judge Austin A. King ruled that there was probable cause to believe that Joseph Smith, Hyrum Smith, Lyman Wight, Alexander McRae, Caleb Baldwin, and Sidney Rigdon were guilty of treason. On December 1, 1838, Joseph Smith and his companions were sent to Liberty, the seat of Clay County, Missouri, to await a trial in the spring. They remained in the Liberty Jail for the next five months. One resident of Liberty later described the arrival of the Latter-day Saint prisoners at the jail: "The inhabitants of Liberty, and many from the surrounding country, were out to witness the entrance of the prisoners into the place, and many, on that occasion, expressed their disappointment that the strangers should so much resemble all other men of prepossessing appearance . . . one by one, the tall and well-proportioned forms of the prisoners entered. . . . Joseph Smith was the last of the number who lingered behind. He turned partly around, with a slow and dignified movement and looked upon the multitude. Then turning away and lifting his hat he said in a distinct voice, 'Good afternoon gentlemen.' The next moment he passed out of sight."[170]

Liberty Jail was destined to become one of the most sacred places in Church history, but its initial appearance filled the prisoners with dread and foreboding. The walls of the jail were four feet thick, consisting of limestone and oak. There was only one way in and out of the jail—through thick double iron doors at the top of a short flight of stairs. The jail consisted of two floors: a top floor with two windows, each with thick iron bars to prevent escape, and a dungeon below. In the center of the top floor there was a trapdoor—the only entrance to the lower floor. The dungeon was a 14-foot by 14.5-foot space just 6.5 feet high. The walls and floor of the dungeon were built entirely of stone, with just two windows, 2 feet wide and 6 inches high, with a heavy iron bar running through them horizontally.[171] During their stay, the prisoners' diet consisted of foul food, which the prisoners said were "vittuals of the coarsest kind and served up in a manner which was disgusting."[172] Joseph and his companions slept on dirty straw mattresses on the floor.[173]

Alexander McRae, one of the prisoners, later recalled several attempts to poison the prisoners, including one incident which left them "sorely afflicted, some being blind two or three days, and it was by much faith and prayer that the effect was overcome."[174] Occasionally, the prisoners spent time in the upper floor of the jail. Hyrum Smith met his infant son, Joseph F. Smith, for the first time during a visit to the jail.[175]

In a hearing in January 1839, Sidney Rigdon was released on bail, but Joseph Smith and the rest of the prisoners were remanded back to the jail. Discouraged by the outcome of the trial, the prisoners tried to escape from the jail on February 7. Hyrum Smith forced his way out of the door. The jailers quickly recaptured Hyrum and the other prisoners, firing a shot but not injuring any of the inmates.[176] A few weeks later, the prisoners attempted to escape again by breaking through the wooden inner walls of the prison. However, when they reached the outer layer of rock, their tools broke. While they were seeking outside assistance, their plan was discovered, and security at the jail was increased.[177]

Joseph described the conditions in Liberty Jail in one of the letters written during his incarceration as follows: "We are kept under a strong guard, night and day, in a prison of double walls and doors, proscribed in our liberty of conscience, our food is scant, uniform, and coarse; we have not the privilege of cooking for ourselves, we have been compelled to sleep on the floor with straw, and not blankets sufficient to keep us warm; and when we have a fire, we are obliged to have almost a constant smoke. The Judges have gravely told us from time to time that they knew we were innocent, and ought to be liberated, but they dare not administer the law unto us, for fear of the mob. But if we will deny our religion, we can be liberated."[178]

The travails of the prisoners were exacerbated by the distressing news of the forced exodus of the Church from Missouri. Joseph wrote several tender letters to Emma Smith, empathizing with her suffering. In March 1839, Joseph wrote, "Dear Emma, I very well know your toils and sympathize with you. If God will spare my life once more to have the privilege of taking care of you, I will ease your care and endeavor to comfort your heart. I want you to take the best care of the family you can."[179] The five months Joseph Smith and his associates spent in Liberty Jail rank among the most trying times in the Prophet's life, but the suffering experienced in Liberty Jail also sanctified and transformed the site into one of the holiest locations in Church history.

The Prophet and his fellow prisoners left Liberty in April 1839, but Latter-day Saint fascination with the location and the trying episode of the imprisonment remained. The structure was used as a jail until about 1856, when it was deemed unsafe for human habitation. In the years following it was utilized as an icehouse, a testament to the prisoner's recollection of freezing temperatures within its walls.[180] In 1887, with its roof partially collapsed and its walls crumbling, it was visited by the Prophet's son, Joseph Smith III, then the president of the Reorganized Church of Jesus Christ of Latter-day Saints (RLDS). Joseph III was moved during the visit, later writing, "In humility I am led to raise my heart in thanks to God that I, the son of one of those men imprisoned in that dreary and desolate jail am permitted to live quietly . . . not far from those scenes of violence and persecution."[181] One of Joseph III's associates subsequently heard rumors about the location of the door of the jail, tracked it down, and placed it in the RLDS museum in Graceland College, Iowa. From there it was transferred to the RLDS (now Community of Christ) temple in Independence, Missouri, where the door is currently on display. The door is 29 inches wide, 63 inches high, and 3 inches thick.[182]

In 1903 a private residence was built over the ruins of the jail by Homer R. Stephens. Stephens kept the original dungeon floor and incorporated many of the stones into the walls of his new home. In 1939, the home was purchased by The Church of Jesus Christ of Latter-day Saints. It was subsequently renovated to serve as a missionary home.

In 1949, a missionary couple arrived to serve as custodians of the jail and answer questions. In the early 1960s, the frame home was torn down and replaced with a visitors' center. The heart of the new center was a rotunda featuring a recreation of the jail built on its original stone floor.[183] Over time, the structure has become a vital symbol of the purifying power of trying times. Elder Jeffrey R. Holland noted, "Most of us, most of the time, speak of the facility at Liberty as a 'jail' or a 'prison'—and certainly it was that. But Elder Brigham H. Roberts, in recording the history of the Church, spoke of the facility as a temple, or, more accurately, a 'prison-temple' . . . in what sense could Liberty Jail be called a 'temple'—or at least a kind of temple—in the development of Joseph Smith personally and in his role as a prophet?" He continued, "Every one of us, in one way or another, great or small, dramatic or incidental, is going to spend a little time in Liberty Jail—spiritually speaking . . . But the lessons of the winter of 1838–39 teach us that *every* experience can become a *redemptive* experience if we remain bonded to our Father in Heaven through that difficulty. These difficult lessons teach us that man's extremity is God's opportunity, and if we will be humble and faithful."[184]

13. Joseph Smith Handkerchief

– Church History Museum –

One of the most prominent themes in the revelations given to Joseph Smith is the restoration of miracles, in particular the power of healing the sick. In an early revelation given to the Prophet, the Lord cautions to "require not miracles except I command" but does make an exception for "casting out devils and healing the sick" (D&C 24:13).[185] In another revelation, given in 1832, the Lord declares that Apostles called in God's name "shall do many wonderful works, in my name they shall cast out devils, in my name they shall heal the sick" (D&C 84:67–68).[186] The power to heal was seen by the Saints as an important connection to the labors of Christ and his disciples.

One of the most dramatic recorded incidents of healing occurred in the summer of 1839, after Joseph Smith joined the Saints following his travails in Liberty Jail. After their forced exodus from Missouri, the refugee Saints regrouped on the banks of the Mississippi River near Commerce, Illinois. When the Saints arrived in Commerce it was little more than a malarial swamp. Joseph renamed the city Nauvoo, from a Hebrew word meaning "beautiful." Joseph's optimistic expectations were offset by the awful conditions found in the swamp as mosquitoes infected hundreds of Saints with malaria.[187] Wilford Woodruff later wrote, "The large number of Saints who had been driven out of Missouri, were flocking into Commerce; but had no homes to go into, and were living in wagons, in tents, and on the ground. Many, therefore, were sick through the exposure they were subjected to. Brother Joseph waited on the sick, until he was worn out and nearly sick himself."[188] So many Saints fell ill that Joseph gave up his home for the care of the sick and was living in a tent pitched in his yard. Joseph Smith's history from this time reads, "About this time, sickness began to be made manifest itself, much amongst the brethren, as well as among the inhabitants of the place, so that this week and the following was generally spent in visiting the sick, administering unto them, some had faith enough, and were healed, others had not."[189]

According to Elder Woodruff, on the morning of July 22, 1839, Joseph "arose reflecting on the situation of the Saints of God in their persecution and afflictions, and he called upon the Lord in prayer, and the power of God rested upon him mightily." Joseph began first with the sick inside and surrounding his house. Then, accompanied by Sidney Rigdon and several apostles "he went through among the sick lying on the bank of the river, and he commanded them in a loud voice, in the name of Jesus Christ, to come up and be made whole, and they were all healed." Next Joseph crossed the Mississippi River in a ferry boat, arriving at the home of Brigham Young, another victim stricken with illness. Joseph healed Brigham and asked Wilford to accompany him to the next house. Joseph then crossed the public square and entered the home of Elijah Fordham, another stricken Saint. Elder Woodruff then records the following exchange:

When we entered the house, brother Joseph walked up to Brother Fordham, and took him by the right hand. . . . He saw that Brother Fordham's eyes were glazed, and that he was speechless and unconscious. After taking hold of his hand, he looked down into the dying man's face and said:

"Brother Fordham, do you not know me?" At first he made no reply; but we could all see the effect of the Spirit of God resting upon him. He said again: "Elijah, do you not know me?" With a low whisper, brother Fordham answered, "yes!" The Prophet then said, "Have you not faith to be healed?" The answer, which was a little plainer then before was: "I am afraid it is too late. If you had come sooner. I think it might have been." He had the appearance of a man awaking from sleep. It was the sleep of death. Joseph then said, "Do you believe that Jesus is the Christ?" "I do, brother Joseph," was the response. Then the Prophet of God spoke with a loud voice, as in the majesty of the Godhead: "Elijah, I command you, in the name of Jesus of Nazareth, to arise and be made whole!" The words of the Prophet were not like the words of man, but like the voice of God. It seemed to me that the house shook from its foundation. Elijah Fordham leaped from his bed like a man raised from the dead. A healthy color came to his face, and life was manifested in every act.[190]

Elijah Fordham not only left his bed, but accompanied Joseph and the other leaders as they continued to minister to the rest of the sick in the community. Elder Woodruff later noted of Fordham, "In a few minutes more he would have been in the spirit world, had he not been rescued. Through the blessing of God, he lived up till 1880, in which he did in Utah, while all who were with him on that occasion, with the exception of two, are in the spirit world."[191]

Joseph continued to heal throughout the remainder of the day. While waiting for a ferry boat to return home, the Prophet was approached by a man who was not a Latter-day Saint but had heard of Joseph's miraculous healing power. The man told Joseph about his twin children, just five months old, who fell ill and were near death. The Prophet at first said he would visit the children, then paused and turned to Elder Woodruff and said, "You go with the man and heal his children." He took a red silk handkerchief out of his pocket and gave it to Wilford, instructing him to wipe their faces with the handkerchief when he administered to the twins. He added, "As long as you will keep that handkerchief, it shall remain a league between you and me." Joseph's instructions paralleled a passage from the book of Acts where "God wrought special miracles by the hands of Paul" and healed the sick through handkerchiefs sent from the Apostles (Acts 19:11–12). Elder Woodruff adds a simple coda to the story: "I went with the man, and did as the Prophet commanded me, and the children were healed. I have possession of the handkerchief unto this day."[192]

The miraculous healings helped to stem the tide of illness in Nauvoo but did not stop them completely. The notation in Joseph Smith's history for July 22 reads simply, "The sick were ministered unto with great success, but many remain sick and new cases are occurring daily."[193] Elder Woodruff's narrative account was written in 1881, long after the event took place, but he did record a shorter version of the events in his journal at the time of the healings. His journal for July 22, 1839, reads, "Joseph was in Montrose and it was a day of God's power. There was many sick among the Saints on both sides of the river and Joseph went through the midst of them taking them by the hand and in a loud voice commanding them in the name of Jesus Christ to arise from their beds and be made whole and they leaped from their beds made whole. By the power of God Elder Elijah Fordham was one among the number and he with the rest of the sick rose from his bed and followed Joseph from house to and it was truly a time of rejoicing."[194]

The handkerchief stayed with Wilford Woodruff throughout the remainder of his life. One entry in his journal from May 1857, reads, "My daughter Phebe had a very severe attack of inflammation of the lungs or something like plurisy. She could not breathe, ownly with great difficulty. We holstered her up in the bed and she would catch her breath like a person strangling. She was so for several hours. We anointed her, laid hands upon her, and rebuked the disease. I finally got Joseph Smith's silk handkerchief which he gave me in 1839 and said it should ever remain as a league between us as long as I should keep it. I laid it upon her stomach. . . . In the evening she became some better and slept some."[195] The handkerchief eventually passed from the Woodruff family to the custody of the Church, where it now resides in the Church History Museum as an emblem of the restoration of spiritual gifts to the world in the last days, including the gift of healing.

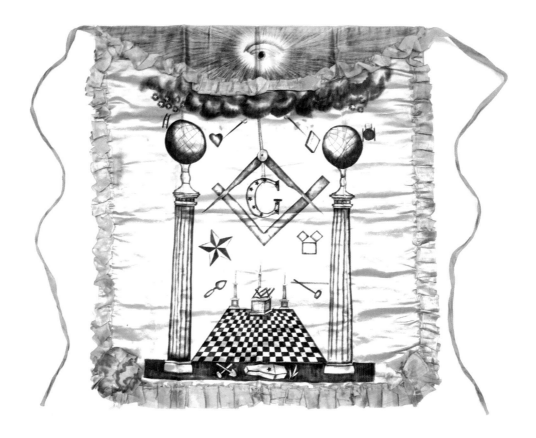

14. Joseph Smith's Masonic Apron

— *Community of Christ Library* —

The founding of Nauvoo allowed the Saints a fresh start, but they brought with them fears and the shared trauma of the persecutions from Missouri and Ohio. Construction of the Nauvoo House and other initiatives signaled a new effort on the part of the Saints to reach out to groups around them. Church leaders attempted to gather allies to prevent a recurrence of the hostilities they faced in Missouri. A number of important Church leaders, including Hyrum Smith, Heber C. Kimball (an Apostle), John Smith (the Prophet's uncle), Newell K. Whitney (a bishop), and George Miller (another bishop) already belonged to the fraternal organization of the Freemasons, so reaching out to the group seemed like a natural way for the Saints to recruit important and influential allies to help with their recovery.[196]

Few organizations in the history of the world have inspired as much speculation, suspicion, and rampant conspiracy creations as the Freemasons. Originally known simply as Masonry, Freemasonry is a fraternal organization organized into groups known as lodges and is designed to encourage men to pursue a moral life. Freemasons participate in rituals not shared with outsiders, where lectures and morality plays are used to initiate new members into the order. All Freemasons are required to believe in a supreme being, though most come from varying religious backgrounds. A number of prominent Americans, including George Washington and Benjamin Franklin, were members of Masonic fraternities. Freemasonry in the United States was in a steep decline during the 1830s due to the alleged murder of William Morgan, a man who threatened to publish masonic secrets. The number of lodges in the United States declined dramatically after the Morgan scandal. For instance, in New York, Masons operated 480 lodges with 20,000 members in 1825, the year Morgan disappeared. By 1835, only 75 lodges with 3,000 active members remained in the state.[197] Anti-masonic sentiment was rampant during the period, and when the Book of Mormon first appeared, many assumed its references to "secret combinations" referred to the Freemasons.[198]

The origins of Masonry are unclear. Many Masons believe the origins of their practices stretch back to the Old Testament, though there are no known Masonic documents before about A.D. 1400. The earliest known minutes of a Masonic lodge date to around two hundred years later. The title of Mason is derived in part from the Masonic initiation rites, which utilize a story about the construction of Solomon's temple.[199] While Masons do not openly discuss their rituals with the uninitiated, what is known of them parallels many existing rituals found throughout Christianity.[200] Masonic rituals likely began in medieval England, though over time they appear to have adapted rituals and other concepts from Christianity and a number of esoteric fraternities. Some Masons believe the rituals trace as far back as Solomon's temple or even to Adam.[201]

In June 1841 several Church members who were also Freemasons submitted a request for a lodge in Nauvoo.[202] Shortly after the establishment of the lodge, Joseph Smith, Sidney Rigdon, and forty other

Latter-day Saints petitioned for membership in the order. The Nauvoo Lodge began holding regular meetings in January 1842. In March of the same year, the leader of the Freemasons in Illinois, Abraham Jonas, sent a letter giving instructions that "should the ballot be unanimous in favor of said Smith and Rigdon at a full meeting of said Nauvoo Lodge—then and in that case—the said lodge is authorized to confer the three degrees of ancient York Masonry on the said Joseph Smith and Sidney Rigdon—as speedily as the nature of the case will permit."[203] Joseph was inducted into the Masonic fraternity and received the Masonic rites on March 15, 1842.[204]

Several weeks later, on May 3, 1842, Joseph began preparations to introduce a selected group of men into a new order of the priesthood. The Prophet's history records his plan for "instructing them in the principles and order of the Priesthood, attending to washings, anointings, endowments and the communication of Keys pertaining to the Aaronic Priesthood, and so on to the highest order of Melchisedec Priesthood, setting forth the order pertaining to the ancient of Days, and all those plans and principles, by which any one is enabled to secure the fulness of those blessings, which have been prepared for the Church of the first born, and come up and abide in the presence of the Eloheim in the Eternal worlds."[205] On this first day, nine men received the ordinances that modern Latter-day Saints still refer to as "the endowment."[206]

Because of the close proximity in time between Joseph Smith's induction into Masonry and his introduction of the endowment ordinances, many scholars have linked the two events together. Similarities do exist between the Masonic rites and the temple endowment, and it is possible that Joseph Smith may have been inspired by or adapted certain parts of the Masonic ceremonies to meet his needs. Several contemporary members of the Church recorded conversations with Joseph in which he remarked to them that the rites of the Masons represented a corruption of divine ordinances. Benjamin Johnson, a close friend of the Prophet during this time, recalled, "He [Joseph] told me Fremasonry, as at present, was the apostate endowments, as sectarian religion was the apostate religion."[207] Heber C. Kimball made similar comments, writing in a letter to fellow Apostle Parley P. Pratt, "There is a similarity of priesthood in Masonry. . . . Br. Joseph says Masonry was taken from priesthood but has become degenerated. But many things are perfect."[208] Commenting on the possibility of a connection between the ceremonies of the Masons and the temple endowment, historian Steven Harper wrote, "What if the divine restoration was not wholly new but like the restoration of an old house, where the restorer keeps all that's useful and charming and replaces or refurbishes all that's broken weak, or no longer useful? . . . It requires a logical leap to bridge the evidentiary gap between *similarity*, which was obvious to those who knew both Masonry and the endowment, and *dependence*, which is assumed—not known."[209]

At the same time, a number of dissimilarities between the endowment and the Masonic rites existed. Freemasonry was intended to be an exclusive fraternity consisting of only a small group of select members. Joseph intended for the endowment to be given to all of the Saints ready to receive it. The Prophet's history from the day the first nine men received the endowment reads, "There was nothing made known to these men, but what will be made known to all the Saints of the last days, so soon as they are prepared to receive, and a proper place is prepared to communicate them, even to the weakest of Saints."[210] A key illustration of this desire came when the Prophet introduced the endowment ceremonies to women. Other than a few obscure groups in France, Freemasons never introduced women into their ceremonies.[211] In addition, though the endowment shared some forms of procedure and symbolism with the Masonic ceremonies, it told a completely different story with a message centered on redemption through Jesus Christ. The Masonic ceremonies spoke of Hiram of Tyre and Solomon's temple; the endowment cast Adam and Eve as representatives of all men and women in a cosmological journey through God's plan of salvation. The content of the endowment consisted more wholly of material revealed to Joseph Smith through his labors to translate the Bible and the book of Abraham than anything in the Masonic rites.

While Joseph Smith continued to introduce the temple ordinances, the size of the Nauvoo Lodge continued to grow. By October 1842, the lodge consisted of 253 members. By comparison, the total number of all Freemasons in Illinois outside of Nauvoo was 227. Two additional units opened in 1843, and growth of the Nauvoo Lodge began to alarm other Masonic fraternities. Additional lodges organized by Latter-day Saints opened across the Mississippi River in Iowa, bringing the total number of Latter-day Saint Masons in Illinois and Iowa to almost fourteen hundred. The lodges in and around Nauvoo attempted to reach out to their Masonic brethren, but tensions continued to rise, with Masons from other lodges accusing the Saints of politicizing Freemasonry and mixing it with religion. Masons outside Nauvoo also charged that Joseph Smith and Sidney Rigdon became master Masons too quickly, and that the rapid increase in the numbers of the Nauvoo Lodge was carried out improperly.[212] One Masonic history from the time recorded that Illinois Masons began to develop a "well-founded fear that within a short time the Mormon Lodges, if allowed to continue, would become more numerous than all others in the jurisdiction, and thus be able to control the Grand Lodge."[213]

Relationships with the lodges outside of Nauvoo eventually became so acrimonious that the Masons revoked the charters of the lodges in and around Nauvoo and suspended their activities.[214] When

Joseph Smith and Hyrum Smith were martyred in Carthage Jail, many members of the Church accused local Masons of complicity in the killings. An unsigned editorial appearing in a Church newspaper, *The Times and Seasons,* declared that Joseph and Hyrum "were shot to death, while, with uplifted hands they gave such signs of distress as would have commanded the interposition and benevolence of Savages or Pagans. They were both masons in good standing. . . . Joseph's last exclamation was 'O Lord my God!'"[215] Many Church members at the time speculated that Joseph Smith's last plea was a Masonic cry for help, a question impossible to ever fully answer.[216]

Several months after the deaths of Joseph and Hyrum, the Illinois Grand Lodge permanently withdrew fellowship from all Latter-day Saint Masons. At the same time, the Masonic leadership of Illinois declared the murders of Joseph and Hyrum Smith as a "source of shame to the commonwealth." On April 10, 1845, Brigham Young moved to suspend all Masonic activities in Nauvoo, effectively ending an institutional affiliation between the Saints and the Masons.[217] Joseph's Masonic apron, used in the initiation rites in Nauvoo, remained behind with Emma and his family when the Saints began their exodus to the West. It became a family heirloom, passed down through the generations, now residing in the archives of the Community of Christ. It serves as an emblem of a time when the Saints reached out to the outside world for connection, and instead found a pathway connecting them to a larger spiritual world.

15. Hyrum Smith's Martyrdom Clothing
– Church History Museum –

On June 27, 1844, shortly after five o'clock in the afternoon, a mob burst into Carthage Jail and murdered the Prophet Joseph Smith and his brother Hyrum Smith. With this event, the Prophet and Patriarch of the Restoration sealed their testimonies of the restored gospel with their blood.[218] Though killed in cold blood, their legacy has endured, and the message of the Restoration has spread throughout the world. As President Gordon B. Hinckley observed, "Joseph Smith died . . . at Carthage Jail . . . but his work has grown in magnitude, strength and power, and will continue to do so. . . . The testimonies which were sealed . . . now nurture the faith of people around the world. God bless the memory of Joseph Smith and Hyrum Smith who died here."[219]

The martyrdom clothing of Hyrum Smith is a precious artifact that tells a detailed story of the events that occurred on that fateful day in Carthage. "These artifacts are perhaps the most intimate remembrance of the martyrdom of Joseph and Hyrum Smith: they are the clothes Hyrum was wearing when he was killed, the watch he carried in his pocket that day, and a pair of sunglasses he owned.

They show the bullet holes and bloodstains that tell of his death at the hands of an angry mob."[220]

On June 24, 1844, a few days prior to the martyrdom, Hyrum and Joseph made the decision to voluntarily go to Carthage and surrender themselves to the authorities in order to prevent further conflict in Nauvoo. John Smith, Hyrum's oldest son, recorded that "he saw his father come in the house, and take his good watch out of his pocket and hang it on the peg by the washstand. . . . He went into the other room and changed his clothing and put his older watch in his vest pocket." Hyrum then came out, said goodbye to his family, and rode off toward Carthage with Joseph. The clothing that Hyrum changed into that day consisted of a homespun linen shirt, a vest with a back and a front, and a pair of homespun wool trousers.[221] One modern observer described that "Hyrum's vest was of a unique pattern of silk weave and his buttons were of bone. The vest was laced in the back. . . . Hyrum's trousers had a front flap that buttoned up on either side. . . . The shirt had very fine stitching at all seams and was gathered at the cuffs, which were held together by links."[222] Hortense Smith, wife of emeritus Church Patriarch Eldred G. Smith, Hyrum's great-great-grandson, noted that "not only are they homespun, but they're all handsewn. Every stich in them was with a needle and thread."[223] Hyrum would be martyred in this clothing three days later, in the upper room in Carthage Jail.

After the martyrdom, Willard Richards reported finding six wounds in Hyrum's body: (1) a wound on the left side of his nose, (2) a wound under his chin, (3) a wound through his lower back, (4) a graze wound to his breastbone, (5) a wound just below the left knee, and (6) a wound on the back of the right thigh. Four of these are confirmed by defects in Hyrum's clothing, and evidence of the nose wound is provided by the remaining bloodstains in the clothing.[224]

On the front right shoulder of the shirt, one can see the bloodstains from the wound in Hyrum's nose. John Taylor recounted that on the day of the martyrdom, he was sitting at one of the jail's front windows when he saw men with painted faces coming around the corner of the jail. As he got up and went to the door, he found Hyrum and Willard Richards braced against it, holding it closed. As the mob swarmed up the stairs to the upper room, a shot was fired through the door. It struck Hyrum on the left side of the nose, and he fell back, exclaiming, "I am a dead man!" (D&C 135:1). Hortense and Eldred G. Smith proposed that in order for Hyrum to be hit on the left side of the nose, he would likely have been bracing the door with his left shoulder, which means his head would have been turned to the right. When he was struck by the musket ball that came through the door, he fell back with his head still turned to the right, which is why the large bloodstain is on the right shoulder of his shirt, although he was hit on the left side of the nose.[225]

The wound on Hyrum's back has been subject to much debate—no one is quite sure how or when it happened. But there are holes that match up through the right side of his vest, pants, shirt, and underwear. This ball entered his lower back on the right side, traversed his abdomen, and struck the pocket watch in his right vest pocket with enough force to smash the crystal and ceramic face.[226] Both Willard Richards and John Taylor claim that the ball came from the window and hit Hyrum in the back just after he was struck in the face.[227] According to Joseph L. and David W. Lyon's research, this is a possible but rather unlikely explanation, given the distance, the angle from the ground to the window, and the poor accuracy of smoothbore military muskets.[228] Another possibility was presented when Eldred G. Smith suggested that in the commotion after Joseph Smith was shot and fell out the window someone turned Hyrum over and shot him through the back.[229] However, John Taylor could see Hyrum's body from where he was hidden across the hall in the cell, and he later declared that the body had not moved.[230] Furthermore, if the wound had been made at such a close range, there would have been powder burns or residue on the light-colored fabric of Hyrum's vest, of which there are none. A third possibility for this wound was proposed by Joseph L. and David W. Lyon:

> Remember that Hyrum Smith was pushing against the door with his left shoulder. When he was shot through the face, he stood up, releasing pressure on the door. The door swung partway open, striking his left shoulder and turning him to face away from the door, exposing the right side of his back to the opening. One of the attackers, with his musket held under his right arm about 49 inches above the floor, fired through the door opening and the ball struck Hyrum Smith in the back. The force of the ball then turned him another 180 degrees, and he fell to the floor with his head away from the door.[231]

The other marks on Hyrum's clothing show the wounds to his chest, knee, and thigh. These wounds probably occurred after he had fallen to the floor and were made by attackers firing from the door. A ball grazed his chest as he lay on the floor, and another hit the front of his left leg, just below the knee. When he fell, Hyrum's right leg must have fallen outward, exposing the back of the leg to the musket fire, where a ball struck him on the back of the thigh.[232]

Hyrum's clothes and the marks and stains they carry are important because they physically record the martyrdom of Joseph Smith and Hyrum Smith. Brigham Young touched on the significance of this martyrdom when he wrote, "For they killed the prophets . . . ; and they have shed innocent blood, which crieth from the ground against them. . . . Many have marveled because of his death; but it was needful that he should seal his testimony with his blood, that he might be honored and the wicked might be condemned" (D&C 136:36, 39). Joseph and Hyrum's willing sacrifice certified what they knew to be true. Of the two brothers, John Taylor wrote, "[Joseph] lived great, and he died great in the eyes of God and his people; and like most of the Lord's anointed in ancient times, has sealed his mission and his works with his own blood; and so has his brother Hyrum" (D&C 135:3).

16. PEPPERBOX PISTOL

– Church History Museum –

In the last moments of his life, with his brother Hyrum already slain by the bullets of assassins, Joseph Smith took up a pistol and defended himself and his friends. Faced with a mob of more than two hundred vigilantes attacking the jail he was held in, the Prophet fought back. The exchange of gunfire between Joseph and his assailants has left behind it a number of difficult historical questions. Can a person be a martyr if they fight back against their murderers? Did the Prophet's actions wound or kill any of the mob members attacking the jail? Even identifying the pistol used by Joseph Smith in Carthage Jail presents a tantalizing historical mystery—one that is still not entirely settled and most likely will never be to everyone's complete satisfaction. Nevertheless, the stories and evidence surrounding the pepperbox pistol used in Carthage Jail also illuminate a number of issues about the death of Joseph and Hyrum Smith, and the nature of historical inquiry.

Accounts both hostile and friendly to Joseph Smith confirm the use of the pistol in Carthage Jail. Confronted by dozens of mobocrats outside and inside the jail, Joseph made the decision to fight back. Willard Richards, an Apostle in the jail with Joseph Smith, records the following: "A ball was sent through the door which hit Hyrum on the side of his nose, when he fell backwards. . . . Joseph looked towards him, and responded 'O dear! *Brother Hyrum!*' and opening the door two or three inches with his left hand discharged one barrel of a six shooter (pistol) at random in the entry from whence a ball grazed Hyrum's breast. . . . Joseph continued snapping his revolver, round the casing of the door into the space as before, three barrels of which missed fire, while Mr. Taylor with a walking stick stood by his side. . . . When the revolver failed, we had no more fire arms, and expected an immediate rush of the mob."[233]

In his account, John Taylor, the other apostolic survivor of the martyrdom, emphasized that Joseph did not appear to be acting in the spirit of rage or vengeance when he picked up the pistol. "I shall never forget the deep feeling of sympathy and regard manifested in the countenance of Brother Joseph as he drew nigh to Hyrum, and, leaning over him, exclaimed, 'Oh! My poor dear brother Hyrum!'" Taylor continued, "[Joseph], however, instantly arose, and with a firm quick step, and a determined expression of countenance, approached the door, and pulling the six-shooter left by Brother Wheelock from his pocket, opened the door slightly, and snapped the pistol six successive times; only three of the barrels, however, were discharged."[234]

Several members of the mob reported the shots fired from the pistol as well. William R. Hamilton, one of the youngest members of the Carthage militia at the time of the murders, recalled that "those in the hall had tried several times to push [the door] open, Smith having shot at them by putting the muzzle of his old English pepperbox revolver through the opening at the side of the door (made by their efforts) and firing four shots into the hall."[235] John Taylor recalled with some uncertainty, "I understood that two or three were wounded by these discharges, two of whom, I am informed, died."[236] Later Church historian B. H. Roberts cited John Hay, a young man living in Hancock County, who believed the shots fired from the pepperbox pistol struck three men, two in the upper arm and a third in the face. Hay's account reads, "Joe Smith died bravely. He stood by the jamb of the door and fired four shots, bringing his man down every time. He shot an Irishman named Wills, who was in the affair from his congenital love of the brawl, in the arm; Gallagher, a Southerner from the Mississippi Bottom, in the face; Voorhees, a half-grown hobbledehoy from Bear Creek, in the shoulder; and another gentleman, whose name I will not mention, as he is prepared to prove an alibi, and besides stands six-foot two in his moccasins."[237] It is difficult to verify the accuracy of Hay's account, since it is tinged with sarcasm, but B. H. Roberts believed that though none of the wounds were immediately fatal, one man may have later died from an arm wound.[238]

How did the pepperbox pistol make it into the hands of Joseph Smith on the fateful day of his murder? Apparently, the pistol belonged to John Taylor, who tried to get the weapon into Joseph's hands when the Prophet initially left Nauvoo, crossing the Mississippi River in an effort to avoid further conflict. Taylor recruited Cyrus H. Wheelock, a Church member in Nauvoo, to accompany Joseph on his journey. When Joseph returned to face charges in Carthage, John Taylor accompanied him to the jail. Wheelock visited the prisoners on the morning of the martyrdom and was able to pass by the guards while concealing the pistol in his overcoat pockets. John Taylor later recalled, "Cyrus Wheelock came to see us and when he was leaving drew a small pistol, a six-shooter, from his pocket, remarking at the same time; 'would any of you like to have this,' Br. Joseph immediately replied, 'Yes, give it to me.' Whereupon he took the pistol and put it in his pantaloons pocket."[239]

However, the true identity of the pepperbox pistol is a mystery still unsettled in our time. Recent historical scholarship points to no fewer than three different pistols claimed to be the actual item used in Carthage Jail. The most well-known is an Allen &

Thurber .36 caliber dragoon-sized pepperbox pistol with a dog leg grip. The pistol was on display at the Church History Museum in Salt Lake City from 1984 to 2015 and is probably the most photographed of the three pistols. It has a silver memorial escutcheon on the right handle reading, "Joseph Smith held this when Martyred June 27th, 1844."[240] Though the dragoon pistol is the most well known of the three, however, there are serious reasons to doubt that it is genuine article from Carthage Jail.

First the dragoon pistol is decidedly not a "small pistol" as John Taylor described it. The weapon was intended to be carried by dragoon soldiers riding on horseback. Its weight (33 ounces) and its size would have made it very difficult for Cyrus Wheelock to smuggle it into the jail unnoticed. The weapon visibly deforms clothing when placed in a pocket. In addition the pistol uses an internal lock mechanism not patented until February 27, 1845, well after the martyrdom. Although it is possible, it is unlikely that the pistol was fashioned before the patent was given. This pistol also has a complicated provenance. According to some accounts the pistol was given to Joseph Smith by Miner R. Deming, a brigadier general in the Illinois State Militia. The account adds that Deming passed the pistol on to Joseph Smith while he was in the jail, then retrieved it after the martyrdom. Deming was then elected Sherriff in Hancock County and brought a number of mob members to justice. During the trial of Hyrum Smith, the story is that Deming was confronted by Samuel Marshall, a physically imposing anti-Mormon. In the lobby of the courthouse Marshall attacked Deming, who drew the pistol and fired a single fatal shot, killing Marshall. From there the weapon was turned over to a deputy sheriff, then passed through a number of relatives before it was given to Lyman Wood, a Latter-day Saint from Springville, Utah, who was passing through Hancock County. Wood gave the pistol to the Salt Lake Museum and Menagerie, which was taken over by the Church in 1878. The pistol has remained in continuous Church custody since that time.

A second pistol, a photograph of which is featured in this chapter, is an Allen & Thurber Grafton-style pepperbox pistol, with a 3.39 inch, six-shot barrel that fires .32 caliber bullets. Joseph Johnstun, a firearms historian, has confirmed from internal evidence that the pistol was manufactured in late 1841 or early 1842. It also has an engraving on the right side of its handle that reads "J.T." indicating it may have been owned by John Taylor. We do not know when this pistol was donated to the Church History Museum, but documents created in 1943 read, "These were in John Taylors [sic] possession at the time of the martyrdom of Joseph Smith." The pistol also lacks a cap guard to prevent the percussion caps from falling off the gun. This may explain why the weapon misfired three times during the attack on the jail. It is also much smaller than the dragoon pistol, making it easier for Cyrus Wheelock to conceal when he entered the jail. There is documentation indicating the pistol was found in the room after the attack on the jail and returned to John Taylor, still in Carthage recovering from his wounds.[241] In his account of the martyrdom, written in 1856, John Taylor wrote of the pistol, "I have it now in my possession."[242]

For many years the location of this pistol was unknown. Some believed it was stolen. It was rediscovered in 1996 when Dave Packard, a volunteer researcher for the Church museum, found it in a Church property in Nauvoo. Upon close examination the museum staff became convinced it was likely the pistol used in Carthage Jail. It has been on display in the Church museum since 2015.[243]

A third pistol is claimed to be the weapon used in Carthage Jail as well. It is owned by a private collector in Utah. There is less evidence for the origin of this pistol, but some claims indicate it was taken from the jail by Charles Fancher, who is said to have been in the attacking party. Fancher took the gun with him when he migrated west with a company of immigrants from Arkansas. The Fancher party was massacred by Latter-day Saint militia and Native Americans at Mountains Meadows in 1856. Supposedly the pistol was taken from Fancher's body by John Higbee. The present owner does not hold this provenance, and the pistol's lock mechanism is of the same 1845 patent as the dragoon pistol, making the weapon an unlikely candidate for the gun used in Carthage.[244]

Setting aside the complicated story of the true identity of the pistol, the last question remains: If Joseph Smith defended himself, is he truly a martyr? This question is more academic and philosophical than anything else. There are few among us who, when confronted with similar circumstances, would not have used any nearby weapon to defend ourselves. Though Joseph may have sensed his approaching demise (see D&C 135:4), the fact that he was not alone in the jail may have made him feel a moral obligation to protect his friends who were with him. Joseph did not use the weapon until after Hyrum was murdered and it was clear the mob was determined to take their lives. It can be argued that Joseph's actions in firing the pistol saved the lives of Willard Richards and John Taylor. The mob most likely needed time to remove their wounded from the narrow hallway. Further, knowing their intended victims possessed a means to protect themselves may have kept the mob from directly entering the room and shooting the men at close range. Prophets in all ages have acted at times to defend themselves and their friends without forfeiting their right to be called Christians, disciples, or martyrs. Faced with overwhelming odds, Joseph Smith's actions demonstrated his true character—not as man afraid of death but one who would fight for, protect, and if necessary, lay down his life to protect his friends.

17. DAGUERREOTYPE OF EMMA SMITH AND DAVID HYRUM SMITH

- Community of Christ Library -

A beautiful photo turns tragic when one knows of its place in Emma and Joseph Smith's history. Less than a year before the photo was taken, Joseph was martyred, leaving Emma four months pregnant and widowed. The young child in Emma Hale's arms, David Hyrum Smith, was born five months after Joseph's martyrdom. The circumstances of the martyrdom are an enigma. The Prophet Joseph Smith, who had planned upon his first arrest to escape to the east, was, by some accounts, coaxed back by a letter from Emma.[245] An examination of the correspondence between Joseph and Emma, especially in these crucial hours, reveals at least one truth: Joseph cared deeply for his family, and Emma cared just as much for Joseph and her children.

On June 12, 1844, Joseph and seventeen others received charges for arrest stemming from the earlier destruction of the *Nauvoo Expositor* printing press. On the evening of May 22, Emma was seeing to the needs of her family and household when she heard men arrive at her home whom Joseph had earlier sent with a letter for Governor Ford. "Joseph called Hyrum, John Taylor, Willard Richards, William Phelps, William Marks, and others to his room" where one of them read Ford's response aloud.

Joseph paced the room as the letter was read. "There is no mercy—no mercy here," he cried. "No," Hyrum responded, "just as sure as we fall into their hands we are dead men."[246] After brief counsel, Joseph and Hyrum determined to cross from the Iowa side of the Mississippi River and travel east to Washington to place their appeal directly before President Tyler.

Joseph's "grief at leaving his family was deep. As he walked out of the house, Emma saw him pull his handkerchief from his pocket to cover his tears."[247] Porter Rockwell rowed Joseph, Hyrum, and several other men across the Mississippi and returned the following morning with a letter that Joseph had dictated early that morning for Emma. The close of the letter reads,

> Do not despair—If God ever opens a door that is possible for me I will see you again. I do not know where I shall go, or what I shall do, but shall if possible endeavor to get to the city of Washington. May God almighty bless you and the children. . . . My heart bleeds. No more at present. If you conclude to go to Kirkland, Cincinnati, or any other place, I wish you would contrive to inform me, this evening.[248]

As Emma tried to figure out her plans so as to inform Joseph of them by nightfall, she was faced with difficult options. On the one hand was the safety of the Saints in Nauvoo; on the other, the safety of her husband. Her concern for the latter was lessened somewhat by news from Joseph's trusted attorney, James W. Wood, who "arrived with a pledge from Governor Ford for her husband's safety and fair trial."[249] That night Emma sent Joseph her reply.

Emma's letter reached Joseph at one o'clock on June 23. Joseph read it and then handed the letter to Hyrum, indicating to Hyrum that his course would be to leave to the east. Reynolds Cahoon and Hiram Kimball snapped, calling Joseph a coward. "If my life is of no value to my friends, it is of none to myself," Joseph responded, then asked Hyrum what they should do. "'Let's go back and give ourselves up, and see the thing out,' he answered." Joseph was contemplative. Then, gazing on his stalwart brother, he replied, "If you go back, I will go with you, but we shall be butchered."[250] On that 23rd day of June, Hyrum and Joseph crossed the river to return to Nauvoo.

Some historians assume that Emma's letter caused Joseph to return to Nauvoo, but as it has never been quoted and was read by only Joseph and Hyrum, we can only assume its content by second-hand accounts. The diary of William Clayton gives a noteworthy intimation: "Emma sent messengers over the river to Joseph and informed him what they intended to do and urged him to give himself up inasmuch as the Governor had offered him protection." But even this is uncertain, for Emma later remarked to a friend, "When [Joseph] came back I felt the worst I ever did in my life, and from that time I looked for him to be killed."[251] Had Emma in fact encouraged Joseph's return, she had not in the least expected it.

At six o'clock the following morning, June 24, after a brief return home, Joseph left his family and headed for Carthage. One witness recalled Joseph turning to Emma and asking, "Emma, can you train my sons to walk in their father's footsteps?" Emma, then mother of four and four months pregnant, was overcome with grief to think of raising the children on her own and requested of Joseph a final blessing. Joseph, with little time, instructed her to write the best blessing she could and he would sign it upon his return.

Emma's requested blessing, probably written in the quiet hours of that evening, read in part, "I particularly desire wisdom to bring up all the children that are, or may be committed to my charge, in such a manner that they will be useful ornaments in the kingdom of God, and in a coming day arise up and call me blessed. . . . I desire with all my heart to honor and respect my husband as my head, to ever live in his confidence and by acting in unison with him retain the place which God has given me by his side."[252]

Joseph would be killed early the next morning. When Lorenzo Watson appeared at Emma's house to inform her of her husband's death, "she reeled in horror." John P. Greene, attempting to comfort Emma, assured her "that the sorrow she bore would be the crown of her life. Emma lifted her head and replied, 'My husband was my crown.'"[253]

Later that afternoon, Emma went to see Joseph's body. She "kneeled down, clasped him around his face, and sank upon his body. Her children gathered around their weeping mother, and the dead body of a murdered father, and grief that words cannot embody seemed to overwhelm the group."[254] At age thirty-nine, Emma was a widow with four children and one on the way.

Five months later, on November 17, 1844, four months after her fortieth birthday, Emma gave birth to her son, David Hyrum Smith. Eliza Snow, who came to visit Emma shortly after his birth, composed a poem for the child:

Sinless as celestial spirits—
Lovely as a morning flow'r
Comes the smiling infant stranger
in an evil-omen'd hour

Thou may'st draw from love and kindness
All a mother can bestow;
But alas! on earth, a father
You art destin'd not to know![255]

During the seventeen and a half years of their marriage, Emma and Joseph "had lived in at least a dozen homes across fives states. During these years, they had buried six of their eleven children."[256] With the loss of her dear husband—her crown—Emma underwent intense grief that would last the rest of her life. The years that followed were not easy, but at least one of the desires in her written blessing was granted: in coming years her children would rise up and call her blessed. In 1893, young Joseph III wrote the following of Emma: "My mother was . . . of the purest and noblest intentions . . . was absolutely fearless where the right was concerned; and was a just and generous mother. It's needless to say that we *loved her*."[257]

18. GREEN FLAKE'S PIONEER MEDAL

– Church History Museum –

O n July 19, 1897, near the fiftieth anniversary of the entry of the first members of the Church entering into the Salt Lake Valley, the *Deseret News* reported: "Two pioneers called at the *News* office today; one was a colored man named Green Flake, who claims to have been in the first wagon through Emigration Canyon, and moved to Idaho after living in Utah 49 years. He is now 70 years of age."[258] In fact, Green Flake was one of three African Americans in the Vanguard pioneer company, along with Oscar Crosby and Hark Lay.[259] Today, as part of a growing worldwide faith, members are comfortable with a multiracial Church, though many often picture the early membership of the Church as consisting of Europeans from the Northern United States or Western Europe. In reality, the racial history of the Church is as complicated as the racial history of the United States, evidenced by Green Flake's honored, but relatively unknown, role in the Vanguard Pioneer Company.

Green Flake was born January 6, 1828, though the exact place of his birth is still not entirely settled. The *Salt Lake Tribune* printed in 1897 and again in 1903 that Green was born in Mississippi, though other records indicate he was "born into slavery on the Jordan Flake plantation in Mads- burr, Anson County, North Carolina." When Green was ten years old, he was given to Jordan Flake, who presented Green as a wedding gift to his son, James. It is likely at this time that Green took the surname of his master, a custom common in Antebellum America.[260] Though Green resided with

James Flake, it appears that Green remained the property of Jordan Flake until 1843 when Jordan deeded Green to his son. The will of Jordan Flake reads, "I, Jordan Flake . . . give to my son James M. Flake, two Negroes, Green and Lyse and three hundred dollars."[3]

James and Agnes Flake owned and operated a plantation on the Mississippi frontier. In the winter of 1843–44, two missionaries from The Church of Jesus Christ of Latter-day Saints knocked on their door. Southern hospitality prevented the Flakes from turning away their visitors, though at first they viewed the message with skepticism. After several weeks, the Flakes became convinced of the truthfulness of the missionaries' message and were baptized. James began to share the message of the restored gospel with all his acquaintances, including his slaves.[261]

Slavery was a reality of the world the early Church was restored into, and Church leaders often spoke with practicality of the proper way of sharing the gospel with slaves and their owners. In an 1836 letter to Oliver Cowdery, Joseph Smith wrote, "All men are to be taught to repent; but we have no right to interfere with slaves contrary to the mind and will of their masters. In fact, it would be much better and more prudent, not to preach at all to slaves, until after their masters are converted: and then, teach the master to use them with kindness, remembering that they are accountable to God, and that servants are bound to serve their masters, with singleness of heart, without murmuring." Recognizing the strong feelings surrounding slavery, Joseph Smith continued, "I do, most sincerely hope, that no one who is authorized from this church to preach the gospel, will so far depart from the scripture as to be found stirring up strife and sedition against our brethren of the South."[262] By the time Green was baptized, Joseph Smith was publicly stating his opposition to slavery, writing in one letter, "While I have knowledge of heaven to guide me, and the riches of eter-

nity to back me, I shall continue to strive for the emancipation of all kinds of slavery, as well as the slavery of sin; yea, until I can exclaim like Caesar: Veni, vidi, vici!"[263]

Green accepted the gospel and was baptized at age sixteen on April 7, 1844, by John Brown, a missionary from Tennessee. Shortly after his baptism, James Flake decided to gather with the Saints to Nauvoo. Before the move, Flake freed all of his slaves, telling them they were at liberty to go where they pleased. However, Green, along with two other slaves, elected to stay with the Flake family. It appears because Green stayed with the Flakes, he retained his status as a slave. Green assisted the Flakes with their move to Nauvoo and helped them build a new home. While in Nauvoo, James Flake arranged for Green to help with several Church projects, and Green's labors were offered as tithing for the Flake family, suggesting Green was still seen as their property. Further, when the Flake family joined the westward exodus, Green was still spoken of as a slave owned by the family. A Flake family history reads, "James M. Flake, who had put his all upon the altar, sent his best slave, Green, with a pair of white Mississippi mules and white-topped mountain carriage, to help the pioneer company to their destination."[264]

Green was a valuable addition to the Vanguard Company when it left Winter Quarters in the spring of 1847 to make the first trek to the Salt Lake Valley. When Brigham Young became severely ill during the final approach through the Wasatch Mountains, he appointed Elder Orson Pratt to take a company of forty-two men to "build bridges and roads as they went." Green was among the men selected to travel with this advance party, engaging in the difficult work of clearing a trail for the remainder of the pioneer company. Green entered the valley with Orson Pratt's company on July 21, 1847, later declaring he was in the first wagon to pass through Emigration Canyon and into the new home of the Saints.[265] Once Brigham Young arrived in the valley, he instructed the company to renew their covenants with God by entering in rebaptism. On August 8, 1847, Green was rebaptized by Tarleton Lewis and reconfirmed by Wilford Woodruff.[266]

In September of 1847, Green was in the company led by Brigham Young who departed from the valley to prepare the rest of the Saints at Winter Quarters to travel to their new home. Green arrived back in the valley with the Flake family in 1848. At some point, Green gained his freedom, though the exact circumstances remain unknown. While scouting for new colonization sites, James Flake was killed in an accident in 1850. Following James' death, his widow, Agnes, relocated the family to the new Church settlement in San Bernadino, California. According to one source, she left Green behind in Utah as a form of tithing. In 1854, Amasa Lyman wrote a letter on behalf of Agnes Flake asking "if it was possible to . . . receive any help by way of the Negro man she left," adding that they had means to "purchase the Negro and pay for him."[267] Green never rejoined the Flake family. According to one family member, Green "worked for two years for President Young and Heber C. Kimball, and then got his liberty."[268]

In 1848, Green married Martha Crosby, another African-American Church member from Mississippi. Green and Martha established a homestead in present-day Midvale, Utah, cultivating a farm and raising cattle. They had two children, Lucinda and Abraham, and remained in the Salt Lake Valley for more than forty years. Throughout his life, he remained a devoted member of the Church. He attended the Union Ward, worked in a rock quarry for the building of the Salt Lake Temple, and is credited with helping build the first chapel outside of Salt Lake City. Flake family tradition maintains that Green received the Aaronic and Melchizedek priesthoods, though there are no written records indicating he was ever ordained.[269]

In 1885, Martha passed away and Green moved to Gray's Lake, Idaho, to live with the family of his son, Abraham. When the fiftieth anniversary of the Vanguard Company came in 1897, Green was among the handful of survivors still living. Green participated in the festivities surrounding the pioneer jubilee. A Salt Lake newspaper recorded, "A feature in the celebration at Union, Salt Lake County, was a pioneer carriage driven by Mr. Green Flake, colored, who drove President Young's carriage across the plains in 1847."[270] Green also received the small medal shown at the beginning of this chapter with his name engraved on the back of it.

Green Flake's legacy reflects the complicated nature of race relations in the nineteenth century and the vital role of African Americans in the history of the Church. Green died in full devotion to the gospel, with one Salt Lake newspaper recording, "The deceased was a faithful Latter-day Saint, and to his dying day bore testimony of the divine mission of the Prophet Joseph Smith."[271] Green's story is also a reminder that God "inviteth all to come unto him and partake of his goodness; and he denieth none that come unto him, black and white, bond and free" (2 Nephi 26:33).

The Plough that was used by Elder Wᵐ Carter to plough the first half ACRE in SALT LAKE VALLEY, July 1847. Also the first furrow in Sᵗ George City, Feb. 1862.

19. WILLIAM CARTER'S PLOW

– Church History Library –

William Carter was born in the ancient market town know as Ledbury near the border of Wales and England. He went to school, grew up, and was educated in the same village, eventually becoming a glass blower and an apprentice in a blacksmith shop. One day while he was working in a forge in Ledbury, he heard some beautiful singing. Leaving his work, he went to the door but could not see where the singing was coming from. That night while he was walking home, he encountered an Elder from a new faith who invited him to attend a meeting in the evening. William gathered several family members and attended the meeting, where he was introduced for the first time to the teachings of The Church of Jesus Christ of Latter-day Saints. Immediately after the meeting he asked the Elders to baptize him. He was cautioned to wait until he could learn more about the gospel. William replied, "If I should wait a year, I would not be any more ready than I am now." A few days later, despite the strong objections of several family members, William was baptized.[272]

Soon after, William emigrated to America. He landed in Quebec, Canada, and then made his way across the continent. He arrived in Nauvoo, Illinois, on July 11, 1841, barefoot because his shoes were worn out. As his small company arrived in the city, the Prophet Joseph Smith rode up to greet the company. When he asked William, who was only nineteen, "Boy, what are you here for?" William replied, "For the Gospel's sake." Over the next few years he bought a little farm near the city, and assisted in building the Nauvoo House and the temple, alongside serving in the Nauvoo Legion. He also met and fell in love with Ellen Benbow. They were married in Nauvoo on December 5, 1843.[273]

A few years later the Carters joined the forced exodus from Nauvoo. In the spring of 1846 William was selected to join the Vanguard Company to the Salt Lake Valley. He hesitated to join the company when his wife became seriously ill. Seeking Brigham Young for counsel, the Prophet told William, "Go, Brother Carter, and I promise you in the name of the Lord, that your wife will recover and follow you out to the West." Obedient to President Young's counsel, William departed with the Vanguard Company, his wagon third in line.[274]

As the Vanguard Company approached the Salt Lake Valley, William was chosen to be one of the members of the advance company, the first to enter the valley. When he arrived in the valley, he found a land dry and burnt by the scorching summer heat. One group of men had already broken a plow while attempting to cut a furrow in the hard ground. William took a shovel, cut an opening into a nearby creek, and watched as the clear mountain water spread across the rock ground. Then, on July 23, 1847, shortly after Elder Orson Pratt dedicated the land to the Lord, William Carter plowed the first half-acre of ground at a site near present-day Third South and State Street in Salt Lake City. Even before Brigham Young and the rest of the company arrived in the valley, the first potatoes had been planted. The first irrigation and plowing, farming techniques critical to the settlement of the West, began with William Carter's work that Friday morning.[275]

In 1861, fourteen years later, William was asked to colonize the St. George area. Arriving in a place even more arid than the Salt Lake Valley, William nevertheless went ahead with his work. he used the same plow to cut a furrow from a nearby stream to the area where the pioneers were camping. He remained in St. George, helping construct the first Latter-day Saint temple in the West, before his death in 1896 at the age of 75.

20. 1849 "Mormon Gold" Coin
– *Smithsonian National Museum of American History* –

The phrase "the kingdom of God" means something different to modern Latter-day Saints than it did to their pioneer forbearers. The early Saints often saw their destiny in millennial terms, looking forward to the time when "Christ will reign personally upon the earth" (Articles of Faith 1:10). This impulse reached its peak when the Saints fled the boundaries of the United States in an attempt to create a new kingdom in the West. The literal intention of the pioneers was to set up their own kingdom and operate under their own government. In deliberations of the Council of Fifty after the death of Joseph Smith, Brigham Young declared: "But I tell you in the name of the Lord when we go from here, we will exalt the standard of liberty and make our own laws. When we go from here we don't calculate to go under any government but the government of God."[276] The vision of the Saints fleeing persecution was nothing less than an independent kingdom with its own laws, symbols, and even its own money.

From the beginning of the colonization of the Great Basin, the Church was deeply involved in the spiritual and temporal welfare of the Saints. The theological system revealed in the Restoration presented a unity of nature, social welfare, and the work of God. An early revelation to Joseph Smith declared, "Verily I say unto you that all things unto me are spiritual, and not at any time have I given unto you a law which was temporal; neither any man, nor the children of men; neither Adam, your father, whom I created" (D&C 29:34).[277] When the pioneers first arrived in the Salt Lake Valley, one of the most pressing problems was the shortage of proper coin and currency. By one account, "about $50" was the sum total of currency brought with Brigham Young and the Vanguard Company in 1847.[278] Naturally, Church leaders set about addressing the problem.

One advantage working in favor of the Church was the involvement of members of the Mormon Battalion in the discovery of gold at Sutter's Mill, California. Several members of the battalion participated in early mining operations in California, and took with them money and gold dust they secured in California when they arrived in the Salt Lake Valley. The Church even called about twenty young men to travel to California to mine gold. Battalion veterans brought quantities of "gold dust" to Utah, but it proved to be a difficult medium for accurate trading and bartering. The dust was measured sometimes in weight and other times in "pinches," described by one expert as "the amount of gold dust that could be raised between the thumb and the forefinger." Given the lack of precision in such measurements, it soon became clear that Church leaders would need to melt down the gold to mint their own coins. "Valley coins" were minted under the direction of Church leaders in 1849, 1850, and 1860.[279]

Brigham Young, John Taylor, and John Kay collaborated to create the design of the first coins produced. Engraved on the coins was the phrase "Holiness to the Lord," encircling a symbol of the priesthood, a three point Phrygian crown over the all-seeing eye of God. The Phrygian crown was a common symbol of liberty in the nineteenth century, frequently associated with the French Revolution. The symbolism of a people seeking liberty from an oppressive government was potent.[280] On the opposite side was a depiction of clasped hands, a symbol of friendship, encircled by the words "pure gold" and the denomination of the coin. The coins were minted in values of $2½, $5, $10, and $20, and were produced at the Church mint located near the pres-

ent-day Joseph Smith Memorial Building.[281] The coins were produced from December 1848 through 1851. By one estimate, the mint coined around $70,000 in gold pieces during this time.[282]

Even while the gold pieces were being coined, paper currency was a necessity in the early Utah Territory. In December of 1848, the crucibles producing the gold coins cracked, creating a temporary halt in production. In place of the coins, paper currency called "valley notes" were issued, backed 80 percent by the gold dust in the local treasury. These handwritten notes were stamped with the official seal of the Twelve Apostles, consisting of the three-pointed Phrygian crown and the all-seeing eye found on the coins and encircled by the initials PSTAPCJCLDSLDAOW, which stood for "Private Seal of the Twelve Apostles, Priests of The Church of Jesus Christ of Latter-day Saints, in the Last Dispensation All Over the World." According to another source, the initials on the seal may have also stood for "Patience, Sobriety, Truth, Affection, Prudence, Charity, Justice, Constancy, Love, Duty, Solidity, Long-suffering, Diligence, Amiability, Toleration, and Worth."[283]

The need for currency was so great that Church leaders began to circulate a supply of notes from the Kirtland Safety Society, printed more than a decade earlier. The notes bore the signatures of Joseph Smith, cashier of the Kirtland Society, and Sidney Rigdon, president of the society. The notes proved to be a convenient medium of exchange, easily and cheaply introduced. They also pleased Church leaders who saw their reissue as a fulfillment of "a prophecy by Joseph Smith that one day they would be as good as gold." The notes were countersigned by Brigham Young, Heber C. Kimball, and Newell K. Whitney. At the same time Truman Angel, the Church architect, made a press to print another series of currency, marking the first printing carried out in the Utah Territory.[284]

The minting of "valley coins" came to an end in early 1852. With the authority of the United States increasing in the western regions of North America, the secular influence of the Latter-day Saint kingdom declined. Outside of the Latter-day Saint spheres of influence the coins began to be devalued. The journal history of the Church noted in 1850 that "the $20 gold pieces coined in the valley were passing in St. Joseph for $18.00."[285] Church leaders took umbrage at the devaluation of the coins. The *Deseret News* sarcastically noted, "If Valley coin in exchange, is not as valuable as goods, at the current prices offered in our market, we recommend our friends to keep their coin, and not insult their neighbors with such miserable trash as virgin gold."[286]

Throughout the 1850s the availability of "valley currency" decreased as Church leaders abandoned the gold missions to California, choosing instead to keep the urgently needed manpower closer to home. By 1851 most of the Latter-day Saints in the gold field had relocated to Utah, diminishing the flow of gold dust into the territory. Lack of Church leadership in the areas near the gold fields meant almost no collection of tithes and offerings, further limiting the influx of gold. Finally, as the federal government continued to exert greater influence over the western territories, the "valley currency" became more and more anachronous, even to the point where it began to affect the credit of the Church. As the Kingdom began its integration into the Republic, its emblems began to fade as its independence waned.[287]

A last attempt to produce Church coinage came in 1859 after a supply of gold dust from Colorado made its way to the Utah Territory. Brigham Young asked J. M. Barlow, a local jeweler, to prepare a new $5 coin. The result was a more refined and elaborate design for the coin. One collector notes, "No other gold coins of this era are more impressive, including those made at the United States mint."[288] On one side the coin was designed with a crouching lion and a small stretch of water in the foreground. Engraved near the edges of the coin was the phrase "Holiness to the Lord" written in the Deseret Alphabet, along with the date 1860. On the reverse side was an eagle with outstretched wings, a beehive on its chest, and its talons holding an olive branch and a set of arrows. Another version of this coin with slight variations, including a series of three mountains behind the lion, was also minted around the same time. The example in this chapter is the same pattern as the gold coins were, but minted in copper.[289]

No more coins were minted after this time. On June 8, 1864, the US Congress passed a law forbidding the private coinage of gold.[290] Nearly two centuries later, only a small handful of the currency minted in the valley remains in existence. In 2017, several of the 1849 coins, along with a page of the original manuscript of the Book of Mormon, were put on display by the Smithsonian Institution in Washington, DC, in an exhibit focusing on the role of religion in American history. Displayed alongside such items as George Washington's christening robe, Thomas Jefferson's creative edit of the Bible, *The Life and Morals of Jesus of Nazareth,* and 1654 Torah scroll, the coins serve as an important reminder of the role of the Saints in the settlement of the American frontier.[291] They also serve as witness of a time when the Church was more than just an ecclesiastical organization, but a literal kingdom in the West.

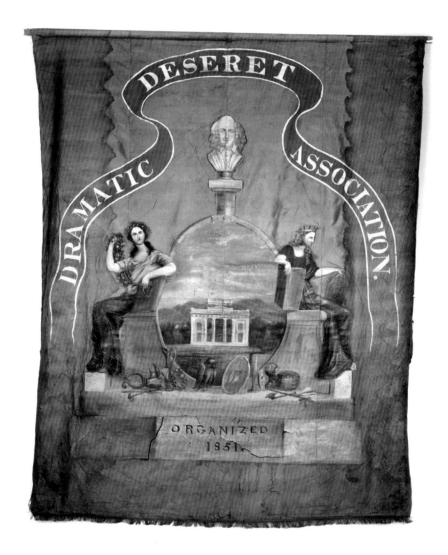

21. BANNER OF THE DESERET DRAMATIC ASSOCIATION

— Church History Museum —

The tradition of involvement in the arts, including theatre, has been with the Latter-day Saints since the early days of The Church of Jesus Christ of Latter-day Saints. Joseph Smith introduced drama to the Saints in Nauvoo, where he formed a dramatic company known as the Nauvoo Dramatic Club.[292] With the assassination of Joseph and Hyrum Smith in June 1844 and the following exodus of the Saints from Nauvoo, all theatrical activities were put on hold. In the fall of 1850, however, once the Saints had found a home in Salt Lake City, a new company, the Musical and Dramatic Association, was organized by members of the former Nauvoo Brass Band.[293] The company performed a number of plays in the Old Bowery.[294]

In 1851, the Old Bowery was torn down, and the building materials were used to build the first tabernacle. With no place to perform, the Musical and Dramatic Association disbanded. But Brigham Young would not stand for the inactivity, and with his urging, members of the old company reorganized and named the new club the Deseret Dramatic Association (DDA).[295] On January 1, 1853, a new building for the DDA was dedicated and became known as the Social Hall. Made of adobe and a shingle roof, the hall could hold an audience of up to 350. "Soon after the dedication of Social Hall, a bust of Shakespeare was placed above the stage."[296] This is likely the bust that can be seen presiding over the Social Hall in the banner of the association. Two Greek muses, likely Melpomene and Thalia, or tragedy and comedy, complete the scene on the banner.[297]

The Deseret Dramatic Association performed in the Social Hall for the next nine years as an amateur company putting on plays for the amusement of the community. Despite their amateur status, the group was praised for their plays.[298] One spectator remembered, "I never saw an amateur company equal it. Some of the performers were stars in their line. . . . The scenery was superb, the orchestre [sic] not to be excelled, the director, an Italian by birth, D. Ballou, worthy of great praise."[299] Another recalled, "We still remember the sensations of pleasure which we experienced at witnessing the performances at that elegant little hall. Everyone gave way to unrestrained enjoyment, for all felt at home."[300] Undoubtedly, the building of the Social Hall and the activity of the DDA meant much to the Latter-day Saints and helped continue the tradition of the arts in the Church.

22. Brigham City Cooperative Pie Safe

– Church History Museum –

In the minds of some Latter-day Saints, the law of consecration is generally thought of as a failed social experiment from Joseph Smith's time. At other times it is spoken of as a law meant for the Saints to live only after the return of Christ to the earth, when conditions of scarcity and want no longer apply. However, the early Saints never gave up on consecration. Throughout Joseph Smith's lifetime, numerous attempts were made to find a way to live the principles of the law of consecration. After the Saints relocated to the western regions of North America, their longing to live the law and fulfill their obligations to the poor and needy resurfaced. In every generation, consecration took on a different form, but the principles endured. In the West, a rebirth of consecration occurred in a small city at the hands of Lorenzo Snow, and this small cooperative community served as a model for the United Order movement launched by Brigham Young.

In 1864, during a conversation with Brigham Young, Elder Snow counseled about how he might ensure the "moral, spiritual, and financial interests of the Saints in Brigham City." Elder Snow later recalled, "I stripped myself and put on the harness for the conflict, so I could say to this people, Come and follow in my footsteps. They have felt the influence of this until prejudice and opposition have been gradually giving way, and moving along, step by step, we have succeeded in arriving at a position of some prominence in spiritual and financial union."[301]

Lorenzo Snow's success in Brigham City came not from a literal application of the instructions given in the Doctrine and Covenants but rather by adapting the principles of the law of consecration. It started simply with the organization of a cooperative general store—a joint stock enterprise that Elder Snow and three others launched with about 3,000 dollars. The store became a success through a combination of persuasive sermons and the reduction of shares to only five dollars each. Elder Snow later recalled, "A good spirit . . . prevailed, and a desire to build up the kingdom of God and work for the interests of the people, outweighed all selfish considerations; hence, consent was granted by all the stockholders to establish home industries and draw dividends in the kinds produced."[302]

The businesses linked to the cooperative continued to multiply. A leather-goods department was added a few years later, followed by a woolen factory, which in turn necessitated an increase in the size of the sheep herds owned by the co-op. The number of sheep owned by the organization increased from 1,500 to 5,000 and then grew to 10,000, which created a dependable supply of wool. Along the way, the co-op added a herd of 1,000 cattle to supply an associated meat market. According to one study, "by 1874 virtually the entire economic life of this community of 400 families was owned and direct-ed by the cooperative association." Forty different departments operated by the cooperative provided each household with its food, clothing, furniture, and other necessities. The pie safe featured at the beginning of this chapter, a simple cabinet deigned to protect pies from insects and interlopers while they cooled, was built by the members of the coop-erative.[303] Lorenzo Snow modestly commented, "I do not for a moment consider that we are worthy to be called a people of the United Order, but we are slowly progressing toward that position." Brigham Young felt differently, observing that "Brother Snow has led the people along, and got them into the United Order without their knowing it."[304]

Inspired in part by the cooperative in Brigham City, Brigham Young set about spreading the principles of the law of consecration through-out all settlements in the Latter-day Saint sphere of influence in the West. Cooperative institutions were launched in a number of settlements in antic-ipation of the full return to the law of consecration. In an 1869 sermon, President Young declared, "This cooperative movement is only a stepping stone to what is called the Order of Enoch, but which is in reality the order of Heaven." While the ideal was to live after the manner of the ancient people of the city of Zion, Brigham believed in flexibility as to how the principles of the order were implemented, preaching, "Now suppose we had a little society or-ganized . . . after the Order of Enoch—would you build our houses all alike? No." One writer observed the different approaches to the United Order during this time, stating, "The Orderville United Order was communal, the Brigham City Order was cap-italists, and Kanab had two Orders existing simul-taneously—one communal and one collective."[305] In Brigham's mind, communities combined labor to ensure everyone received proper food, clothing, and care, but also education and cultivation in the higher things. "Have our historians, and our differ-ent teachers," he admonished, "teach classes of old and young, to read the Scriptures to them; to teach them history, arithmetic, reading, writing, and painting; and have the best teachers that can be got to teach our day-schools."[306]

Among the United Orders launched in Southern Utah, a collection of fourteen rules was circulated to govern the behavior of the members of the United Order. A sampling of these rules highlights the religious nature of the orders—they were designed not just for economic advantage but also to assist the Saints in their quest to live a godly life:

Rule 1. We will not take the name of Deity in vain, nor speak lightly of His character or of sacred things.

Rule 4. We will treat our families with due kindness and affection, and set before them an example worthy of imitation; in our families and intercourse with all persons, we will refrain from being contentious or quarrelsome, and we will cease to speak evil of each other and will cultivate a spirit of charity toward all.

Rule 8. That which we borrow we will return according to promise, and that which we find we will not appropriate to our own use but seek to return to its proper owner.

Rule 10. We will patronize our brethren who are in the Order.

Rule 12. We will be simple in our dress and manner of living, using proper economy and prudence in the management of all entrusted to our care.[307]

The United Orders launched during this time met with varying degrees of success, though most never achieved the success of the Brigham City cooperative. The first official United Order was organized in February 1874 in St. George, Utah. The last known United Order authorized by the Church was organized at Cave Valley, Chihuahua, Mexico, in 1893. During the time between the first and the last United Orders, more than 200 iterations of it appeared in communities in Utah, Idaho, Wyoming, Nevada, and Arizona, though most were short-lived. In Brigham City and other places such as Orderville, these communal experiments lasted more than a decade, but in most places the United Orders failed within a year or two. At least one Order, a joint enterprise of the Logan Second and Third Wards, continued on into the twentieth century, finally ending in 1909.[308]

Several factors led to the end of this great experiment in consecration. One factor identified was the hesitation of the wealthier citizens of the territory to fully commit to the order. Another factor was the increasing amount of persecution faced by Church members from merchants and businessmen of other faiths who were wary of being shut out if the United Order was fully implemented. Perhaps the most important factor was the death of Brigham Young, the greatest proponent of the United Order experiment, in 1877. One historian reflected, "There is something awesome in the spectacle of Brigham Young attempting to organize a communal commonwealth. The sheer scale of the undertaking imposed problems of a magnitude that makes it hardly comparable to small self-selected communes characteristic of nineteenth-century American communitarianism. There is, in addition, a marked poignancy in the vision of President Young, aging and in ill health, putting all his resources to the task of realizing in his lifetime the vision of Joseph Smith—and failing."[309]

The Brigham City Cooperative reached its peak level of expansion in 1877, the year Brigham Young passed away. In the years immediately following, it suffered a series of reverses due to natural disasters and man-made persecutions. The most serious blow came in December 1877, when the woolen mill operated by the co-op was destroyed by fire. The co-op went into a steep decline and never fully recovered, though it persisted for more than a decade. In November 1895, the Brigham City co-op went into receivership. The last document in the director's minute book was signed by Lorenzo Snow, who oversaw the communal experiment from its birth to its death. The last entry in the minute book for the Brigham City co-op, recorded more than a decade before its final closure, attributes to Elder Snow a speech which serves as an affecting coda for a noble experiment: "Because of losses and disasters . . . we have discontinued some of our enterprises and curtailed others. Yet for a period of fifteen years, our union has prevented division in mercantile business; say nothing about many other things which have been done by our union, and I have nothing to regret of all we have accomplished. We have kept out our enemies, and in all these matters we did them by common consent."[310]

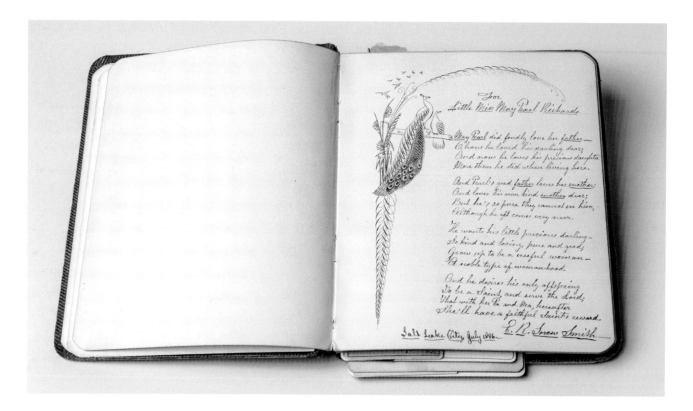

23. ELIZA R. SNOW POEM

– *Private Collector* –

◆

As a poet, Eliza R. Snow is almost without peer in the history of the Church. She produced nearly four hundred poems during the six decades of her life as a member of the Church. She witnessed and participated in many of the key events of the Restoration and used her gifts to record many of them firsthand. Her friend Emmeline B. Wells wrote, "There has scarcely been an event in the history of the Church which has not been faithfully delineated by her gifted pen." At one point, Joseph Smith designated Eliza as "Zion's Poetess," and in the later decades of her life, visitors to the Utah Territory described her as "Zion's poet-laureate."[311] Her poems covered profound subjects, such as the nature of God, the mission of Jesus Christ, and the sacred covenants of the gospel. However, while her pen was often employed to chronicle the history of the Restoration, or to explain its doctrines, it was also ready at hand to comfort a suffering child.

Eliza was born in 1804 and spent most of the early years of her life in Mantua, Ohio. Though she grew up in a religious home, Eliza was reluctant to commit to any specific church until 1828, when she committed to primitive Christianity as taught by Alexander Campbell, Walter Scott, and Sidney Rigdon. A few years later, Rigdon was converted by the Book of Mormon and introduced Eliza to Joseph Smith. Eliza's mother and several sisters immediately joined the Church, but Eliza hesitated. In 1835 she was baptized after receiving her own revelatory witness. She moved to Kirtland, later writing, "I bade a final adieu to the home of my youth. To share the fortunes of the people of God." From her baptism onward, Eliza's fate was inextricably tied to the fortunes of the Church of Jesus Christ.[312]

Over the next few years, Eliza was at the forefront of the some of the most challenging and trying events in Church history. She witnessed the apostasy of many important Church leaders during the Kirtland Banking Crisis, the expulsion of the Saints from northern Missouri in 1838, and the formation of the Relief Society in Nauvoo. On June 29, 1842, Eliza was sealed to Joseph Smith "for time and eternity, in accordance with the Celestial Law of Marriage which God has revealed," as she described it. Eliza maintained a close relationship with Joseph Smith whom she identified as "my beloved husband, the choice of my heart and the crown of my life." After Joseph's death, she was sealed to Brigham Young and lived with him for the remainder of her life, serving as a close counselor and confidant. Beginning in 1880, after the deaths of Brigham Young and Emma Smith, Eliza used the name Eliza Snow Smith as her public identification, and that name appears on her headstone.[313]

Almost a year and half after Joseph's martyrdom, Eliza published a poem in the November 15, 1845, issue of the Nauvoo *Times and Seasons* titled "My Father in Heaven." The poem became her most significant doctrinal contribution to the Restoration because of its expression of the concept of a Mother in Heaven. It reads in part:

> *I had learn'd to call thee father*
> *Through thy spirit from on high*
> *But until the key of knowledge*
> *Was restor'd, I knew not why.*
> *In the heav'ns are parents single?*
> *No, the thought makes reason stare;*
> *Truth is reason—truth eternal*
> *Tells me I've a mother there.*

Eliza's poetry about a Mother in Heaven stood as a primary statement of Church doctrine on the subject for decades. It was quoted by several prophets, including Wilford Woodruff, Joseph F. Smith, and Gordon B. Hinckley as an illustration of the doctrine. Wilford Woodruff once commented, "With regard to our position before we came here, I will say that we dwelt with the Father and with the Son, as expressed in the hymn, 'O My Father,' that has been sung here. That hymn is a revelation, though it was given unto us by a woman—Sister Snow. There are a great many sisters who have the spirit of revelation. There is no reason why they should not be inspired as well as men."[314] Eliza later eschewed credit for the revelation, saying the teaching came from Joseph Smith and she was "inspired to use [her] Poetical gift and give that Eternal principal in Poetry."[315]

While Eliza's poetry was often employed to explain and defend the doctrine of the Saints on the public stage, it was also used in personal, private settings to comfort and console. Pictured here is a poem Eliza wrote for May Pearl Richards, the daughter of Lorenzo Mauser Richards, and the granddaughter of Elder Franklin L. Richards.[316] Eliza was close with the Richards family and wrote the poem to console Pearl, who had lost her father in an accident three years earlier. At the time Eliza wrote the poem, Pearl was only six years old, but she was still grieving over her father's death. The poem, never published during Eliza's life, was written in a private autograph book owned by Pearl, which she kept as a keepsake for the rest of her life. In the poem, Eliza depicts Pearl's departed father as watching over his daughter from the other side of the veil:

> *He wants his little precious darling—*
> *So kind and loving, pure and good;*
> *Grow up to be a useful woman—*
> *A noble type of woman-hood.*

The poem was never read or known publicly until it was included in a complete collection of all of Eliza's known works published in 2009.[317] It lacks the grand themes of some of Eliza's other works, though it does reflect her abiding faith in a life beyond death and the eternal love found within a righteous family. It also demonstrates how versatile Eliza was, using her talents to elucidate some of the most profound revelations of the Restoration but also to console a grieving child.

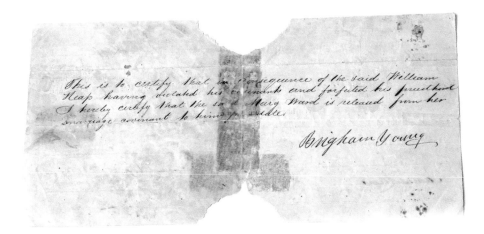

24. Cancellation of Sealing Form, 1858

– *Private Collector* –

One of the most unique aspects of Latter-day Saint theology is the emphasis placed on family and marital relationships.[318] Belief in the enduring nature of family relationships is one of the most powerful and comforting doctrines taught in the restored gospel. However, these doctrines can also be a source of distress for those who feel they don't meet the ideal. As divorce became more prevalent in the latter part of the twentieth century, it became more common for Church leaders to address the topic and offer comfort and solace. In a strange way, it is also comforting to know that complexities in family life are not unique to modern-day Church members. From the earliest days of the Church, the aspirational theology of enduring marriages in the next life was accompanied by a practical approach to marriage and family relationships. Especially in the complex marriage system of the Saints in the nineteenth century, pragmatic measures to end a marriage existed and were often employed by early Church members.

Latter-day Saints often preferred to work out marital conflicts with ecclesiastical leaders rather than civil courts. This occurred, in part, because of the questions of legality surrounding plural marriages and the prominent role the Church played in the everyday lives of the Saints. For a time, Brigham Young heard all marriage disputes. After the arrival of the Saints in the Great Basin, bishops and high councils dealt with each case, then forwarded their recommendations to Brigham Young for his approval.[319] Church historian Leonard Arrington, who read thousands of letters related to this topic, concluded that "although not an advocate of divorce, Brigham was nevertheless fairly liberal in granting it, especially in cases of plural marriages."[320] Brigham also explained on several occasions that divorces were given to women, not to men. When one man wanted to divorce his current wife to marry another woman, Brigham sternly wrote back, "If Bro. Jas. [omitted] really wants to marry, he had better take his old wife and keep her instead of giving a divorce. It is the woman's place to apply for a divorce and not the man's." Brigham's first advice usually was for counseling and reconciliation, but he at times ended a union for reasons including, "habitual drunkenness, willful absence for more than one year, impotency after marriage, conviction for felony, brutal conduct, incompatibility, &c." [321] In addition to this, Church leaders recognized that plural marriage could be challenging for women and made divorce an option for those who were unhappy in their marriages.[322]

Over time, Brigham Young began to feel overwhelmed by the continual family disputes brought to his attention and began relying more and more on the existing Church court system to settle disputes. Councils urged forgiveness and repentance more often than divorce. In one case, the combined authority of the Council of Seventy, the Twelve, and the First Presidency worked together to persuade a husband whose runaway but repentant wife sought his forgiveness for her past acts. Divorce was seen as a last resort. Paul Dredge, a scholar of Church courts wrote, "Unless there was constant physical abuse or complete abandonment, the thought of divorce or separation did not even enter the minds of most Mormons in the nineteenth century."[323]

In spite of these efforts, there were times when divorce was considered the best alternative. In 1856, Brigham Young approved a divorce when a bishop recommended it "on the ground that [JL] don't know enough to keep a wife—too big a fool. He is not fit to have a wife—for three years I caution all the girls against him. He had no just cause to put away his wife."[324] On another occasion, a husband was granted a divorce because his wife "did cause great mental distress to plaintiff by calling him a black devil and other bad names, and by saying that she did not love him and the she never should."[325] Church leaders also recognized the use of divorce when spouses became completely estranged from each other. Mary Ann West, a convert who traveled from Britain to Nauvoo, wrote in her petition, "I was married in England to a man by the name of Sheffield, he did not treat me well, and so I left him before I came to America. I was not divorced from him; never have been divorced from Mr. Sheffield; left him because he drank too much, and did not treat me right." Church leaders recognized the irreconcilable differences in the case and granted Mary Ann's request to marry another man.[326]

Though Church leaders are no longer involved in the legal functions of ending marriages, ecclesiastical leaders still play an important role in serving as counselors to struggling couples, and the First Presidency still oversees the cancellation of sealings.[327] The Church position on divorce remains similar to its stance in the nineteenth century. Church leaders see divorce as undesirable but necessary in some cases. President Dallin H. Oaks taught, "When a marriage is dead and beyond hope of resuscitation, it is needful to have a means to end it. . . . All who have been through divorce know the pain and need the healing power and hope that come from the Atonement. That healing power and that hope are there for them and also for their children."[328] The existence of a divorce form from the pioneer era, signed on the front by the divorcing couple and their ecclesiastical leaders, and on the back by a prophet of God, serves as a potent reminder of the complexities of human relationships in any era. It is also a reminder of the healing power of Christ, then and now.

25. DESERET ALPHABET READER
– L. Tom Perry Special Collections, Brigham Young University –

Although The Church of Jesus Christ of Latter-day Saints is presently limited to an ecclesiastical kingdom, during the millennial reign of Christ, "the kingdom of God will be both political and ecclesiastical."[329] It is in this light that President Brigham Young viewed the Church when he spoke of its potential to "influence and improve all aspects of life:"[330] political, economic, religious, and educational. "We will continue to improve the whole science of truth," he stated, "for that is our business; our religion circumscribes all things, and we should be prepared to take hold of whatever will be a benefit and blessing to us."[331] For Brigham Young, the Deseret Alphabet was one means of furthering the kingdom of God.

The idea for the Deseret Alphabet began with Brigham Young, who was, at the time of its development, not only president of the Church but also governor of Utah Territory. He was bothered by the inconsistencies and incongruity of the English language and saw a phonetic alphabet as the most fitting solution: "We may derive a hint of the advantage to orthography, from spelling the word eight, which in [a phonetic] alphabet only requires two letters instead of five to spell it, viz: AT."[332] Brigham Young proposed that an orthographic alphabet would not only be cheaper to print due to its concise language and abbreviated characters but would also significantly decrease the requisite time for immigrants and young children to obtain a knowledge of the English language.[333]

While Brigham Young is often accredited with the impetus for the Deseret Alphabet, the idea of revising language symbols and creating phonetic characters stemmed from a larger movement of orthographic reform that had its roots in the eighteenth and nineteenth centuries. The movement was led by such orthographic reformers as "John Hart, Alexander Gill, Benjamin Franklin, and Noah Webster,"[334] but the reformer to have the greatest influence on the Deseret Alphabet was a British phonologist named Isaac Pitman. Pitman designed a "phonetic system that consisted of having a character for every sound in the English language"[335] and developed a well-known shorthand system that he began to teach in 1837.

Among the avid disciples of Pitman's shorthand system was a man named George D. Watt. While living in England, he came in contact with missionaries from The Church of Jesus Christ of Latter-day Saints and became, shortly thereafter, the first Latter-day Saint convert in Great Britain. Watt followed the Latter-day Saints to America and, upon arriving in Nauvoo, began teaching classes in phonology. Among his many students was the Apostle Brigham Young.

When Watts left for his mission to England in 1846, Brigham Young sent him a letter "indicative of [his] strong interest in a new orthographic system."[336] He asked Watt to procure two hundred pounds of phonotype to print a small book for the benefit of the Latter-day Saints and to send it to Winter Quarters.[337] While the Latter-day Saints were beginning the journey West, Brigham Young's vision for them had expanded far beyond the struggles of the plains to encompass their future society and education.

Shortly after arriving in the Salt Lake Valley, Brigham Young organized a board of regents from the University of Deseret to discuss his idea for orthographic reform. The members of the board had difficulty agreeing whether to use the current Roman symbols differently or to create an entirely new set of symbols. In December 1853 they reached a consensus; the result was the Deseret Alphabet.

The alphabet's characters turned out to be neither phonetic adoptions nor Roman copies. Theories have been proposed that characters were taken from Egyptian symbols found on the gold plates or that they were derived from Pitman's phonetic system. "However, a comparison of Deseret Alphabet characters and other alphabets suggests that, although there may be some similarities, the Deseret Alphabet is for the most part original,"[338] and a majority of scholars believe George D. Watt to be their primary creator.

While most of the characters of the alphabet were original, the letters *C, D, L, O, P, S,* and *W* of the Roman alphabet were incorporated. To these seven, thirty-one characters were added, resulting in a thirty-eight-character system, with the only difference between capital and lowercase characters being size. The characters themselves were kept simple, since it was decided by the Board of Regents that they "not have any tops, tails, or dots . . . so that the type would last longer without wearing out."[339]

Four months after the creation of the alphabet, on April 10, 1854, Brigham Young issued the Eleventh General Epistle of the Presidency of The

Church of Jesus Christ of Latter-day Saints regarding the new alphabet:

> The Regency have formed a new Alphabet, which it is expected will prove highly beneficial, in acquiring the English language, to foreigners, as well as the youth of our country. We recommend it to the favourable [*sic*] consideration of the people, and desire that all of our teachers and instructors will introduce it in their schools and to their classes. The orthography of the English language needs reforming—a word to the wise is sufficient.[340]

Eight months following this epistle and a year after the alphabet's creation, in December of 1854, Brigham Young introduced the alphabet to the territorial legislature. The following spring of 1855 it was taught to the clerks of the Church Historian's office, and, for a short time after its introduction, some of the Church records and a number of *Deseret News* articles were written using the new alphabet.[341] The cessation of its use correlated with the coming of Johnson's Army and the Utah War, which may have led to the seeming abandonment of the alphabet in the late 1850s.

In the mid-1860s, however, interest in phonography revitalized the abandoned alphabet, and Brigham Young initiated the motion to print it, charging Orson Pratt in 1868 with the task of preparing some elementary texts. Pratt finished the task in 1869, making two alphabet readers and also transliterating the entire Book of Mormon into the Deseret Alphabet.

Around the time of the Deseret Alphabet's revival, Brigham Young made mention of it in the October 1868 general conference, recommending it to the Latter-day Saints. "It will be the means of introducing uniformity in our orthography," he said, "and the years that are now required to learn to read and spell can be devoted to other studies."[342]

Though it was encouraged and promoted by some Church and educational leaders, the Deseret Alphabet generated little interest among most teachers and students. Not only was the cost of printing prohibitive, but the library of Deseret text was sparse, with only four books available. "Those already literate had little incentive to learn the Deseret Alphabet, while illiterates would have had very little to read."[343] The completion of the transcontinental railroad in 1869 dissolved interest even further by bringing many people to Utah who were not members of the Church and who had little interest in the new alphabet.[344] In 1877 with the death of Brigham Young, "the Deseret Alphabet lost its most powerful advocate."[345] When he died, the Deseret Alphabet died with him. The Deseret Alphabet experiment cost the Latter-day Saints more than twenty thousand dollars and had lasted roughly fourteen years, from 1853 to 1877.

Despite the alphabet's ultimate failure to subsist among the Latter-day Saints, learning the Deseret phonetic system was as easy as Brigham had assured. For instance, "a previously illiterate missionary wrote letters home after only six lessons . . . [and] Hosea Stout, Thales Haskell, and others kept diaries in the Deseret Alphabet."[346] And because pronunciation, which determined spelling, varied, many of these texts are valuable resources for linguists and historians in determining the pronunciations of the early Latter-day Saints.

Because of its commendation given in such formal church settings as general conference, and its recommendations in church publications, some may have seen the alphabet as a divine mandate, and thus its end as a failure of the prophet or of the work of the Lord. But for Brigham Young and others, it was the means of fulfilling the commandment to "do many things of [our] own free will and bring to pass much righteousness."[347]

26. LEAH WIDTSOE'S BABY BLESSING DRESS

– Church History Museum –

In April 1830, Joseph Smith received revelation on the subject of the naming and blessing of children, along with many other topics central to the founding of The Church of Jesus Christ of Latter-day Saints. This revelation, which would later be recorded in the twentieth section of the Doctrine and Covenants, states, "Every member of the church of Christ having children is to bring them unto the elders before the church, who are to lay their hands upon them in the name of Jesus Christ, and bless them in his name" (D&C 20:70). Leah Widtsoe's baby blessing dress symbolizes this commandment to name and bless children as well as the long tradition of this ordinance in the Church.

The blessing of children was not a new concept when the Lord revealed this commandment to Joseph Smith. In Mark 10:14, Jesus Christ commanded His disciples to "suffer the little children to come unto me, and forbid them not: for of such is the kingdom of God." He then "took them up in his arms, put his hands upon them, and blessed them" (Mark 10:16). When Christ ministered to the Nephites in ancient America He "took their little children, one by one, and blessed them, and prayed unto the Father for them" (3 Nephi 17:21). Joseph Smith was also known to give blessings to children. Oliver Cowdery records that at a conference in Ohio on April 21, 1834, Joseph Smith "laid hands on certain children and blessed them in the name of the Lord."[348]

The naming and blessing of children became a regular part of services in the restored Church. Typically performed by the father of the child on fast Sundays, this ordinance, though not a saving ordinance, is a commandment from God that enables children to receive blessings and protection from the Priesthood.[349] Leah Widtsoe, daughter Alma Dunford and Susa Young and granddaughter of Brigham Young, received a name and a blessing in the manner laid out in this manner shortly after her birth on February 24, 1874. Her baby blessing dress symbolizes the importance of baby blessings and the long-standing doctrinal tradition of naming and blessing children.

27. SALT LAKE TEMPLE DOORKNOB AND ESCUTCHEON

— *Church History Museum* —

⬥───────────────────────────────

The Salt Lake Temple is one of the most recognizable symbols of The Church of Jesus Christ of Latter-day Saints. Built over a period of forty years, it stands as a witness of the sacrifices of the early Saints and their work to build a new home in the mountains of the western United States. It is also a masterwork of symbolism. From its inception, building took the symbolism of the earlier temples built in Kirtland and Nauvoo, reinterpreting them and providing a new collection of figurative expressions on the exterior of the temple to accompany the symbolic ceremonies performed in the interior of the temple. From angelic statue on its highest tower, to the earthstones just above the ground, every symbol on the temple is calculated to teach the principles of the gospel of Jesus Christ.

One of Brigham Young's first actions after the arrival of the Vanguard Company in the Salt Lake Valley was to identify the location for the construction of a temple. The question of survival in the arid land delayed start of construction by several years, but on April 6, 1853, the corner of the temple was laid, and construction began. After several stops and starts, including burial of the temple foundations during the Utah War, the temple gradually rose over a period of decades. The battlements were finished in 1886, and the capstone was put in place on April 6, 1892, with the interior and final dedication happening one year later, in 1893.[350]

Truman Angell served as the architect for the temple, though major contributions of the design of the building came from Brigham Young. When the cornerstone of the temple was laid, President Young declared that he had seen in vision five years earlier that the temple would have six towers, symbolizing the heads of the Aaronic and Melchizedek Priesthoods. At the same time, Brigham appears to have given Angell a fair amount of freedom on the architecture and symbolism of the temple. At one point Brigham remarked, "Brother Joseph often remarked that a revelation was not more necessary to build a Temple than a dwelling house; if a man knew he needed a kitchen, a bedroom, a parlor, etc. he needed no revelation to inform him of the fact; and I and my brethren around me know what is wanted in a Temple, having received all the ordinances therein." Seeking a synthesis of a wide variety of architectural and symbolic traditions, Angell, along with several "art missionaries" traveled to Europe to find inspiration of the temple.[351]

One critic of the earlier Nauvoo Temple, Illinois Governor Thomas Ford, described Latter-day Saint architecture and symbolism as "a piece of patchwork, variable, strange, and incongruous."[352] Ford's description of a patchwork missed the point of one of the key tenets of Latter-day Saint thought—a coming together of ideas from different traditions. "Our religion drinks up all truth," Brigham Young declared in 1859, "and the Lord God Almighty will gather unto Zion all the intelligence and wisdom that has ever been realized among men."[353]

It is difficult to be too definitive about the symbolism on the exterior of the temple. At least in part, symbols are meant to be malleable as teaching tools, allowing the learner to draw the desired lesson based on their spiritual progression. At the same time, some symbolism in the temple was definitively stated by Brigham Young. According to William Ward, Truman Angell's assistant, Brigham Young's first sketch of the temple was a simple rectangle with three circles on each end. "There will be three towers on the east, representing the President and his two Counselors, also three similar towers on the west representing the President Bishop and his two Counselors," Brigham explained to Ward. He continued, "The towers on the east the Melchizedek Priesthood, those on the west the Aaronic priesthood [sic]."[354]

Other symbols on the temple exterior have a wider and more varying interpretation. Many visitors notice the familiar shape of Ursa Major (the Big Dipper) carved into the central tower on the west-facing side of the temple. At one point, Truman Angell explained the present of the Big Dipper was meant to remind the Saints that the lost can find their way with the help of the priesthood. The all-seeing eye is a symbol commonly found on early temples of the Restoration and throughout the pioneer period. This symbol is depicted on the Salt Lake Temple underneath the image of a pleated veil, representing the view of God on His children from the other side of the veil. The temple sunstones, moonstones, star-stones, and even Saturn-stones, are intended to evoke reflection about the degrees of glory and the nature of the universe. Hugh Nibley once remarked, "A temple, good or bad, is a scale-model of the universe."[355]

Though symbols vary in interpretation, the most important function of temple symbolism is to point the faithful toward Jesus Christ. Even the smallest details of the temple reinforce the centrality of Christ in Latter-day Saint theology. The escutcheon plates on the door themselves contain a small bas-relief of a door, tying to the numerous place in the scriptures where Jesus referred to Himself as the gate or the doorway to salvation (see John 10:9). Above the door on the escutcheon is an arch featuring a prominent keystone. During the period when the temple was under construction, Elder Erastus Snow referred to ordinances as a keystone, declaring, "This new and everlasting covenant reveals unto us the keys of Holy Priesthood and ordinances thereof. It is the grand keystone of the arch which the Lord is building in the earth. . . . It completes the exaltation and glory of the righteous who receive the everlasting Gospel." Just above the keystones are the years of the temples construction, 1853 to 1893, the forty-year period itself reminiscent of the period the Israelites wandered in the wilderness without a permanent home (see Deuteronomy 2:7). Above the numbers is an emblem of clasped hands, a common symbol on the temple exterior. The hands possibly represent fellowship and community, as well as a covenant relationship with the Lord.[356]

Even the doorknobs to the temple contain important symbolism. The center of the doorknob contains a beehive, one of the most ubiquitous symbols from the pioneer era. A symbol of industry and co-operation, beehives place the temple in the context of pioneer Utah. It was used in spiritual architecture such as the St. George and Salt Lake temples, and in secular settings, such as the seal of the University of Utah and the state of Utah. It hearkens back to Deseret, the original name of the Saints' idealized state in the western United States, a name in the book of Ether meaning "honeybee" (see Ether 2:3).

The doorknob also contains words emblazoned on every temple built by the Latter-day Saints: "Holiness to the Lord." These words were found on the original crown worn by the high priest of Israel (see Exodus 28:36) and was also found on the Kirtland and Nauvoo temples. The care taken to sculpt the phrase into something as ordinary as a doorknob demonstrates the commitment of the pioneer Saints to consecrate their lives to God. It is also a partial fulfillment of the prophet Zechariah's prophecy that in the Millennium even the bells on horses would bear the phrase "holiness to the Lord" (Zechariah 14:20). Elder D. Todd Christofferson reflected on the tendency to make seemingly secular things holy in the pioneer era of the Saints: "The pioneer Saints in these valleys affixed that reminder, 'Holiness to the Lord,' on seemingly common or mundane things as well as those more directly associated with religious practice. It was inscribed on sacrament cups and plates and printed on certificates of ordination of Seventies and on a Relief Society banner. 'Holiness to the Lord' also appeared over the display windows of Zion's Cooperative Mercantile Institution, the ZCMI department store. It was found on the head of a hammer and on a drum. 'Holiness to the Lord' was cast on the metal doorknobs of President Brigham Young's home. These references to holiness in seemingly unusual or unexpected places may seem incongruous, but they suggest just how pervasive and constant our focus on holiness needs to be."[357]

Brigham Young commented on the need for holiness during "a dedicatory prayer, presenting the Temple, thus far completed, as a monument of the saints' liberality, fidelity, and faith," explaining, "Thirty years' experience has taught me that every moment of my life must be holiness to the Lord, resulting from equity, justice, mercy, and uprightness in all my actions, which is the only course by which I can preserve the Spirit of the Almighty to myself."[358] Given the emphasis of the pioneer Saints on holiness, it is fitting that to enter the temple built as a monument to their sacrifice, one must first touch a fixture with the words "Holiness to the Lord" emblazoned on it.

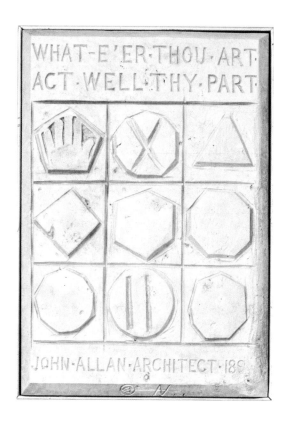

28. "What E'er Thou Art, Act Well Thy Part" Stone

– Church History Museum –

When David O. McKay became president of The Church of Jesus Christ of Latter-day Saints (1951–1970), he dismissed the notion that there was any hierarchy, status, or station associated with callings in the Church. He taught that all assignments are equal in the Church and that each Latter-day Saint is accountable for his responsibilities no matter the station. This idea was conceived when he was serving a mission (1897–99) as a young man in Scotland. As a missionary, David O. McKay was experiencing the common feelings of homesickness and discouragement. On March 26, 1898, instead of tracting (an activity which he often admitted in his missionary journal that he disliked), he and his companion, Peter G. Johnston, were sightseeing at the Stirling Castle. On their way back to their apartment they had rented that morning, they passed a home under construction with an inscription carved in the stone arch over one of the windows.[359] The quotation, thought to be from Shakespeare, read, "What E'er Thou Art, Act Well Thy Part."[360] President McKay internalized the message of those words and felt that his reading those words was inspired. He recorded the feelings he had at the time in his journal:

I said to myself, or the Spirit within me whispered, "You are a member of The Church of Jesus Christ of Latter-day Saints. More than that, you are a representative of the Lord Jesus Christ. You accepted the responsibility as a representative of the Church." Then I thought [about] what we had done that morning. We had been sightseeing. We had gained historical instruction and information, it is true, and I was thrilled with it . . . However, that was not missionary work. . . . I accepted the message given to me on that stone, and from that moment we tried to do our part as missionaries in Scotland.[361]

The stone's message had a profound impact on the young missionary. He took this experience as a sign that he should remain in the mission field and do his part well. There and then, he decided he was not acting very well the part of a missionary, and so he rededicated his efforts to the work, vowing to act as the best missionary he could for the rest of his mission. His entire missionary experience improved dramatically from that time forward. He also determined that whatever responsibility might come his way in the future, he would do his very best.[362] Thus, this experience not only changed David O. McKay's perspective as a missionary but also reminded him throughout his life to perform each duty to the best of his abilities.[363]

This quote discovered on a stone in Scotland would also become one of the mainstays of President McKay's teachings during the sixty-three years he spoke in general conference. President McKay consistently taught that each Latter-day Saint is important to The Church of Jesus Christ of Latter-day Saints, no matter how small or large his part may be, and that when one Latter-day Saint neglects his duties, the equation for the success of the Church is hindered and the outcome reduced. Through his repetition of this message, President McKay hoped Latter-day Saints would incorporate this slogan into their lives. Church members became well-acquainted with not only the quotation and the teachings associated with the mantra but with the stone mantel itself.

The large stone window lintel, which measures thirty-seven inches high, twenty-six inches wide, and five inches thick, was designed by a nineteenth-century Scottish architect named John Allan in 1898. Allan was known throughout Scotland for his unusual designs and often included carved inscriptions on buildings like the one that David O. McKay encountered. The particular design found on the "What E'er Thou Art, Act Well Thy Part" stone is known as the magic square. In this design, there is an arrangement of numbers in a square grid; each number appears once, and the sum in any direction is the same. This particular square has different symbols and shapes to represent numbers, such as a hand symbolizing five or a triangle representing three. The symbols are incised within the nine squares, and each row adds up to eighteen. The square would lose its "magic" if any of the numbers were changed. Each one is vital to the whole and irreplaceable.[364] Numerically, the "magic square" demonstrates the same message as the Shakespeare quotation.

When David O. McKay joined the Quorum of the Twelve Apostles in 1906, he began to share his experience with the John Allan arch.[365] Missionaries who were sent to Scotland were shown the building where the plaque had been and were told about President McKay's experience. This was done in the hopes that they too might be inspired by the slogan. When David B. Haight was serving as the Scottish Mission President (1963–66), he felt that the stone's message was so important to missionary work that he had a replica of the arch made and sent to the Language Training Mission Center in Provo, Utah.[366] This replica is still found today in the foyer of the Missionary Training Center in Provo, Utah.

Tracing how the original stone made its way to Salt Lake City is a bit controversial because there are several different accounts of its travels. In the biography *Mark E. Peterson*, author Peggy Preston Barton states that when Elder Mark E. Peterson was in Wales to dedicate the Merthyr Tydfil chapel in 1963, he also visited Scotland and inquired about the stone. Barton states that it was Elder Peterson who arranged to have the arch shipped to Salt Lake City, where it was put on display.[367]

In a different account, historian Susan Easton Black taught that a couple of alert missionaries noticed that the building on which the arch was located was being demolished. She shared that these missionaries went to the contractor and asked if they could have the stone with the inscription. The contractor figured it was one less stone for him to haul away and was happy to let the missionaries have the arch. With the assistance of some local members, the Elders loaded the stone onto a truck, took it to Edinburgh, and deposited it on the mission home lawn. After a few years, the stone was then sent to Utah.[368]

However, according to the Church History Museum, when the building that contained the original stone was torn down, the stone was lost for a time. Years later, some missionaries recognized the inscribed stone, which had been incorporated into a stone fence in their proselyting area. Knowing of its meaning and importance to President McKay, the Scottish mission presidency acquired it and placed it on the mission home grounds, where it remained until 1970. After President McKay's death, the stone was sent to Salt Lake City to be included among his artifacts and displayed in various locations.[369]

Despite the uncertainty about how the original stone got to Salt Lake City, it has been in the Church History Museum since 1984. Two replicas of the stone are on display on the grounds of the Scotland/Ireland Mission Home and at the Missionary Training Center (MTC) in Provo, Utah.[370] Each new missionary at the MTC in Provo who has seen the "What E'er Thou Art, Act Well Thy Part" stone may have pondered what new significance the inscription on the block of stone has for them.

Over the years since the stone found its permanent home in the Church History Museum, General Authorities have periodically reminded Latter-day Saints of David O. McKay's experience with its message.[371] And even for the "Millennial Generation," President Russell M. Nelson and Elder Quentin L. Cook have reinstated the message anew. In a CES devotional given in 2012 Elder Cook retold the story of President McKay and the stone and then admonished, "Your generation, born in the 1980s and early- to mid-1990s, is currently referred to as the 'Millennial Generation.' Some commentators are skeptical about what your generation will accomplish. I believe you have the background and the foundation to be the best generation ever, particularly in advancing our Father in Heaven's plan."[372] This milestone experience in the life of David O. McKay has become a milestone in the history of the Church, and the inscription found on the stone will continue to be a mantra in the lives of Latter-day Saints.

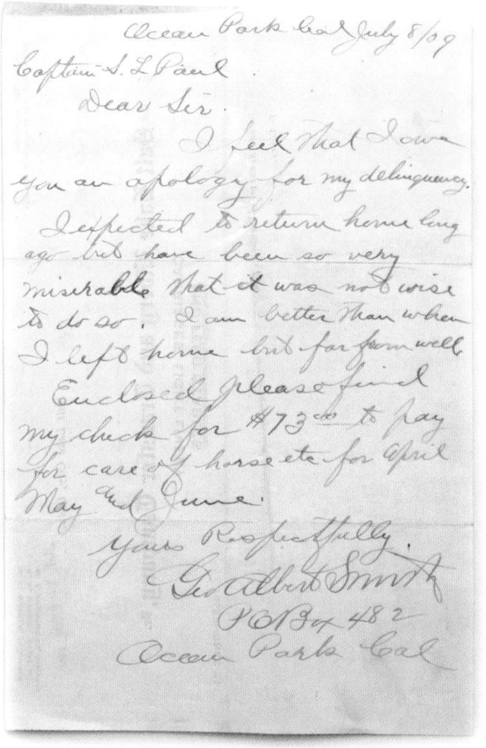

Ocean Park Cal July 8/09

Captain S. L Paul.

Dear Sir.

    I feel that I owe you an apology for my delinquency.

I expected to return home long ago but have been so very miserable that it was not wise to do so. I am better than when I left home but far from well

Enclosed please find my check for $73⁰⁰ to pay for care of horse etc for April May and June.

    Yours Respectfully.

Geo Albert Smith
PO Box 482
Ocean Park Cal

29. GEORGE ALBERT SMITH'S LETTER WHILE RECOVERING FROM MENTAL BREAKDOWN

– Private Collector –

George Albert Smith wrestled with many physical and emotional issues starting early in his life. At just thirteen, he received his patriarchal blessing, which told him he would become a "mighty prophet."[373] This great future responsibility perhaps put pressure on a personality that lent itself to obsessiveness and anxiety. Being called as an apostle at the young age of thirty-three also advanced George Albert's problems. Constant travel as a church leader, averaging more than 30,000 miles a year, presented difficult situations for him. Frontier life could not accommodate his unique and fastidious habits, such as using several towels to wash his face and hands or a sensitivity to odors.[374] He was a frail man with a weak body and a delicate digestive system. He suffered from sleep disturbances as well as hypersomnia. Depression and anxiety also plagued him. He had a very sensitive and compassionate heart and always felt responsible to help people with their problems. Because his office was accessible to the general public, anyone could come and ask an apostle for help. This became a problem when he carried the burdens of many who came to see him. Though George Albert had a good work ethic, his high-strung personality caused him to struggle with the idea of taking a break from work. He did not have an outlet such as sports or music to relieve his stress, and he continually struggled with the idea that resting from work meant shirking his duties in the Church.[375] A wide range of emotional, mental, and physical problems all contributed to a three-year period of depression, discomfort, and discouragement.[376]

While there has never been a definitive diagnosis of his health problems, doctors today have speculated on what George Albert could have been experiencing; the diagnoses range from hepatitis curitis or hyperthyroidism to multiple sclerosis or some kind of lead poisoning. Whatever the medical condition, George Albert's nervous breakdown caused him to be incapacitated, both physically and emotionally. He could not serve as a church leader and was unable to communicate through speech. Leading up to and during this dark period in his life, he received advice from a variety of people encouraging him to take a break. Several doctors ordered him to rest, but he often ignored their advice. His own wife worried about his fragile health, but because of her own lack of emotional strength, she sometimes added her burdens to his already heavy shoulders.[377]

In January 1909, when a streetcar neglected to stop for him, "he ran to the depot with a heavy coat and valise. He caught the train but felt that he had been unwise for overexerting himself." He felt his heart was weak and visited the doctor's office when he got home. The diagnosis was a healthy heart, but he needed to take a rest. Ignoring the doctor's advice, George Albert continued at a feverish pace. During the next few weeks, he drove through several "raging blizzards" to stake conferences, and by February 24, his throat was causing him a lot of trouble. The next night, he awoke in pain from head to toe. Dr. Gamble looked at him and diagnosed him with la grippe (a type of influenza).[378] Though la grippe was an awful virus, it was not the root of his problem. All during March, his nervous tension continued and he was depressed and discouraged, feeling he was not able to do any work. [379] Fellow apostles administered to him, and his wife, Lucy, hovered over him. Group prayers were offered in his behalf, but he continued to be in a state of nervous exhaustion.[380] George Albert himself once wrote that he felt strong spiritually but weak physically. He was de-

pressed with the fact that the harder he worked, even for a good cause, the sicker he became.

In April, he attended the first session of general conference but missed the rest of the sessions. Things were not getting better. He realized that he could not get the rest he needed as a member of the Quorum of the Twelve Apostles living near Church headquarters. So it was decided he would go to Ocean Park, California, to recuperate.

George Albert arrived in Ocean Park—near Santa Monica, California—on April 13, where he rented a little house by the beach for twenty-five dollars a month. Things were dramatically different for him in Ocean Park. There were no meetings, no visitors, and no speeches. Instead, he spent time sleeping and walking on the beach. That spring, his life was filled with fervent prayers and priesthood blessings.[381] However, throughout the summer, there was no improvement, and it seemed that the Lord was turning a deaf ear to all the petitions sent to heaven in his behalf. His sleep was troubled, his nerves were on edge, his skin blistered, his ribs felt very weak, and his stomach was upset.

It was during this time that he wrote this letter. Written on July 8, 1909, to Captain S. L. Paul (who was caring for one of George Albert's horses in Salt Lake City), it is one of the few communications we have where he admitted his illness and low spirits. As he states in the letter, he had thought that his stay in California would be shorter and had "expected to return home long ago, but [was] so very miserable that it was not wise to do so. He then observed, "I am better than when I left home but far from well."[382]

His health would take another turn for the worse on August 24, when, seeking some relief from the monotony of bed rest, he decided to take a swim out into the ocean. All went well until he started back. He was about halfway to shore when a double-headed wave struck him, burying him under the water.

George Albert could not get himself back to shore and was rescued by a neighbor. He caught a nervous chill and had to go directly to bed. "That was as near drowning as I ever want to be," and his narrow escape haunted him for days.[383] With his new aversion to the ocean, he decided he wanted to go home, and he left for Utah on August 28. A few weeks later, on September 13, Dr. Samuel Allen concluded George Albert must have a strained heart muscle and prescribed a full year of absolute rest.[384]

With a year of bed rest facing him, George Albert decided to go to the better climate of St. George and arrived there on November 6. A short time later, George Albert went to bed and remained in a pitiful condition. For five months, he did not leave his bed and never changed out of his bedclothes. Even arranging his bedclothes caused him a nervous chill or a fainting spell. Never before had he experienced unanswered prayers to this degree. George Albert

still felt depressed, inadequate, and neglectful of his church responsibilities.

However, a turning point eventually came, starting in the form of a dream where George Albert declared to his grandfather his faithfulness to the Smith name throughout his life. This dream helped remind George Albert of his self-worth.[385] Soon after, George Albert experienced a change when he succumbed to the Lord's will, even acknowledging that it might mean leaving his weak mortal body. This submission in prayer was the turning point in George Albert's life.[386] Health problems continued, and public speaking was still a struggle, but George Albert eventually learned how to handle the bouts of depression or anxiousness. After his three-year period of despair ended, he learned how to trust in the Lord and fight his emotional and physical problems with power from God.

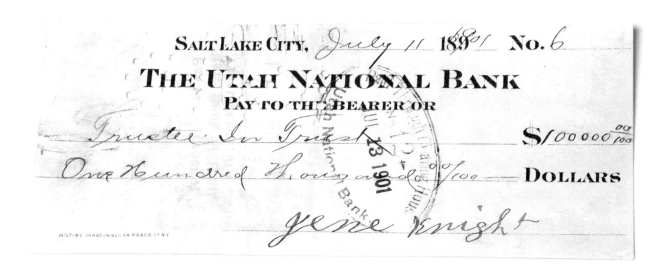

30. Jesse Knight Check

– Private Collector –

Jesse Knight was the scion of one of the most famous families in the history of the Church. His grandfather, Joseph Knight, hired Joseph Smith as a farmhand even before the young seer received the gold plates and began his prophetic career. The Knights were among the first converts to the Church: Jesse's father, Newel Knight, was baptized in May 1830, less than a month after the Church was organized. The first miracle of the Church involved the Knight family when Joseph Smith cast a devil out of Newel "not by man, nor by the power of man, but it was done by the power of God, and by the power of Godliness."[387] From that point on the Knights stayed at the side of Joseph Smith, enduring trials as they were forced from Kirtland to Missouri to Nauvoo, where Jesse was born on September 6, 1845. Despite his illustrious heritage, as a young man Jesse found himself estranged from the Church, uninterested in actively serving in it, and seemingly destined to lead a life outside of the faith. However, through a miraculous series of events, Jesse not only returned to Church activity but became a key figure in saving the financial future of the Church.

Jesse's estrangement from the Church may be linked to the death of his father when he was less than two years old. Newel Knight was among the stalwarts of the faith, and he left Nauvoo when the call came to travel west. During the exodus from Nauvoo, his family was forced to winter at Ponca, Iowa, where Newel died after a short illness on January 11, 1847. Jesse's mother, Lydia, was able to eventually bring her family to Pottowattamie, where she spent several miserable years before she was able to emigrate to the Salt Lake Valley in 1850.[388] Jesse lived a difficult and hardscrabble life on the frontier. He found work as a teamster, traveling throughout the West. As a young man he also displayed an impulsive demeanor. When his toe was partially smashed in an accident, Jesse placed his foot on a block of wood and chopped off the troublesome digit, not realizing that the pain would subside, but an amputated toe was lost forever.[389]

Jesse married Amanda McEwan and began raising a family but remained indifferent toward religion. He even joined the anti-Mormon Liberal Party. To the distress of his family, he did not set foot in a house of worship for fifteen years. He refused to baptize his children, telling them to wait until they were older and to decide for themselves.[390] When he was in his forties, his mother paid him one last visit before her death. Noting her silence on the subject of religion, Jesse challenged his mother: "Mother, how is it you are not preaching to me as you usually do?" She replied, "Jesse, I have prayed in the [St. George] temple for my children many times and on one occasion the Lord made known to me that I was not to worry about you any more, and that you would one day understand for yourself." Jesse answered, "Mother, I know you must be mistaken, for I'm further from the Church now than I have ever been before."[391]

Jesse's religious awakening came a few months later when his youngest daughter, Jennie, became deathly ill. The water on Jesse's ranch was contaminated by a dead rat. Jennie, only two years old, ran such a high fever that doctors told the Knights she would soon pass away. When his wife decided to call the local elders from the Church, Jesse stopped her, saying, "No, it would be hypocritical, now that the doctors have given her up, for me to resort to such a thing," adding, "I have no faith in the Church." Amanda replied, "I have, and think my feelings should have consideration at such a serious moment." Jesse backed down and the elders soon arrived. After they gave Jennie a blessing she immediately rose up from her bed and commented on the flowers placed in the window.[392] She made a full recovery, but another of the Knights' children, eighteen-year-old Minnie, soon became very ill. Minnie told her parents that when Jennie became ill, she prayed and asked God to take her life and spare her sister. She believed she would die thirty days from the time she became sick and, true to her prompting, passed away thirty days later. She was the only child of the Knights who had been baptized.

Jesse was twisted in knots by the miraculous healing of one of his daughters, only to lose another so soon after. He remembered that when Minnie was a baby she became deathly ill with diphtheria. At the time, Jessie promised God that if his daughter was spared, he would return to church and serve faithfully. She was healed, but in the following years he did not keep his promise. Reflecting on her death, he wrote, "How keenly I felt the justice of her being taken from us!" He pleaded with God for forgiveness, later writing, "My prayer was answered and I received a testimony."[393] From that time forward, Jesse lived as a committed Latter-day Saint, as did his family. Another of his daughters, Inez, even became one of the first two female missionaries of the Church.[394]

The sincerity of Jesse's conversion was evident in the way he conducted his business affairs following the incident. Jesse became involved in mining, even following spiritual promptings to help him find the places he should dig. When he offered a partnership to Jared Roundy, an expert miner, Roundy replied, "I do not want an interest in a damned old humbug like this." Roundy relented, and Jesse used his response to craft the official name for the venture: the Humbug Mine. In July 1896, silver was discovered in the Humbug Mine, leading to a series of ventures making Knight one of the wealthiest and most influential men in Utah. With success after success, Jesse soon became known as "the Mormon Mining Wizard."[395]

To facilitate his mining ventures, Knight built several towns, the first being Knightsville, located a few miles southeast of present-day Eureka, Utah. The terms he set for his employees were generous, with Knight declaring he would "raise their wages without being asked; he would not run a boarding house and require them to patronize it, as often done in other places; and would arbitrarily take nothing out of their wages for hospital funds, insurance fees, or other purposes; nor would he permit his superintendent or foreman to question any man as to his religion." At the same time, Jesse asked for the right to fire any employee using his wages to purchase alcohol or neglecting to support his family. He also paid his workers twenty-five cents more than the wages in other mines so they could attend church on Sundays without sacrificing their earnings. Knight went on to build similar mining communities at Silver City and Spring Canyon, Utah. Other miners sometimes referred to the communities as "the Sunday School Mines," but the company town founded by Knight created healthy, peaceful environments, especially compared to other mining towns.[396]

Near the beginning of the twentieth century, when the Church was nearly financially exhausted from its long and difficult struggles with the government over plural marriage, Jesse Knight became an unlikely rescuer of the Church's finances. Knight's son recalled that just before the discovery of the Humbug Mine his father told him he was sure they would find ore and that with their earnings "someday we would save the credit of the Church."[397] Just a few months later President Wilford Woodruff arose in a priesthood meeting and explained "that the Church was in very straightened circumstances financially." This condition, President Woodruff continued, was brought about "on account of the Federal Government confiscating Church property and through other oppressing anti-Mormon laws passed by Congress." The situation was so dire that President Woodruff made a special request asking the bishops in the meeting to return to their wards and ask any members of means to make temporary loans to the Church. On his way to the meeting, Joseph R. Keeler, bishop of the Provo Fourth Ward, heard an audible voice declare, "Jesse Knight will lend the Church $10,000."[398]

Bishop Keeler immediately went to the home of "Uncle Jesse" to seek help, informing Knight of what President Woodruff said at the meeting. Keeler tried to find a way to bring up the subject but, he recalled, "Before I could ask him whether he would make the loan, he said instantly, 'Yes, I'll lend the Church $10,000.00 and I'll see the Cashier this afternoon and have a check ready for you tomorrow." The next day Bishop Keeler took the check to the First Presidency in Salt Lake City. When he handed the check to President Woodruff, Bishop Keeler noticed that "it appeared to me that a great weight was lifted off his mind." President Woodruff later told him the check was the means of saving the credit of the Church.[399]

On another occasion Elder Heber J. Grant, then a member of the Quorum of the Twelve Apostles, approached Knight to ask for $5,000 to assist a few Church members in debt. Knight at first declined, seeing the problems as the result of a private venture and none of his responsibility. When Elder Grant mentioned asking another person to pray before they donated, Knight asked Elder Grant why he had not asked him to pray about the decision. "Because you refused altogether to do anything," Elder Grant replied. Knight went home that night and prayed, receiving an impression that he should not only loan Grant the money, but double the amount of the loan. The next time "Uncle Jesse" saw Elder Grant he commented, smiling, "When you ask me for another contribution I'll pay it without stopping to pray."[400]

Jesse Knight's generosity helped save the Church during the lean years of the early twentieth century. He made his contributions without fanfare or publicity. His own son, who became his biographer, did not know about the credit-saving $10,000 until well after his father's death, when Bishop Keeler related the story to him. Likewise, the check shown at the beginning of this chapter, dated July 11, 1901, written to the Trustee in Trust, and signed on the back by Lorenzo Snow, the president of the Church, was unknown to the public in Jesse Knight's lifetime. This check, written for $100,000 instead of $10,000, may represent a vital donation given by a repentant businessman who saved the Church from financial ruin.

31. *Jesus the Christ* Manuscript

– *Private Collector* –

In the early twentieth century, Latter-day Saints went through a transitional process as they moved closer to mainstream American culture. There was a renewal of faith since the end of plural marriage removed barriers from Latter-day Saints in developing relationships with and learning from leaders and scholars of other Christian churches. In the nineteenth century, a grand Christian tradition emerged as several Victorian-era biographies of Jesus Christ became popular. Works such as Alfred Edersheim's *The Life and Times of Jesus the Messiah* (1883), Frederic W. Farrar's *The Life of Christ* (1874), and J. Cunningham Geikie's *Life and Words of Christ* (1877) gained widespread readership among Victorian Christians. Latter-day Saints, long seen as a peculiar people by their Christian peers, became eager to enhance their knowledge of Christ and share with the world the unique set of truths they possessed concerning the mission of the Messiah. One Latter-day Saint's response to the Victorian biographies of Jesus was a work that was both old-fashioned in its scriptural approach and radical in its embrace of Restoration scripture. This work was James E. Talmage's *Jesus the Christ*, published in 1915.[401]

James E. Talmage was a British immigrant who arrived in the United States in 1876. He attended school at Brigham Young Academy in Provo and then trav-eled to the eastern states, where he received training in chemistry and geology at Lehigh University and Johns Hopkins University before returning to Utah. Talmage eventually became the president of LDS University (the early forerunner of LDS Business College) in Salt Lake City and then president of the University of Utah. During his academic career, he became well known as a scientist, educator, author, and administrator. He also became well known for his gospel scholarship. While he was president of LDS University, the First Presidency asked him to give a series of lectures on the doctrines and teachings of the Church. Gathered into one book, these lectures were published in 1899 as *The Articles of Faith.* In the following years, Talmage was asked by Church leaders to prepare a new edition of the Pearl of Great Price, which was published in 1902, and then to give a series of lectures in 1904 on the life of Jesus Christ. He became one of the leading intellectuals among Latter-day Saints, publishing *The Great Apostasy* (1909), *The House of the Lord* (1912), *The Story and Philosophy of Mormonism* (1914), and *The Philosophical Basis of Mormonism* (1915).[402]

In December 1911, he was called as a member of the Quorum of the Twelve Apostles. Even with his wide experience as a scholar and a teacher, Talmage was still overwhelmed by his call to serve as an Apostle. At the time of his call, he recorded in his diary, "I feel that I would shrink from the responsibility, and hesitate, even if I did not actually decline; but I hold myself ready to respond to my call made upon by and in the Priesthood. . . . I pray for the strength to honor this divine calling. The brethren testify to one that the call is from the Lord. To it I respond with prayerful trust."[403] With a new commission to serve as one of the special witnesses of Christ in all the world, Elder Talmage began searching for ways to share the Latter-day Saints' unique witness of Christ.

In the summer of 1914, Talmage met with the First Presidency and was invited to prepare a book based on the lectures he had given a decade earlier on the life of Christ. He was given specific directions to prepare the book "with as little delay as possible"

and was even granted the special privilege of the use of an office in the Salt Lake Temple to allow him to focus as much as possible on preparing the book. Talmage prepared the manuscript in an impressively short span of time, presenting the manuscript to the First Presidency on April 19, 1915, just seven months and five days after he began writing. The entire original manuscript was written in longhand with a pencil. Because of Talmage's remarkable speed in completing the manuscript, stories are still told about how he never left the temple while he was preparing the book. His journal, however, reveals that he carried out a full slate of apostolic responsibilities in addition to his writing. On April 19, 1915, Talmage wrote in his journal, "Finished the actual writing of the book 'Jesus the Christ' to which I have devoted every spare hour since settling down to the work on September 14th last. Had it not been that I was privileged to do this work in the Temple, it would have been at present far from completion. I have felt the inspiration of the place and have appreciated the privacy and quietness incident thereto."[404]

While Talmage authored the book, it was also a uniquely collaborative work among the leaders of the Church. Talmage held weekly reading sessions for all of the General Authorities, who offered suggestions and revisions for the work. One central question Church leaders wrestled with was whether the book should be structured as a tool for educating children or as a work for mature adults to study the life of Christ. After discussions among the leaders of the Church, Talmage recorded: "As was intended the work is being prepared for our people in general, and is not adapted for use as a text book for immature students."[405] Talmage labored constantly to revise the work based on suggestions and input from other Church leaders, as evidenced by the markups present in the manuscript shown above.

Talmage was not a trained biblical scholar, but in preparing the manuscript and his earlier lectures, he immersed himself in the literature of his day related to biblical studies. He frequently cites Farrar, Edersheim, and Geikie in the manuscript, and his work mirrors their efforts in many ways. In the early twentieth century, higher biblical criticism was becoming more popular, and Talmage took a moderate, mostly literal approach toward the scriptures. He incorporated new scholarship into his work with moderation. For instance, though he primarily quoted from the King James Version of the Bible, Talmage also quoted from the 1881 Revised Version of the Bible, a newer work including more recent discoveries and alternative readings, more than twenty times in the manuscript. He also wrote candidly about some of the complexities of biblical interpretation. When he tackled the problem of determining the actual hour of crucifixion, he observed: "All attempts to harmonize the accounts [between the synoptic Gospels of Matthew, Mark, and Luke with the Gospel of John] in this particular have proved futile because the discrepancies are real."[406] The result is a study both forward-looking and old-fashioned at the same time.

While Talmage followed the general pattern laid down by Victorian writers, he also offered a radical departure from their writings by including the additional witnesses of Restoration scripture. The subtitle of the book boldly proclaims it as "A Study of the Messiah and His Mission according to the Holy Scriptures both Ancient *and Modern*" (italics added). The chapters outlining the narrative found in the New Testament Gospels are followed by chapters titled "Ministry of the Resurrected Christ on the Western Hemisphere" and "Personal Manifestations of God the Eternal Father and His Son Jesus Christ in Modern Times," detailing the First Vision of Joseph Smith and the appearance of the Savior in the Kirtland Temple. The final chapter, "Jesus the Christ to Return," walks the reader through prophecies of the Second Coming found in biblical sources, Book of Mormon sources, and modern prophecy, sharing Elder Talmage's witness of the Resurrection. Though the work showcases biblical scholarship and human reason to expound on the mission of Christ, it is a work without doubt, ending with Elder Talmage's assurance to the faith that "forever shall they reign, kings and priests to the Most High, redeemed, sanctified, and exalted through their Lord and God—JESUS THE CHRIST."[407]

When *Jesus the Christ* was published in 1915, it was endorsed by the First Presidency—Joseph F. Smith, Anthon H. Lund, and Charles W. Penrose—who issued the following statement: "We desire that the work, 'Jesus the Christ,' be read and studied by the Latter-day Saints, in their families, and in the organizations that are devoted wholly or in part to theological study. We commend it especially for use in our Church Schools, as also for the advanced theological classes in Sunday Schools and priesthood quorums, for the instruction of our missionaries, and for general reading."

Elder Talmage continued writing and kept his unique office in the Salt Lake Temple until his death in 1933.[408] At the time of his passing, Elder Melvin J. Ballard, a fellow apostle, reflected: "He produced many volumes that shall be read until the end of time, because that which he has written is so clear and so impressive that it shall ever be among the cherished treasures for those who love the works of God. Yet these contributions he gave freely to the Church without any earthly reward."[409]

A century later, *Jesus the Christ* is still published by the Church and remains the most widely read single volume study of the life of Christ among the Latter-day Saints. Coming at a time when the Saints were still transitioning from being an isolated society toward becoming a part of society at large, *Jesus the Christ* demonstrated the Christian centrism of the Latter-day Saints while also showing the Church's unique contributions to the world's knowledge of the Messiah.

32. 1830 MEISSEN VASE

– General Relief Society Building –

O n October 3, 1956, President David O. McKay offered a dedicatory prayer for the new General Relief Society building in Salt Lake City, Utah. The entire building was built at the heart of Temple Square and dedicated to the Relief Society of The Church of Jesus Christ of Latter-day Saints. Like many of the Church's chapels of the past, this building was financed independently; uniquely, however, it was specifically financed and furnished by women. This building was conceived as more than just a place to house leaders or to conduct the administration of the auxiliary—it was to be a symbol for every woman who participated or would participate in the Relief Society, especially for those who participated in the financial plan that brought it about. Sacrifices made by individual members of the Relief Society from around the world were at the heart of financial fundraising for this building. A Meissen vase made in 1830 that is now on display in the General Relief Society building was a gift from some women of the Church, chosen for the new building to represent faith and sacrifice.

From the organization of the Relief Society in 1842, women of the Church desired and were promised a building to call their own. While in Nauvoo, Joseph Smith assigned the Relief Society "a lot belonging to the Church and a house on it which could be repaired and made useful."[410] However, when Joseph Smith was martyred and the Saints left Nauvoo, the organization of the Relief Society was abandoned, along with their hopes of a building. The Relief Society was eventually reestablished in December of 1867, but it was not until 1896 that a Relief Society building was once again discussed. On October 3, 1896, General Relief Society President Zina D. H. Young presented the possibility of such a meeting place. Given approval by President Lorenzo Snow and the First Presidency, women of the Church began a five-year fundraising campaign to bring their dream to life. As they approached their goal, however, the Relief Society was again disappointed as they discovered that their new building was to become the Presiding Bishopric's building instead, in which they would be given offices.

Finally, years later, at the conclusion of World War II, the time seemed right to renew the dream of a headquarters for Relief Society. And so, at the first postwar conference, in October 1945, General Relief Society President Belle S. Spafford called for a vote on a proposal to erect a Relief Society building to "more adequately house the general offices, the Temple-Burial Clothes Department, the *Magazine*, the Welfare, and other departments. . . . Like one great wave, thousands of uplifted hands unanimously voted in the affirmative."[411] Spafford remarked two months later in December 1945, "As we are [entering] upon a second century of Relief Society, a strong and growing organization rich in the blessings of the Lord, this seems the right and appropriate time to bring to fruition this dream of the past, to erect a building that shall stand a monument to Latter-day Saint women and a credit to the Church."[412]

With President George Albert Smith's approval, the General Relief Society Presidency initiated a year-long fundraising campaign that commenced on October 2, 1947. Each local organization within the stakes was responsible for submitting a sum of money equal to five dollars for each member enrolled in the Relief Society. Women who were not members of the Relief Society were also welcome to participate if they desired. Any excess contributed was to cover contingencies, furnishings, and equipment. To meet any additional costs, the general board hoped that Relief Society members and nonmembers alike would contribute amounts larger than the quota. They also encouraged families to join together in making memorial gifts for loved ones, deceased or living.[413] Branch Relief Societies and Church missions (except for those in Europe, which were struggling to recover from World War II) were expected to participate in the fundraising in accordance to the advice of their presiding leaders.[414]

The Relief Society planned to raise an unheard-of five hundred thousand dollars, which in 2018 dollars would equal approximately $5.48 million.[415] Considering the economic effects of World War II, it seemed an impossible undertaking, but the general board's hopes were met and exceeded as the sisters of Relief Society immediately pulled together to accomplish this tremendous task.[416] The great bulk of the money that was raised over that year came from individual donations earned by sisters through what was referred to as the "close and dear friend of Relief Society—'Hard Work.'"[417] The sisters sold bread, cakes, pies, flowers, aprons, and other items of clothing. In one case, a sister saved nickels and dimes and meant her donation as the ultimate Christmas gift. Others put off personal purchases. It was the golden wedding anniversary gift for another. Many dollars donated represented the labor of individual sisters' hands—aprons made, cakes baked, evenings spent caring for a baby, or days given to domestic service.[418] The year from October 1947 to October 1948 was filled with much sacrifice and many achievements as women earned money for this great cause.

Although the European sisters could not send money to contribute to the building fund, due to strict laws following World War II, they did send objects.[419] As Sarah Dockstader Heaps observed, "These sisters from formerly war-torn countries . . . sent gifts to beautify the building."[420] Indeed, "many of the exquisite furnishings, lamps, tables, vases, paintings, needlecraft, wood-carvings, pieces of sculpture work, models of ships, canoes, etc., dolls and figurines, as well as books for the library, desk sets, cabinets, etc. have been gifts to the building," either from individuals, families, stakes or missions, or other groups.[421] These gifts represented many nations, both large and small, where women were affiliated with the Relief Society organization. Some gifts represented the native skills of women in their homelands, and these items became a treasure trove for the Relief Society.[422]

One of the most treasured gifts was sent from one of the most war-torn countries. Relief Society sisters from a small branch in Austria wanted to do their part for the building. Because they had little money, they hunted for items in second-hand shops, searching for something to represent the Swiss-Austrian Mission that would be worthy of the Relief Society building. In one shop, Hermine Weber Cziep found a Meissen vase, a surprisingly valuable piece of art. The exquisite porcelain vase that the Austrian sisters found is thirty inches high, covered with ornate figures and blossoms, and was once displayed in a German castle.[423] Beyond this, the sisters found the vase to be a perfect symbol of their shared sisterhood since it was made in 1830—the year that The Church of Jesus Christ of Latter-day Saints was organized.[424]

Considering the history and value of Meissen porcelain, finding a Meissen piece in a second-hand shop was surprising and even miraculous. Meissen (or Meißen), Germany, is where the first white European porcelain was manufactured in 1708. Previously, only the Chinese had discovered the formula for the true hard-paste porcelain that was so valuable.[425] As such, when German-born Johann Friedrich Böttger successfully produced white porcelain, it was a significant discovery because wealthy Europeans had been paying fortunes to import porcelain from China. With the development of the Meissen Porcelain Manufactory in Albrechtsburg Castle, in Meissen, Germany, however, Europeans had much easier access to porcelain, and the popularity of Meissen porcelain quickly skyrocketed.[426] As the first hard-paste porcelain manufactured in Europe, the Meissen porcelain style dominated European porcelain for much of the eighteenth century. Interestingly, their mark of two crossed swords is one of the oldest trademarks in existence.[427] Although they no longer dominate the porcelain market, the Meissen Manufactory still exists (although it has since moved) and continues to be one of the most famous European producers of porcelain.[428] The artistry and fine quality of their porcelain makes Meissen porcelain still desirable and valuable today.

As the Swiss-Austrian sisters exemplified, every aspect of the Relief Society Building was completely done by women, from the planning of the building, to the fundraising, to the construction and furnishing. It is a tribute to Relief Society women that such a great feat was accomplished with relative ease. Through their unique financing and fundraising, the Relief Society women brought about "a home of the heart of Relief Society of which every Relief Society member is a part. A home containing the loveliest offerings of the world-wide sisterhood. Unitedly, through sacrifice . . . the Relief Society Building stands an ensign to women."[429]

33. NORTH AFRICAN CAMPAIGN WORLD WAR II SACRAMENT TRAY

– Church History Museum –

When World War II struck, many members of The Church of Jesus Christ of Latter-day Saints were called to service. Despite difficult circumstances, they demonstrated their commitment to worship God. As Latter-day Saint servicemen met on all fronts of the war, military officials were astonished at their "initiative and ability" in conducting their own worship services.[430]

The Church played a substantial part in helping these Latter-day Saint servicemen find ways to participate in the sacrament by organizing groups and designating group leaders to conduct services "wherever sufficient numbers of Latter-day saint servicemen could be found."[431] With lack of available chapels, however, many of these group leaders were forced to make do with less conventional means of worship. They transformed bombed-out buildings, fox holes, pup tents, and open fields into sanctuaries where they could gather to partake of the emblems of the sacrament.[432] For sacrament trays and cups, they would use what they could find or fashion them out of spent shell casings, canteens, or available lumber.

Elder L. Tom Perry fondly remembers a green footlocker that was used to house their sacramental objects while he was serving in the war. Finding a tent in which to hold church services, he and others made benches, a pulpit, and a sacrament table out of any piece of lumber they could find. "And under the sacrament table we placed that special green footlocker. The contents included a wooden plate, a wooden sacrament tray, a card containing the sacrament prayers, and several boxes of small paper cups." Years following his service, Elder L. Tom Perry remarked, "The contents of the green footlocker represented all we held dear. As we gathered each week on the Lord's day, opened our footlocker, and used the contents to prepare, bless and pass the sacrament, it was a spiritual and uplifting experience that renewed our faith and gave us hope for the days ahead."[433]

Such sentiment is echoed by a number of servicemen who, over the years since the war, have told their stories of Church meetings in the Pacific Theater of World War II. One such story is told by serviceman Buddy Spears, who served in the South Pacific theater. In a letter to President Samuel O. Bennion of the Seventy he wrote, "We made our sacrament cups from 20-millimeter shells cut off to about an inch in length. The tray for them is of oak wood with a polished brass handle. Bread trays, and a bowl to wash our hands before ministering, we made from aluminum casings in which 5-inch shells are stored. We are quite proud of the set and feel that it adds much to our meetings."[434]

Servicemen E. James Carlson and Robert L. Backman likewise recall employing spent shell casings as their group's sacrament cups, while another group in Guam passed the water around in a canteen. Every man would rotate the canteen slightly before taking a sip. Serviceman A. Earl Catmull wrote, "We did not know how many times that cup rotated before it got to all the men."[435]

The commitment and ingenuity of these servicemen to have means for holding and passing the sacrament is reflected in one set of trays made for services in North Africa in 1942. Constructed by a tank mechanic, Lavell Miller, who had become active in the Church shortly before the start of his military service, the water trays were made out of tank parts that had been hammered down into thin sheets of metal with holes cut to fit the sacrament cups, and the bread trays were made from thin sheets of copper.[436]

Ingenuity was portrayed not only in the means for administering the sacrament but in the sacrament emblems themselves. Lacking proper bread, and sometimes even clean water, servicemen made do with what they could take from their rations and other food on hand. Serviceman Lloyd Miller recalls a solitary sacrament meeting that was composed of just himself and a dear friend in which a lemon drink the servicemen termed "battery acid" was substituted for the water, and cookies that came in their K-rations made do for the bread.[437] Elder Neal A. Maxwell of the Quorum of the Twelve Apostles wrote of a similar experience: "I had a C-ration biscuit and rainwater for my sacraments. That proves it is not the ingredients, but the spirit."[438]

Many servicemen wrote of the strong spirit that was present despite, or perhaps because of, their humble circumstances. One serviceman, Robert L. Backman of the Seventy, wrote of his experience as a group leader. In lieu of a chapel, he found a bombed-out house in which to hold their meeting. "The only thing standing were the walls, but it gave us a little bit of privacy. I scrounged some ammunition boxes and formed a pulpit and sacrament table from those. I found some spent shell casings and some little wild flowers that had survived all the battles, and set them up for a little bit of atmosphere. . . . [The men] sat on their steel helmets because that was the only thing they had to sit on. . . . We enjoyed some of the most spiritual services I have ever attended in my life. I will never forget, as we partook of the sacrament, the priests knelt at the table and could not get through the prayers because they were so emotional."[439]

By the end of the war, nearly one hundred thousand members of the Church of Jesus Christ were in active military service.[440] Many recall these humble sacrament meetings as life-changing and unforgettable.[441] But these moments were impactful not just for the servicemen directly involved. Many of the materials that the servicemen left behind when going home or being stationed elsewhere were then gratefully used by others. Some servicemen built chapels on the islands that had none. Elder L. Tom Perry shared that after a while of meeting in a tent, he and his comrades were finally able to construct a chapel. "When our duties on the island were complete, we boarded a ship and moved on to another assignment. Our green footlocker remained in the chapel for others to use."[442]

Whether it be a chapel or a sacrament tray, each portrays the devotion of these servicemen to the sacred emblems of the sacrament. On the bottom of his homemade copper sacrament tray, serviceman Lavell Miller inscribed, "The Church of Jesus Christ of Latter-day Saints," along with the year and place, hearkening back to a tradition that was common among the early pioneers. During the early years in Salt Lake under Brigham Young's administration, "the pioneer Saints . . . affixed . . . 'Holiness to the Lord' on seemingly common or mundane things as well as those more directly associated with religious practice, such as sacrament cups and plates."[443] They believed that all things denote holiness to the Lord and thus can be made holy. All throughout the Pacific and European theaters, the Latter-day Saint soldiers and servicemen of World War II were making even emblems of war to denote holiness to the Lord.

34. THE CHRISTUS ON TEMPLE SQUARE

— North Visitors' Center, Temple Square, Utah —

The *Christus* statue in the rotunda of the North Visitors' Center on Temple Square is one of the most recognizable objects associated with the Church. Standing at more than eleven feet and weighing almost 12,000 pounds, the marble statue, though closely tied to the image of the Church, is actually a replica of a statue held in a Lutheran Church of Our Lady in Copenhagen, Denmark. [444]

The original *Christus* statue by Danish sculptor Bertel Thorvaldsen (1768–1844) was commissioned by the Lutheran Church in 1820.[445] There are many stories and theories about Thorvaldsen's inspiration while creating the statue, particularly about the decision to sculpt the arms in the now-iconic out-stretched position. One story suggests that Thorvaldsen's friend, Herman Ernst Freund, inspired the position when he made the same pose as he was trying to encourage Thorvaldsen, who felt lost on how to sculpt the arms.[446] Though no one knows what the impetus for the positioning of the statue's arms was, President Spencer W. Kimball felt that Thorvaldsen was divinely inspired in his creation of the statue itself. Upon visiting the church in Copenhagen and viewing the *Christus* along with Thorvaldsen's *Twelve Apostles*, he stated, "The man who created these statues was surely inspired of the Lord. The beauty and majesty of the *Christus* are wonderful. While Thorvaldsen was doing his work here, in 1821 to 1844, Joseph Smith was doing his work in America. Thorvaldsen didn't have the gospel as did Joseph Smith, but he had the Spirit. He must have been inspired to create these statues of Christ and the apostles. He was trying to bring them to life." [447]

President Stephen L Richards of the First Presidency had a similarly inspiring experience when he saw the statue in Copenhagen in 1950. He would later express his desire to purchase a replica of the statue to give as a gift to the Church.[448] However, it was not until 1957 that President Richards suggested placing a replica in Temple Square.

Separately, the Temple Square Presidency, assigned to improve missionary work on Temple Square, created a plan for guided tours divided into various sites around Temple Square. In this meeting, Richard L. Evans of the Quorum of the Twelve Apostles stated, "You know, the world thinks we're not Christians. Because they see no evidence of Christ on this square. They hear the words, but see no evidence."[449] The Temple Square Presidency, led by Richard L. Evans, wanted to have a "representation" of the Savior that would "make an impact upon the world—one that would be world-known and be received without creating controversy."[450] Marion D. Hanks of the Temple Square Presidency suggested including a spot, site #7, in their guided tour for a statue of Christ and suggested using a copy of Thorvaldsen's *Christus*. In a meeting with the First Presidency, the Temple Square Presidency paused their presentation as they reached site #7 on their map, hesitant of the response since statues of deity were unprecedented in the Church.[451] President David O. McKay, sensing their hesitation, pointed to the map and asked them what site #7 was. The Temple Square Presidency was surprised when President Richards answered for them, saying, "Here is a place for the *Christus*."[452] The Temple Square Presidency and the First Presidency then quickly agreed on using a copy of Thorvaldsen's *Christus*, but they changed the intended location for the statue, instead choosing to place it in the rotunda of what would later become the North Visitors' Center. Soon after this meeting, President Richards commissioned a copy of the statue from a studio in Italy; however, he unexpectedly died on May 13, 1959, before the finished statue reached Salt Lake City in June.[453] Four years later, the statue was placed in the newly built visitors' center, which President McKay dedicated in 1963.[454]

Another copy of the *Christus* was then commissioned by the Church to be featured at the 1964 New York World's Fair at the Mormon Pavilion.[455] The purpose of this statue as the focal point of the exhibit was to "serve as a visual announcement that the Latter-day Saints were indeed Christians."[456] More than six million people visited the Mormon Pavilion and saw the replica of the *Christus* that would become an iconic image associated with the Church.[457] The success of the Mormon Pavilion at the World's Fair set a precedent for the Church's use of the *Christus* statue as a missionary tool. Now, fourteen copies of the *Christus* can be seen by millions at visitors' centers around the world, acting as "special ambassadors" for the Church.[458]

When Elder Dallin H. Oaks unveiled a copy of the *Christus* at the Washington Temple Visitors' Center in 1988, he stated, "I believe that those who visit this site and wonder about the religious beliefs of those they call Mormons will be given a clearer understanding through its presence."[459] He then described an experience he had when he took a friend to

Temple Square to see the *Christus*: "As we emerged and beheld this majestic likeness of the Christus, arms outstretched and hands showing the wounds of his crucifixion, my friend drew a sharp breath." After a few minutes of silence, his friend thanked him for showing him the statue and observed, "Now I understand something about your faith that I have never understood before." Of this experience, Elder Oaks said, "I hope that every person who has ever had doubts about whether we are Christians can achieve that same understanding."[460]

Not only does the image of the *Christus* demonstrate that Church members are Christians, but the statue itself is also meant to draw people closer to Christ.[461] President M. Russell Ballard taught, "This stunning work of art captures the loving, benevolent spirit of the resurrected Lord, His arms outstretched, kindly beckoning all to come unto Him."[462] Elder Bruce R. McConkie also emphasized the statue's spiritual effect as he described what many members and nonmembers alike have felt upon viewing the *Christus*:

> And as we ponder upon the wonder of it all, our gaze and thoughts dwell upon the beatific face and we feel the beckoning power of the outstretched arms. And the marvel in marble seems to breathe the breath of life and say: "I am the way, the truth, and the life." (John 14:6.) "Come unto me, all ye that labour and are heavy laden, and I will give you rest." (Matt. 11:28.) Come unto me and ye shall be saved. Come, inherit the kingdom prepared from the foundation of the world for all who accept me as the Creator and Redeemer. Come, be one with me; I am thy God.[463]

The increasing number of replicas of the *Christus* statue across the world there are emphasizes the Church's focus on Jesus Christ and invites those who see this artwork to come closer to Him.

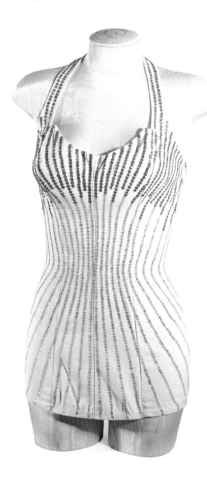

35. THE TEMPLE SWIMSUIT

– Sharon Alden –

The words *swimsuit* and *temple* seem unlikely to go together. However, a swimsuit designed by Rose Marie Reid and the Los Angeles California Temple have a very fascinating connection. On February 3, 1952, President David O. McKay announced a fundraising campaign for the Los Angeles Temple wherein each stake was given a quota to raise.[464] The temple would eventually cost $4 million.[465] As local leaders were trying to raise funds, they came to Rose Marie Reid a second time soliciting a donation after she had already donated. Reid told them she had already contributed as much as she could, but then came up with a fundraising idea. She would design a swimsuit with sequins and pay the women in the Relief Society to hand sew the sequins on each suit. The women could then donate their wages to the temple fund.[466]

At the time, Reid Holiday Togs, Ltd., was the leading swimsuit manufacturer in the United States. How Rose Marie Reid and swimsuits became connected is an equally interesting story. While taking swimming lessons, Rose Marie Yancey met Jack C. Reid, her swimming instructor. The two fell in love and were soon married. Jack, who spent many hours at the swimming pool, disliked the swimsuits of the day that were made of wool, because when they became wet they were heavy and uncomfortable. Thus, Rose Marie decided to make a new swimsuit for Jack. She cut a pair of swim trunks from an old duck-fabric coat and laced the sides for a snug fit. Jack loved his new swimsuit and then encouraged his wife to design a similar suit for the Hudson Bay Department Store. Rose Marie was leery of selling swimsuits but turned to the Lord. As she knelt in prayer and asked if God if He wanted her to make bathing suits, she felt an affirmation. The next day, Rose Marie found some beautiful fabric and designed a woman's swimsuit with laces up the sides. Seeing her designs, buyers for the department store ordered ten dozen men's and six dozen women's suits, and Reid Holiday Togs, Ltd., began.[467]

Rose Marie's suits soon became very popular because they were the first to include brassieres, tummy-tuck panels, stay-down legs, and laces.[468] In the company's first year, it showed more than six styles. In later years, more than 100 styles were shown in one season, and annual sales rose from $32,000 in 1938 to $834,000 in 1946. In 1946, Rose Marie decided to take her company from Canada to the United States. Triumphing over other US swimsuit companies, the company ended up making $14 million in sales by 1958.[469] By 1959, production went up to 10,000 suits a day and worldwide distribution reached forty-six countries, making Reid the largest manufacturer of swimsuits in the world. She was also named one of the *Los Angeles Times*'s 10 Women of the Year in 1955 and in 1958 was awarded Designer of the Year.[470] Rose Marie's popularity grew immensely after the introduction of her swimsuits to the United States. Joan Crawford, Jane Russell, Rhonda Fleming, Marilyn Monroe, and Rita Hayworth all wore her swimsuits in their respective movies or pinup pictures. Marilyn Monroe even gave Rose Marie, "almost as much credit as Mother Nature for her pinup popularity."[471] Rose Marie's designs were at the height of her popularity when

she conceived the idea to raise funds for the Los Angeles Temple with one of her swimsuits.

Inside the factory, the tight-fitting Lastex-fabric white suit with striped lines of brightly colored sequins accenting the contour of the waist and hips became known as "the Relief Society Suit." The suit's design required the sewing on of thousands of sequins. Relief Society sisters of southern California were paid fifteen dollars for each swimsuit. Hundreds of women donated thousands of hours sewing on sequins and Rose Marie, in turn, donated their wages to the temple fund.[472] When the Relief Society met their quota, another problem emerged in how to publicize the swimsuit. The company was not getting as much profit as the temple fund was, so a plan was devised wherein only one of the "temple swimsuits" would be sold in each large city for a certain time period.[473] This strategy worked well, and the design especially became popular when a suit was stolen, and *Life* magazine reported the incident:

A large number of pretty girls have turned up recently in identical models of a pink-sequin-trimmed white bathing suit. Called "Starlight" by its manufacturer, Rose Marie Reid of Los Angeles, and made to sell for $50, the suit had had a limited issue and no extensive promotion. But somehow it managed to get worn in circumstances which made it the season's most photographed swimsuit. Through the medium of a TV program it was seen in millions of U. S. homes. But in one instance the suit did not bring favorable attention. In a Bridgeport, Conn. competition to pick an entry for the Miss Universe contest, an 18-year-old girl named Georgia Poulos appeared in "Starlight," but was eliminated. She then was accused of theft when a department store saw her picture in newspapers and claimed the suit had been stolen from its displays. Miss

Poulos tear-fully explained that she had lacked money to buy the suit and just took it.[474]

Poulos said, "Everyone knew whoever wore this suit would win."[475] The publicity from the stolen suit incident and the *Life* article instantly brought popularity to the "Starlight" swimsuit, and it became one of the most popular swimsuits that year and helped raise the necessary funds to complete the temple.[476]

The suit, which sold for fifty dollars, became one of the most popular styles ever designed. "Among those who wore the suit publicly were Marcia Valibus, Miss Miami Beach of 1959; and [Latter-day Saint] actress Terry Moore. The suit also appeared on Carol Anders in an exclusive Beverly Hills Hilton Hotel fashion show, and on Marie Hermann, queen of the Los Angeles press photographers. Sandy Rosten wore it in Puerto Rico with the Martha Rae traveling troupe at a Marine Corps USO production. And it was seen on the Phil Silvers show when the comical Sergeant Bilko plotted with his men in a scheme to fill the empty suit with a girl."[477] It seemed as though the connection with the temple greatly enhanced sales, and the "temple swimsuit" ended up being the most popular swimsuit ever designed by Rose Marie Reid.

In the 1960s, Rose Marie's business started to decline with the popularity of the bikini. She refused to design a bikini and advocated modest one-piece swimsuits. She left her company in 1962, claiming that the bikini was its "ultimate demise."[478]

However, there would ultimately be one more connection between Reid's designs and the temple when President David O. McKay asked Rose Marie, through Belle Spafford, general president of the Relief Society at the time, to redesign the temple garments so women would feel more comfortable and beautiful while wearing them. Rose Marie discovered while working on the garments that she was related to Elizabeth Warner Allred, the woman who designed the first garments of this dispensation. Rose Marie wondered if the Lord "[kept] that privilege in [their] family."[479]

36. West African Angel Moroni

– Church History Museum –

In the mid-twentieth century the Church began a rapid expansion outside of North America and into more areas around the world. Global expansion was carefully overseen by Church leaders, but the gospel also spread organically in ways no one could have anticipated. As early as 1946, individuals from countries in West Africa began sending requests for missionaries and information about the Church. Over the next decade, hundreds of seekers in Nigeria organized themselves into different independent congregations and began to send requests to Church headquarters for missionaries to teach the gospel and organize the Church in their part of the world. These requests in turn brought about a series of important discussions about Church policies surrounding race, the priesthood, and the global expansion of the Lord's kingdom. While these discussions occurred, faithful believers in countries such as Nigeria and Ghana continued their devotion to the principles of the restored Church, even without the benefit of official Church involvement.[480]

Church leaders began studying the question of sending missionaries and organizing the Church in West Africa starting in 1946, when O. J. Umordak of the Uyo District in Nigeria wrote to the president of the South Africa mission requesting literature and missionaries to teach him.[481] Any attempt to establish the Church in the region was complicated by the Church policy, existing from the mid-1800s until 1978, prohibiting men of black African descent from being ordained to any office of the priesthood and prohibiting black men or women from participating in temple ordinances.[482] In spite of these restrictions, enthusiasm for the teachings of the Church continued to spread in West Africa, and the possibility of great numbers of people joining the Church existed. In 1960, Pastor Itah Akpan of Abak, Nigeria, wrote to Elder Mark E. Peterson, informing him that "all my 18 churches agree to affiliate with you," pleading, "sir I want the church here in Nigeria please."[483]

In response to these requests the First Presidency, at the time consisting of David O. McKay, J. Reuben Clark, and Henry D. Moyle, asked Glen G. Fisher of the South African Mission to visit the people requesting information in Nigeria to find out "whether or not they are really sincere in their desires to become members of the Church and are truly converted to the truths of the Gospel."[484] When Fisher arrived in Nigeria he discovered several groups who had obtained Church literature and organized themselves as best they could with the limited information they possessed. He found one congregation with 125 members using the title "The Church of Jesus Christ, the King, of the Latter-day Saints" and underneath that banner, "Mormons."[485] When Fisher returned he met with the First Presidency, who asked direct questions about the challenges the Church faced in West Africa. When asked what the Nigerians said when Fisher told them they could not hold the priesthood, Fisher responded that they were less concerned with that issue than with receiving more literature and help for constructing chapels. He was impressed with their sincerity and believed if an organization was set up the people could carry on, superintended by Church officials who held the priesthood.[486]

While discussions continued about the best way to proceed with missionary work in West Africa, letters from the region continued to arrive. Adewole Ogunmokun, leader of a congregation in the region, wrote, "My heart will not rest, for it is made up and there is no turning back for me until I achieve my objectives, to be a baptized member of the Church Jesus Christ of Latter-day Saints and to receive the Gift of the Holy Ghost by the laying on of hands by those in authority." Moved by the pleas of Ogunmokun and others, the First Presidency asked LaMar Williams, a representative from the missionary department, to visit Nigeria and tour the region, meeting with many of the congregational leaders who had written to Church headquarters. In October 1961, Williams arrived in the region, accompanied by Marvin Jones, a young missionary assigned to proselyte in South Africa who was temporarily directed to accompany Williams as his traveling companion.[487]

The month-long tour of the region by the two envoys was an illuminating experience. Most of the groups in the area had no correspondence or affiliation with each other, and several different leaders met Williams at the airport. There was some contention over which group the visitors would spend time with first, but once it was settled, Williams and Jones spent several nights teaching in dwellings where their audience spilled out of the doors. The two men, Williams, age fifty, and Jones, age nineteen, spent nights teaching by the light of a kerosene lamp, using a flannel board for visuals, and assisted by a translator, sometimes teaching for nearly two hours. "I recall that the doorway was filled with people," Williams later said, "in every square foot of window there was a face, the children, and the shorter ones down below and the taller ones above."[488] In one meeting an elderly man stood in a congregation and declared, "I am sixty-five years of age, and I am sick. I've walked sixteen miles to be here this morning. I want you to know that I'm sincere, or I wouldn't have done this. I haven't seen President McKay and I haven't seen God, but I have seen you, and I'm going to hold you personally accountable to go back to President McKay and tell him that we are sincere."[489]

When Williams returned to Church headquarters, his findings prompted a discussion among the First Presidency about how to proceed with missionary work in Nigeria. President McKay initially declared his desire to "receive the Nigerian people into the Church with a full knowledge that they will have every blessing of membership excepting the Priesthood." In this plan, missionaries would "take charge of sacrament meetings, administer the sacrament, and will exercise everything pertaining to the Priesthood." Henry D. Moyle expressed concern with the plan, stating, "I don't see how we could ever organize wards and stakes down there. . . . The organization is a problem as well as the priesthood. It is almost inconceivable to carry on the work of a stake without the priesthood." President McKay in turn responded, "We shall help them build their meetinghouses and these meetinghouses will soon be used as school houses in helping the children to read." He even openly mused about giving the local converts the Aaronic Priesthood but not the Melchizedek Priesthood before noting, "I suppose there is no way to differentiate. The Lord will have to do it. . . . Only the Lord can change it [the priesthood policy], but that is what we are facing."[490]

President McKay authorized LaMar Williams to begin preparations for the opening of a mission in West Africa. Williams began his preparations in earnest, but in the meantime, American politics intervened. The Church was subject to widespread criticism in the United States because of its priesthood policy. Some Church leaders worried the publicity surrounding the opening of a mission in West Africa might enflame the tensions in America and intensify pressure for the Church to change its policy. Around the same time, a Nigerian student, Ambrose Chukwu, visited a Church institute in California and after a Sunday service was upset to learn about the priesthood policy. He wrote an angry letter to the *Nigerian Outlook*, a prominent periodical in Nigeria, which caused a maelstrom of controversy throughout the country. The Nigerian Saints responded by posting their own advertisement in the *Nigerian Outlook*, but enough bad feelings existed that Nigerian officials began to refuse American Church officials entrance into the country.[491] These challenges further delayed the mission, and in 1966, a coup to overthrow the government in Nigeria launched the bloody Biafran War, making the region unsafe for several more years. In light of these challenges, President McKay sadly recorded in a First Presidency meeting, "I stated that I think the time has not yet come to go into Nigeria."[492]

During the dark years of the Nigerian Civil War, LaMar Williams maintained correspondence with the groups in the region, though the war caused disruption and scattering among the many Church groups. When the war ended LaMar lamented, "All we could do later was to go back and kind of bring the pieces back together again." The 1978 revelation on priesthood received by President Spencer W. Kimball solved many of the complexities surrounding Church entry into West Africa, and the Church began to move again to establish a presence in the region. In August of 1978, Edwin Q. Cannon and Merrill Bateman were sent by the First Presidency on a fact-finding trip to West Africa. Among the people there, they found many congregations still meeting and even some locals who were already baptized, among them former BYU students, and others converted and baptized in different parts of America. In Cape Coast, Ghana, they found J. W. B.

Johnson leading seven congregations with several hundred members. In one of the small chapels, they discovered a large statue of the Angel Moroni based on a picture appearing on the cover of paperback copies of the Book of Mormon. It was carved out of cement that was allowed to set but not cure so that it could be more easily sculpted. Alongside the statue were pictures of the Bible and the Book of Mormon, portraits of Joseph Smith, and other scenes associated with The Church of Jesus Christ of Latter-day Saints.[493]

Decades later there are now hundreds of thousands of Saints in West Africa, along with two temples—one in Accra, Ghana, and another in Aba, Nigeria—and another soon to be dedicated in the Ivory Coast.[494] The angels on the spires of these buildings testify of the growing strength of the Church in Africa. But a symbol of the faith of the Saints of West Africa that is just as powerful is a smaller, more humble statue of the angel, carved from cement, at a time when the region was torn by warfare and strife, and sanctified by the faith of a people waiting to receive the gospel.

37. INDIAN CHRISTMAS CRÉCHE

– Church History Museum –

One of the most widespread symbols of Christianity is the Nativity scene. Nativities of all sizes, also called creches, are found in private homes and public spaces during the Christmas season. Nativity scenes often become an interesting reflection of the culture that produced them. For instance, in the United States and Western European countries, the Nativity is often depicted in a wooden stable, though it is likely the actual Nativity took place in one of the caves near Bethlehem used to house animals. The Holy Family is often depicted with physical features resembling Western Europeans rather than mirroring the more Semitic features they likely possessed. The scriptural visions of Jesus Christ tend to emphasize an appearance transcendent of race and ethnicity (see Revelation 1:13–15 and D&C 110:1–5), but believers in all cultures also project their cultural values onto people in their sacred texts. In general, depictions of the Nativity among the Latter-day Saints have followed American and Western European depictions, though in recent years, the collection of creches shown on Temple Square during the Christmas season has grown to include depictions of the Nativity from Eastern Asia, South America, Native American, and Maori culture. The inclusion of these displays is one of the encouraging signs of the emergence of a worldwide religion, but it does raise questions about how the restored gospel of Jesus Christ interacts with cultures where Christianity is in the minority. A fascinating case study for these interactions can be found by examining the history of the Church in India.

The history of the Church in India stretches back almost as far as its history in the American West. The first Latter-day Saint missionaries arrived in Calcutta, India, in 1851. Elder Joseph Richards was sent from his mission in England and baptized the first converts in India and ordained several men to the priesthood. He was replaced a few months later when Elder William Willes arrived in December 1851. Elder Willes operated under the direction of Lorenzo Snow, who was serving as the president of the Swiss and Italian missions but saw India as part of his stewardship. Willes found only six members of the Church, and essentially no leadership. He organized the few members in the city, began making plans to publish a gospel tract in the Bengali, Hindi, and Hindustani languages, and began giving public lectures. Over the next few months the small branch grew quickly. A communication to the *Millennial Star,* the Church newspaper in England, reported, "By the beginning of May 1852, the membership to the Church in and around Calcutta had increased to one hundred and fifty, of whom three were Elders, eight Priests, nine Teachers, eight Deacons, and one hundred and twenty-two lay members. By including children belonging to the baptized families, there were more than three hundred Indian Saints of all sizes, colors, and languages."[495]

In August 1852, Joseph Richards returned to the country to assist Elder Willes in the work. The two of them made bold plans to travel to Punjab, nearly 1,000 miles northwest of Calcutta. In what one historian lauded as "one of the great missionary journeys of [Latter-day Saint] history," the two elders traveled more than 620 miles on foot before electing to continue via ox-cart. As they traveled through the Ganges River Basin, the two missionaries immersed themselves in the beautiful and complex history of India, visiting many sacred sites of the Hindu religion, as well as the famous Taj Majal. Along the way they baptized sixteen people. When they reached Agra (800 miles from Calcutta), Elder Richards' health began to trouble him, and he decided to return to Calcutta. Elder Willes continued on to Punjab, but only enjoyed limited success in the region.[496]

Elders Willes and Richards were only two of nineteen missionaries who served in India, Burma, and Siam from 1851 to 1856. By 1856 the missionaries began to be overwhelmed with the challenges of teaching in the region. One missionary composed a scathing assessment of the European population of the country, writing, "The Europeans of India are generally of the aristocracy at home, and entertain such an exalted opinion of themselves, and of human greatness, that it is impossible for a common man to speak to them. . . . If Gabriel from the region of bliss, the presence of God should come, I do not believe that he would attract any curiosity or create any excitement whatever. They would not stop their carriages or look out of their windows to see him." The missionaries also struggled in their labors with the native population, overwhelmed by the linguistic complexity and cultural differences they faced. They struggled to learn some of the local languages, Burmese, Hindustani, Tamil, Telegoo, and Maratha, failing to gain mastery in any. They also struggled to translate the concept of a one true God who is an anthropomorphic being with the Hindu concept of thousands of Gods in all shapes and forms. They also found little common ground or success among the Muslim population of the region. When the last missionary left the region in May 1856, he estimated only about sixty-one members in India and Burma, along with eleven others who had already emigrated to the Salt Lake Valley.[497] Ultimately, the early missionaries failed to establish a permanent presence in the country, despite their noble efforts. Church historian B.H. Roberts offered a stirring tribute their efforts, writing, "There is nothing more heroic in our Church annals than the labors and sufferings of these brethren of the mission to India."[498]

For more than a century organized missionary work ceased in India, though what one historian has called "scattered embryos" occurred throughout the subcontinent. A handful of members joined the Church organically and mostly through their own efforts during this time period. For instance, Mangal Dan Dipty was born into a lineage including Hindu priests, though he himself chose to join the Lutheran Church. In the late 1950s he encountered a book titled

Is Mormonism Christian? Intrigued, he read the book and became interested in the Church. He contacted Church headquarters in Salt Lake City and received other Church literature, including *The Testimony of the Prophet Joseph Smith* and the Book of Mormon. He wanted further information, but there were no missionaries or members in India to teach him. In 1961, Elder Spencer W. Kimball visited Dipty and invited him to travel with him for the next few days. Dipty later recalled that he "was like a sponge soaking up all the gospel lessons [Elder Kimball] taught. . . . On the final day I was ready for baptism. It was noon of the 7th January, 1961 [when] I was baptized by Apostle Kimball in the Yamuna River." Dipty later immigrated to the United States.[499]

Other individual conversions followed in India, but the beginning of an official return to the country came in 1978, when the Edwin and Elsia Dharmaraju family moved to Hyderabad. The move was a return home for the Edwins, who had left India in 1975 to work in Samoa. During their time in Samoa, the family became acquainted with Latter-day Saint missionaries and joined the Church in 1977. A year later the Edwins were set apart as special missionaries for three months so they could return to Hyderabad to teach their family the gospel. In a blessing given by a priesthood leader before his departure, Edwin was told he "would be the Joseph Smith of India." The Edwins wrote to their relatives about their newfound faith and immediately began to teach. By the end of the year eighteen family members were baptized and a branch was organized in Hyderabad. Most of these family members had previously converted to Christian churches, but they represented the first vital foothold of the Latter-day Saints in India.[500]

These encouraging early results led to a gradual re-establishment of the Church in India. In 1993 a mission in India was formally organized. Over the next twenty years reactivation efforts, leadership development, and baptisms led to a tenfold increase in Church membership, even as many members emigrated. In 2012 the first stake was organized in Hyderabad. By 2019 there were four stakes, two missions, and three districts in India, with Latter-day Saints worshipping in forty-five congregations spread throughout the country.[501] In the April 2018 general conference, President Russell M. Nelson felt prompted to announce a temple in Bengaluru, India.[502] In a visit to the country just weeks after the announcement, President Nelson told a gathering of the Indian Saints, "Our plans were to announce six new temples at conference time. The Lord told me on the eve of the conference: 'Announce a temple in India. . . . That was the Lord's doing."[503]

In the midst of encouraging signs, the challenges facing Church members in India are still immense. In 2019 the total membership of the Church in the country was 13,995, making Latter-day Saints .001% of the population, or 1 in 95,960.[504] Just as daunting as the overwhelming size of the population are cultural challenges. As historian Taunalyn Rutherford notes, "In India, the word 'conversion' is charged with meaning and carries the baggage of colonialism and anti-Christian politics." The difficulties as new members navigate the complexities of fusing gospel culture with Indian culture often requires great sacrifice. Hindus who join the Church often experience ostracism from their own families. Church members negotiate patriarchal culture, the caste system, and arranged marriages as they strive to live the tenets of the gospel.[505] Even the family members converted by the Edwins in 1978 noted the cultural pressures present, with one member noting, "Most of [the family] joined because [Edwin] was like the patriarch of the family." Decades later, some family members remain active in the Church, while others no longer attend.[506]

Challenges similar to those in India exist around the world as the Church seeks to become a world religion. The presence of this Christmas creche among the collection of cultural representations of Christ's mission demonstrates the flexibility needed in the future to become a world faith where, as one observer describes it has "found a way to adopt its forms to share its meaning in a panoply of cultures."[507] In this creche, Mary the mother of Christ, in depicted in traditional Indian dress, with a bindi, a small colored dot on the middle of her forehead. The bindi itself is a symbol used in by Hindus and Jains with multiple meanings, but among them as a symbol of the cosmos. In some places in India, the bindi notes the devotion of a married woman to her husband.[508] The wise men are likewise dressed in traditional Indian clothing, while the angel is presented in clothing from Hindu culture. Even the young Christ is depicted with Indian features. This depiction might not be historically accurate, but is it any less correct than depicting the Holy Family with Western European features? The addition of this creche to the collection of the Church shows the inclusion and adaptation possible as more cultures are brought into the family of the gospel of Jesus Christ.

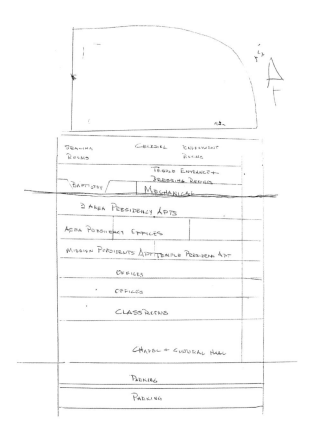

38. HONG KONG TEMPLE SKETCH

- Private Collector -

In the early hours of a mid-July night in Hong Kong, President Gordon B. Hinckley had a vision that would permanently impact the Church's future design of temples around the world. The events leading up to this monumental dream are nothing short of inspired.

The idea of a temple in Hong Kong was, for years, inconceivable. Several factors contributed to this; one was the fact that control of Hong Kong would revert from Great Britain back to China in mid-1997 when a ninety-nine-year agreement between the two countries would expire.[509] Approval for construction of a temple under Chinese control would be more difficult to gain than under British control; this caused the matter of approving a temple

in Hong Kong and selecting a site to become a time-sensitive matter. As 1997 approached, Church leaders met with both British and Chinese government officials, being careful and considerate to both parties in the approval process for a temple.[510]

Hong Kong Church members at the time had to travel incredibly long distances, incurring high expenses, to receive their temple ordinances. In addition to this, temple tape recordings were not available in Asian and South Pacific languages, which meant temple patrons from these areas did not have the opportunity to receive ordinances in their own language.[511] Thus, a temple in east Asia would bless the lives of Church members not only in Hong Kong but in surrounding areas as well.

The Hong Kong Temple would not be officially announced until October 3, 1992, during general conference.[512] However, in early 1991, the First Presidency of the Church instructed the Asia Area Presidency (composed of Monte Brough, Eugene Hansen, and Merlin Lybbert) to discreetly begin looking for an appropriate temple site in Hong Kong.[513] This was a difficult process, as land in Hong Kong is extremely expensive. The Area Presidency compiled a list of potential temple sites; in 1992, President Hinckley, along with Ted Simmons (managing director of Church physical facilities[514]) traveled to Hong Kong for the evaluation of possible locations and selection of a temple site.[515]

On July 25, 1992, President Hinckley, Ted Simmons, and a group of men from the Asia Area Presidency thoroughly inspected each site. Stake President Tak Chung Stanley Wan remembers that President Hinckley gently rejected each of the sites one by one.[516] Downcast, President Hinckley returned to his hotel that evening and retired to bed. Between 2 and 3 a.m., he dreamed concerning the temple site. According to President Hinckley, the voice of the Spirit told him that the temple should be built on property the Church already owned at #2 Cornwall Street in Kowloon Tong, which was currently hosting the mission home and office.[517] President Hinckley describes the dream as follows:

I did not hear a voice with my natural ears, but into my mind there came the voice of the Spirit. It said, "Why are you worried about this? You have a wonderful piece of property . . . in the very heart of Kowloon,

in the location with the best transportation. Build a building of several stories. It can include a chapel and classrooms on the first two floors and a temple on the top two or three floors."[518]

He immediately pulled out a large piece of white drawing paper and sketched a multipurpose temple design. In this sketch, President Hinckley divided a tall tower into several floors, assigning each floor a specific function. The top floor contained sealing rooms, the celestial room, and endowment rooms. Beneath that level, there was the entrance to the temple, a baptistry, and dressing rooms (with some space set aside for mechanical functions). The next sections included three apartments and offices for the area presidency, slightly larger apartments for the mission president and the temple president, two floors dedicated to offices, a floor for classrooms, and a large ground floor chapel and cultural hall. This drawing also included two underground parking levels. President Hinckley later proclaimed, "If ever in my life I felt the inspiration of the Lord, it was with this building."[519]

This was the first design for a temple to house multiple Church functions. All previous temple buildings were built to serve only the needs of the temple itself. However, this design would allow the Church to host temple ordinances and ceremonies, church leader apartments, mission offices, and church meetings all in one building. This was especially apt for Hong Kong, where space is limited and land is expensive.

Early the next morning, President Hinckley called Elder Brough and asked him to cancel all planned site visits for that day and requested that he, Brother Simmons, and Elder Carmack come to the hotel for a meeting. When they arrived per his request, President Hinckley shared his experience from the previous night with them, showing them his sketch to illustrate the concept of a multipurpose temple. When he asked their opinions, Elders Brough and Carmack expressed that although they had never contemplated the idea of a multipurpose temple, "they had a strong conviction that President Hinckley had received inspiration—even revelation—about what the Lord intended."[520]

President Hinckley kept organized notes during this meeting. He first listed their preferences for sites (with Kowloon Tong being first), then jotted down questions and details pertaining to using the Kowloon land. Questions such as "Where would CES go?" and "Where would ward go?" appeared. Under the question "What facilities would be needed?" President Hinckley listed fourteen points (one with six subpoints) concerning the practical aspects of the building. These points demonstrate the thoroughness of these men as they gathered to plan the building of a holy temple; some of these include "express elevators to temple," "foyer, offices, clothing, dressing rooms," and "large apartment for mission president's family." The group carefully considered each aspect of a multipurpose building.

The sketch of the temple was sent to the Church's temple department, who enlarged the design and sent it to Hong Kong officials for approval. Government officials rejected the design because of its height and size.[521] At the request of the Asia Area Presidency (and on behalf of President Hinckley), the temple department reverted to the original design drawn by President Hinckley, and the plans for the temple were quickly approved.[522] President Hinckley eventually gifted his sketch of the Hong Kong Temple to Lynette Brough[523] (Elder Monte Brough's wife).

President Hinckley's concept of a multipurpose temple has had far-reaching effects. The Hong Kong Temple, dedicated in May 1996, has blessed the lives of millions from all across East Asia.[524] This design also paved the way for future multipurpose temples, including the Manhattan New York Temple.[525] This revelation for multipurpose temples was also a precursor to the revelation given to President Hinckley concerning smaller temples, such as the Colonia Juárez Chihuahua Mexico Temple.[526]

This experience demonstrates to the world the power of a receptive prophet. President Hinckley was open to the Spirit; this allowed him to receive revelation that would change and bless the lives of Latter-day Saints globally. He listened to the small voice of the Spirit and, with a piece of paper and some ink, designed a temple for our modern world according to the Lord's knowledge.

39. Sixth-Seventh Ward Pulpit

– Church History Museum –

On May 7, 1950, Thomas S. Monson, at the age of twenty-two, was sustained as bishop of the Sixth-Seventh Ward, located in the heart of Salt Lake City. Significantly, as he was sustained, he stood at the same pulpit where he gave his first church talk at the age of ten.[527] But now, at the age of twenty-two, he was responsible for a large ward of 1,080 members, eighty-five of which were widows and many more who had great financial needs.[528] President Monson remembered, "The magnitude of the calling was overwhelming and the responsibility frightening. My inadequacy humbled me. But my Heavenly Father did not leave me to wander in darkness and in silence, uninstructed or uninspired. In his own way he revealed the lessons he would have me learn."[529] As bishop, he grew to love the individual members of the Sixth-Seventh Ward and established patterns of service that would continue throughout his life of Church service. The ornate pulpit of the Sixth-Seventh Ward meetinghouse represents his time as a young bishop and the lessons that stayed with him long after he was released from this life-altering calling.

Bishop Monson remembered that he learned early on to turn to the Lord in prayer for guidance:

> Every bishop needs a sacred grove to which he can retire to meditate and to pray for guidance. Mine was our old ward chapel. I could not begin to count the occasions when on a dark night at a late hour I would make my way to the stand of this building where I was blessed, confirmed, ordained, taught, and eventually called to preside. The chapel was dimly lighted by the street light in front; not a sound would be heard, no intruder to disturb. With my hand on the pulpit I would kneel and share with Him above my thoughts, my concerns, my problems. Those prayers were always answered in one way or another.[530]

Another object involved in President Monson turning to the Lord in his calling was a painting of the Savior by Heinrich Hofmann. He hung a copy of it across from his desk to look at and help him in his difficult times as a bishop, a habit that he continued in all of his Church callings throughout his life. He said, "I love the painting, which I have had since I was a twenty-two-year-old bishop and which I have taken with me wherever I have been assigned to labor. I have tried to pattern my life after the Master. Whenever I have had a difficult decision to make, I have always looked at that picture and asked myself, 'What would He do?' Then I try to do it."[531]

Often the answer to that question would be to serve an individual. He would prioritize visiting members and often gave blessings to those whom he felt inspired to help as the Savior would have. This, however, was not an easy lesson for Thomas S. Monson to learn. Early on when he was serving as a bishop, a friend asked him to visit his uncle who was in the hospital. Bishop Monson responded that he had to attend a stake meeting but would visit the uncle afterward. During the meeting, he felt impressed to leave the meeting early and go to the hospital. However, he did not want to disrupt the meeting, so he stayed until the meeting concluded. When he finally arrived at the hospital, he was saddened to learn that the patient had been asking for Bishop Monson right before he had passed away. From this experience, he learned the valuable lesson that he lived by for the rest of his life: "Never postpone a prompting."[532]

Thomas S. Monson served as the bishop of the Sixth-Seventh Ward for five years, and in those years he accomplished much and left a strong impact on the ward. The eighty-five widows loved and trusted him. In one well-known story, the trust of one widow is evident. Kathleen McKee left her former bishop a note, which he found after she passed away, wherein she entrusted him with caring for her favorite pet canary, Billie. She wrote, "He isn't the prettiest, but his song is the best." President Monson likened this canary to Kathleen McKee, who, despite trials and burdens of her own, "brightened each life she touched."[533] Certainly, Thomas S. Monson felt this way about all of the widows that he served; he wrote, "While they might feel they benefit by my visit, I know I come away a better man for having spent perhaps a half hour or hour reminiscing with each of these sweet sisters who are in the late years of their lives."[534] Every Christmas, he would visit each widow, often bringing a hen for dinner that he raised himself. He continued these visits long after he was released from his calling as bishop. He cared for each of these widows as they grew older, and he made it a priority to speak at every one of the eighty-five widows' funerals.[535]

In 1967, the Sixth-Seventh Ward meetinghouse was torn down, but Thomas S. Monson ensured that the pulpit was saved. He donated the pulpit to the Museum of Church History and Arts, which would later become the Church History Museum. More than fifty years later in 2009, at the dedication of the Church History Library, President Monson once again spoke at the Sixth-Seventh Ward pulpit, which had been brought in for the dedication ceremony. He stated, "This pulpit is, to me, a cherished remembrance of sacred experiences."[536]

His five years as bishop of the Sixth-Seventh Ward, and the pulpit itself, are reflective of his life as a whole: a life dedicated to serving the individual and loving those he served. President Harold B. Lee observed, "As a young bishop in a ward which required much attention to needy persons . . . he rose to the occasion; and from his intimate association with the problems of the everyday world, he developed a sensitivity which has characterized his life."[537] His time as the bishop of the Sixth-Seventh Ward prepared him for a lifetime of service and love, and the pulpit in the Sixth-Seventh Ward meetinghouse symbolizes the impact that his time as a bishop had on his life.

40. JOSEPH SMITH'S 1832 HISTORY
- Church History Library -

The First Vision of the Prophet Joseph Smith is typically the starting point for students of Church history. This event marked the beginning of a new dispensation and connects the saga of the Saints of the last days with those in the meridian of time. For the ancient and modern Saints, the witness of Jesus Christ and His resurrection shared by prophets then and now connects the grand work across eons of time. After acknowledging the existence of God and the centrality of Jesus Christ and His mission in our faith, the next story we tell is the story of Joseph Smith and his experience in the Sacred Grove. The story works so well because it is so universal. Joseph Smith was more than just the first Latter-day Saint; his story is a pattern every honest seeker of truth can relate to and use as a guide in their own quest to know God. It is a story so central to our conception of God and Christ and emblematic of our approach to Their presence that it has meaning for everyone who encounters the story of the Church of Jesus Christ. Can a story so central, then, ever have anything new added to it? The answer is yes.

In 1965 Paul R. Cheesman caused a sensation in the Latter-day Saint intellectual community when he rediscovered, in the presence of two employees from the Church Historian's office, a new account of Joseph Smith's First Vision.[538] The history, written in 1832, contains the earliest detailed account of the First Vision and is so far the only account written partially in Joseph Smith's own handwriting.[539] While the details and general story of the 1832 account align with the other accounts recorded by the Prophet in his own lifetime, it does contain new details and a more personal approach to the story than the other histories.[540] Cheesman's rediscovery of the early history demonstrates that even the most elemental events of Church history can gain new life as new discoveries are made.

Joseph Smith recorded the four known recitations of the First Vision during his lifetime. The earliest, in 1832, will be discussed in detail in this chapter. Other accounts came in 1835, where Joseph recorded telling the story to Robert Matthews, a false prophet masquerading as "Joshua the Jewish minister." The next account was written in 1838 as part of the Prophet's attempt to record an official history of himself and the rise of The Church of Jesus Christ of Latter-day Saints (see Joseph Smith—History).[541] The last account, written in 1842, was directed toward John Wentworth, the editor of the *Chicago Democrat*, who was writing a history of religions in America.[542] Several of Joseph Smith's contemporaries, such as Orson Pratt and Orson Hyde, published their own versions of the First Vision in Church pamphlets. Other Church members, such as Alexander Neibaur and David Nye White, recorded experiences where the Prophet related the details of the vision to them.[543]

Because of the time of its composition, the 1832 history is among the most intriguing accounts of Joseph Smith's early history. Piecing together the historical context of the account required a consider-

able amount of detective work among scholars, but it also provides a fascinating look at an important period in the Prophet's early ministry. According to the editors of *The Joseph Smith Papers*, the 1832 history was likely written before late September 1832, when the Prophet received a revelation (D&C 84) that "changed [his] lexicon regarding priesthood." Because of this and other factors, scholars have narrowed down the period of composition to a time between July 20 and September 22, 1832.[544] It is possible, however, that the history was recorded earlier than this time period. The history is in the handwriting of Joseph Smith and Frederick G. Williams. Close examination notes that the handwriting of the two alternates back and forth with "little or no correspondence to the narrative progress of the history; the two sometimes alternate inscription mid-sentence."[545] This and other clues indicate that the Prophet and his scribe may have been copying from an earlier document.[546]

If the history was copied from an earlier document, when is it likely Joseph Smith began to record his story? *The Joseph Smith Papers* have speculated that it is likely the history was written by the Prophet during a stay in Greenville, Indiana, early in the summer of 1832. Joseph spent several weeks in Greenville caring for Bishop Newell K. Whitney, who was injured in an accident while the Prophet and a company of Church leaders traveled home to Kirtland, Ohio, from a trip to Missouri. Bishop Whitney was injured when the horses pulling the coach in which the company was traveling became startled and began running. Whitney attempted to jump from the coach, but his foot was caught in a wheel and his leg broke in several places. While the rest of the party moved on, Joseph elected to stay with Bishop Whitney until he was well enough to travel.[547]

The stay in Greenville was a time of loneliness and contemplation for the Prophet. On one occasion he was likely poisoned by someone in the village. He later recorded, "One day when I rose from the dinner table, I walked directly to the door and commenced vomiting most profusely; I raised large quantities of blood and poisonous matter, and so great were the muscular contortions of my system that my jaw was dislocated in a few moments." Bishop Whitney quickly administered to Joseph, who continued, "I was healed in an instant, although the effect of the poison had been so powerful, as to cause much of the hair to become loosened from my head."[548]

The attempt on his life and the frustration of remaining idle in Greenville caused Joseph to deeply contemplate his life and prophetic purpose. Joseph wrote a letter to Emma Smith in which he told her, "My situation is a very unpleasant one, although I will endeavor to be contented, the Lord assisting me." He also added, "I have visited a grove which is just back of the town almost every day where I can be secluded from the eyes of any mortal and there give vent to all the feelings of my heart in meditation and prayer." Joseph also reflected on his history and standing before God. "I have called to mind all the past moments of my life," he wrote, "and am left to mourn and shed tears of sorrow for my folly in suffering the adversary of my soul to have so much power over me as he has had in times past, but God is merciful."[549] It is possible that Joseph's hours of reflection and contemplation in the grove near Greenville caused him to look back to another grove near his boyhood home, and begin the process of writing his own history.

The 1832 account of the First Vision is different from other accounts. It is more private, more poignant, and more personal. While the canonized 1838 account is written to emphasize the importance of the appearance of the Father and the Son to all humanity, the 1832 history focuses on Joseph's personal quest for salvation. "About the age of twelve years my mind became seriously impressed with regard to the all important concerns of the welfare of my immortal soul," Joseph wrote. While mentioning his distress at the "contentions and divisions" of Christian religions, Joseph also "felt to mourn for my own sins and for the sins of the world." In this early recitation of his story, Joseph was not only seeking the true church but forgiveness, recording, "I cried unto the Lord for mercy."[550]

The most controversial part of the 1832 account is Joseph's description of the vision, where he writes, "The Lord heard my cry in the wilderness and while in the attitude of calling on the Lord, in the sixteenth year of my age, a pillar of fire above the brightness of the sun at noon day came down from above and rested upon me and I was filled with the Spirit of God and the Lord opened the heavens upon me and I saw the Lord."[551] Because Joseph makes no mention of the Father and the Son as separate beings, critics often charge that the experience is a fabrication and his theology on the Godhead was undeveloped at this point. This is unlikely given that several months earlier Joseph Smith recorded a vision, now section 76 of the Doctrine and Covenants, which clearly describes the Father and Son as two separate beings. "We beheld the glory of the son on the right hand of God," the February 1832 vision records, adding, "We saw him, even on the right hand of God and we heard the voice bearing record that he is the only begotten of the Father" (D&C 76:20, 23).[552]

Instead of making a theological statement, Joseph's 1832 history underlines the message of salvation given by the Savior. "Joseph, my son, thy sins are forgiven thee," the Lord spoke to him, further admonishing him to "go thy way, walk in my statutes and keep my commandments. Behold, I am the Lord of glory; I was crucified for the sins of the world that those who believe on my name might have eternal life."[553] This early account of the First Vision is more about the salvation of Joseph Smith than the salvation of humanity, and the document gives a sense that even more than a decade after the event, the Prophet was still processing the full meaning of his experience. In this early attempt at historical writing, Joseph may have been mirroring the way other conversion accounts of the time were written.[554] It is also likely the adverse circumstances surrounding the Prophet's stay in Greenville affected the way the account was written. His weeks of contemplation and isolation led to a poignant connection for Joseph. If he was forgiven of his sins in his youth, could he receive the same forgiveness as an adult?

The 1832 account was not published in Joseph's lifetime and was never completed. We do not know the precise reason it was never published. While the 1838 account of the First Vision found in the Pearl of Great Price remains the canonized account of the events, there is power in this earliest written account, as well as the other accounts. The work of the Restoration was not just about the return of ecclesiastical organization, priesthood, or scripture to the earth. The most meaningful revelations come to one's own soul, sometimes in periods of anxiety and depression. President Henry B. Eyring, reflecting on the value of the histories Joseph Smith composed, said, "From studying the various accounts of the First Vision, we learn that young Joseph went into the grove not only to learn which church he should join but also to obtain forgiveness for his sins; something he seems not to have understood how to do." President Eyring continued, "[The First Vision] represents that moment when Joseph learned there was a way for the power of the Atonement to be unlocked fully. Because of what Joseph saw and what began at this moment the Savior was able, through this great and valiant servant and through others that He sent, to restore power and privilege. That power and privilege allows us, and all who will live, to have the benefit of Christ's Atonement work in our lives."[555] In different seasons of our lives, significant events grow and change in meaning. The same is true of the First Vision. Today, Joseph's story provides a pattern for sincere seekers to learn for themselves the true nature of God and the Savior. For Joseph Smith in the summer of 1832, the First Vision was a way of remembering he found salvation and peace in Jesus Christ as a young man, and he could again as an adult.

41. KIRTLAND TEMPLE MORTAR
– Church History Museum –

In December 1832, Latter-day Saints living in Kirtland, Ohio, were commanded through revelation given to Joseph Smith that they were to build a "house of God" (D&C 88:119). This commandment, which would later be published as the eighty-eighth section of the Doctrine and Covenants, was described by Joseph Smith as an "Olieve [sic] leaf which we have plucked from the tree of Paradise, the Lords message of peace to us."[556] This peace that Joseph Smith envisioned would come much later; the Saints suffered through many trials and setbacks in the three years dedicated to the construction of the temple. The construction of the Kirtland Temple, and even the temple mortar itself, represents the sacrifice of early Saints to build a temple and demonstrates the significance of the temple to The Church of Jesus Christ of Latter-day Saints.

Despite receiving this revelation to build a temple as a commandment, the Saints delayed beginning their work on the temple and in turn received a rebuke from the Lord for the delay: "For ye have sinned against me a very grievous sin, in that ye have not considered the great commandment in all things, that I have given unto you concerning the building of mine house" (D&C 95:3). In this revelation given to Joseph Smith on June 1, 1833, the Lord further clarified the purpose of the "house" they had been commanded to build six months earlier: "I gave unto you a commandment that you should build a house, in the which house I design to endow those whom I have chosen with power from on high" (D&C 95:8).[557]

Joseph Smith would later receive further revelation on the details of the building. Frederick G. Williams of the First Presidency wrote, "Joseph [Smith] received the word of the Lord for him to take his two counselors, [Frederick G.] Williams and [Sidney] Rigdon, and come before the Lord, and He would show them the plan or model of the house to be built. We went upon our knees, called on the Lord, and the building appeared within viewing distance, I being the first to discover it. Then all of us viewed it together. After we had taken a good look at the exterior, the building seemed to come right over us"[558] After this unique revelation, construction of the Kirtland Temple began immediately in early June of 1833.

Though the revelation given on June 1, 1833, gave some instruction about the construction of the temple, there were still many questions and decisions to be made on some of the specific details of the building. For example, there was no one in the Kirtland area with masonry skills, and the Saints struggled to realize their plans for the desired brick walls of the temple. The Lord provided a solution to this problem when Brigham Young converted and baptized a skilled mason named Artemus Millet while on a mission to Canada. Millett later wrote that Brigham Young "announced that he had a mission for me. The Prophet Joseph wanted me to go to Kirtland Ohio and take charge of the mason work on the temple as they were going to build a temple there. So I closed out my business there and in April 1834 I moved to Kirtland . . . and I did have full [superintendency] of the building."[559]

Millet suggested that the Saints use stucco for the walls instead of bricks since that would be significantly less expensive. Millet used a building technique called "rough cast" for the stucco, which meant that the temple mortar was made from a "mixture of pebbles, bluish river sand, and other extraneous materials . . . to achieve a textured surface." The stucco on the exterior walls was then painted to "simulate bricks."[560]

Some of these extraneous materials found in the exterior stucco are pieces of dishes and glassware, which is why the "bluish-tinted walls glistened in the light of the sun."[561] Many stories have been perpetuated about the women of the Church at the time donating their fine china to be crushed into the temple mortar; however, Latter-day Saint scholars and historians agree that there are no contemporary accounts or evidence that would suggest that the women sacrificed their fine china to be crushed into the temple mortar.[562] Historian Mark Lyman Staker states that stories about women donating their dishes did not appear until 1935.[563]

The stucco for the walls was mixed with crushed glassware and dishes, but it is likely that the Saints used discarded and broken pieces to make the mortar.[564] Artemus Millet's son recounts that his father sent "men and boys to the different towns and places to gather old crockery and glass to put in the cement."[565] Staker also mentions that archeological digs in Kirtland have found broken china in "nineteenth-century trash heaps," which further suggests that the Saints used already-broken dishes rather than the women sacrificing their best glassware and china.[566] Furthermore, one account from Maybelle Anderson, a child living in Kirtland at the time, states, "I, with other little children, gathered bits of glass and broken dishes which were broken up quite fine and mixed with the mortar used in plastering the temple."[567]Though it is unlikely that women were called upon to sacrifice their treasured glassware and fine china, they sacrificed their time and efforts in aiding to the construction of the temple.

Heber C. Kimball remembers the women "engaged in knitting and spinning, in order to clothe those men who were laboring at the building; and the Lord only knows the scenes of poverty, tribulation, and distress which we passed through to accomplish it."[568] The women were just as involved in the construction of the Kirtland Temple as the men. Lucy Mack Smith wrote that "there was but one main spring to all our thoughts and that was building the Lord's house."[569] The sacrifice of these sisters was acknowledged by Joseph Smith. Polly Angell once described an occasion when she and other sisters were working on making the veils for the temple when Joseph Smith stopped and said to them, "Well, sisters, you are always on hand. The sisters are always first and foremost in all good works. Mary was first at the Resurrection; and the sisters now are the first to work on the inside of the temple."[570]

The construction of the Kirtland Temple was an endeavor that engaged all of the Saints—men, women, and even children sacrificed much to contribute to the work of building a house unto the Lord. In a letter to the Saints, the building committee for the temple, led by Hyrum Smith, wrote, "We are directed, yea, we are under the necessity, to call upon the whole Church as a body, that they make every possible exertion to aid temporally, as well as spiritually, in this great work that the Lord is beginning, and is about to accomplish."[571] The construction of the Kirtland Temple is estimated to have cost somewhere between sixty and seventy thousand dollars, a significant amount for a small church with minimal funds. [572] Though there were only about 150 Latter-day Saints living in Kirtland at the time, the Saints did what was asked of them and sacrificed their money, time, and energy for the construction of the temple.[573] Heber C. Kimball noted that "the whole Church united in this great undertaking, and every man lent a helping hand."[574] Despite many trials, the Saints had faith that the Lord would help them complete this nearly impossible task. Eliza R.

Snow wrote about this faith in spite of difficulties: "The Saints were few in number, and most of them very poor; and, had it not been for the assurance that God had spoken, and had commanded that a house should be built to his name, . . . an attempt towards building that Temple, under the then existing circumstances, would have been, by all concerned, pronounced preposterous."[575] Members of the Church, however, completed construction of the temple, and on March 27, 1836, the first temple in this dispensation was dedicated. The Kirtland Temple dedicatory prayer, given by Joseph Smith, would later become section 109 of the Doctrine and Covenants. In this dedicatory prayer, Joseph Smith said, "For thou knowest that we have done this work through great tribulation; and out of our poverty we have given of our substance to build a house to thy name, that the Son of Man might have a place to manifest himself to his people" (D&C 109:5).

The Lord recognized the sacrifices and accomplishments of the Saints and accepted the temple on April 3, 1836. On that day, Moses, Elias, and Elijah committed priesthood keys to Joseph Smith and Oliver Cowdery (see D&C 110).[576] President Boyd K. Packer of the Quorum of the Twelve Apostles taught that the Kirtland Temple was built as a "holy place" where the restoration of priesthood keys required for temple ordinances could occur. He also spoke of another purpose for the Kirtland Temple: "In addition, this temple had another special but connected purpose. The sacrifice the Saints had made to build it, the spiritual power they had built in the process, and their continued ardent desires to do the Lord's will had fitted them for the spiritual manifestations which would 'endow [them] with power from on high' (D&C 95:8)."[577] The sacrifices that these Latter-day Saints made to construct the temple demonstrate their great faith and prepared them to receive the blessings of the temple.

42. Hawn's Mill Millstone

– Breckenridge, Missouri –

One of the darkest days in the history of the Church occurred on Monday, October 29, 1838, when a militia unit from Livingston County, Missouri, rode into the settlement of Hawn's Mill.[578] They subsequently murdered seventeen Latter-day Saints and wounded fifteen more. The Hawn's Mill Massacre was a graphic escalation of hostilities in northern Missouri between the Saints and their antagonists and remains one of the most severe examples of anti-Mormon persecution in the history of the Church. Today the site of the massacre contains only small marks of what was once a bustling settlement, and the most prominent marker of its existence is found in a small town a few miles to the north. What led to this horrific tragedy?

In 1838 Hawn's Mill was a small but growing community, home of fifteen to twenty mostly Latter-day Saint families. It was also a convenient place to recuperate for Saints migrating from Kirtland to Caldwell County. Many of the victims of the attack were refugees fleeing the collapse of the Church in Kirtland. Some lived in tents, arriving only days before the massacre occurred. Although few Saints lived in Livingston County or Carroll County to the east, Hawn's Mill was close to the borders of these counties and prompted worries that a Mormon population might spill over into non-Mormon territory.[579]

Whether or not the militia that attacked Hawn's Mill knew of Governor Boggs' extermination order is just one of the historical controversies surrounding the massacre. Plans to attack the settlement appear to have been drawn up by the Livingston County militia, led by their commander, Thomas Jennings, before word of the extermination order could have reached them. Prior to the massacre, the militia also made attempts to disarm the Latter-day Saints in the area and entered into a misleading series of peace negotiations designed to lull the Saints into a false sense of security. One local history of the massacre concludes, "Colonel Jennings made the attack on Haun's Mill on his own responsibility, without orders from Governor Boggs, or other superior officer, although it is said that the Governor fully approved what was done afterward."[580]

Another mystery surrounding the massacre centers around the founder of the community and proprietor of its mill, Jacob Hawn. Because the victims of the massacre consisted primarily of Latter-day Saints, most historians assumed Jacob Hawn was a member of the Church. There is no evidence indicating that Hawn or his wife and children converted to the Church, though his brother James appears to have joined. Hawn appears to have been friendly with the Saints and welcomed their business, though he apparently never joined the Church. Even the spelling of Hawn's name has been the subject of controversy. Prior to the 2000s, most histories spelled the name H-A-U-N. In 2010 Hawn's grave was rediscovered in Yamhill, Oregon. Examination of the grave marker revealed the correct spelling was H-A-W-N, and the change has been reflected in recent scholarship.[581]

Another controversy surrounding the massacre has arisen out of conflicting evidence over whether the Saints at Hawn's Mill ignored counsel from Joseph Smith to abandon the settlement and gather to Far West for safety. Several sources indicate that Jacob Hawn met with Joseph Smith in Far West on October 25, five days before the massacre. Hawn was warned by the Prophet to move the families at the settlement to safety in Far West. Hawn is said to have replied, "We think we are strong enough to defend the mill so as to not risk the lives of the citizens." Hawn returned to the settlement and either misunderstood the Prophet's directions, failed to tell the Saints about Joseph's warnings, or deliberately misled them to protect the mill and his own livelihood. According to one resident of the settlement, Hawn "returned and said if we thought we could maintain the mill [it] was Joseph's council for us to do so." Philo Dibble, another Church member, recorded, "While I was at Far West, Brother Joseph had sent word by Hawn, who owned the mill, to inform the brethren who were living there to leave and come to Far West, but Mr. Hawn did not deliver the message."[582] In a discourse given in August 1842, Joseph Smith is recorded as saying, "None had ever been killed who abode by my counsel. At Hawn's Mill the brethren went contrary to my counsel; if they had not, their lives would have been spared."[583] It is unknown whether Joseph was only referring to Hawn, or if he was unaware that the Saints didn't receive his counsel. It does appear inappropriate to blame the massacre on the unwillingness of the Saints at Hawn's Mill to follow the Prophet's directions.

When the attack came on October 30, it was swift and brutal. Joseph Young, the older brother of Brigham Young, had only arrived at the settlement two days prior when the attack came. He wrote, "It was about four o'clock, while sitting in my cabin with my babe in my arms, and my wife standing by my side . . . I cast my eyes on the opposite bank of Shoal creek and saw a large company of men, on horses, directing their course towards the mills with all possible speed." Most of the women and children in the settlement fled into the nearby woods. Amanda Smith recorded, "I took my little girls, my boys I could not find, and ran for the woods. . . . The bullets whistled by me like hailstones and cut down the bushes on all sides."[584]

Many of the men in the settlement ran into the blacksmith shop for cover. Joseph Young recalled, "All at once, they discharged about one hundred rifles, aiming at the blacksmith shop into which our friends had fled for safety; and charged up to the shop, the cracks of which between the logs were sufficiently large to enable them to aim directly at the bodies of those who had fled there for refuge from the fire of the murderers."[585] After killing or wounding most of the men in the blacksmith shop, the militia entered and finished off most of the wounded by closeup shots in the head. Among the victims was young Sardius Smith, Amanda Smith's son, who joined another young boy, Charles Merrick, to beg for their lives before the mob murdered them. One mobber put his gun to Sardius Smith's head and fired, then reportedly declared, "Nits make lice, and if he had lived he would have become a Mormon."[586]

When Amanda Smith returned to the scene, she was overcome with grief, later writing, "My husband and one son ten years old lay lifeless upon the ground and one son six years old wounded very bad, his hip all shot off and to pieces, and all the ground covered with the dead and the dying . . . nothing but horror and distress . . . a dozen helpless widows, thirty or forty orphaned or fatherless children screaming and grieving for the loss of their husbands and fathers, the groans of the dying and wounded; all this put together was enough to melt the heart of anything but a Missouri mob."[587]

Given the uncertain conditions following the attack, there was no time for proper burials. Most of the bodies were collected and hastily buried. One local history of the massacre records that there "was a large unfinished well at the place, and the bodies were gathered up, the women assisting, and borne, one at a time, all gory and ghastly, to this well and slid in from a large plank. All of the corpses were disposed of in this way; then some hay or straw was strewn over the ghastly piles and then a thin layer of dirt thrown on the hay."[588]

The survivors of Hawn's Mill quickly fled the area, and the once promising settlement was abandoned. The millstone in Breckenridge was rediscovered when George Edward Anderson, a Latter-day Saint photographer from Springville, Utah, spent four days in Caldwell County in May 1907 to take pictures of the massacre site. In his journal Anderson recorded, "Crossed the creek and located one of the old millstones, which we worked out of the ground and [then moved it] down to the edge of the creek and made two or three negatives of it, putting an inscription on one side."[589] Anderson took a haunting photograph of the stone with the inscription, "In memory of victims of the Haun's Mill Massacre, Oct 30th 1838."[590] The millstone apparently remained at the site until 1914 when citizens from Breckenridge retrieved the stone and placed it in the city park. A photograph from 1915 shows the stone lying flat on two raised blocks with a sign protruding from the center labeled, "A MILL-STONE FROM HAUN'S MILL WHERE EIGHTEEN MORMONS WERE KILLED IN A BATTLE AND THROWN IN A WELL. OCT. 30 1838."[591] The stone was placed in concrete in 1941 and again in 1987 by the local citizens. In 2001 the city, working with members of the Missouri Mormon Frontier Foundation, renovated the monument, placing a new descriptive marker alongside the stone. The new marker reads:

Mill Stone believed to be From Haun's Mill
(1836–1845)

This relic represents a tragic episode in American religious history. A testament to an enduring need for greater understanding and tolerance between peoples of differing ideologies, including religious beliefs and cultural backgrounds. As a result of miscommunication and feelings of powerlessness to effect change in the way of what they saw as offensive Mormon military actions in Daviess County, Livingston County Regulators and other volunteers, brutally attacked the nearby Mormon settlement of Haun's Mill, on Shoal Creek, 30 October 1838, killing 17 persons, 14 of whom were hastily interred in a partially completed well on the site.

Dedicated May 26, 2001
City of Breckenridge Park Board & Missouri Mormon Frontier Foundation

The Church purchased the site of the Hawn's Mill massacre from the Community of Christ in 2012 and has begun plans for preservation of the site.[592] At the time of this writing, the site is an empty, swampy field next to Shoal Creek, with two small markers commemorating the massacre. The millstone in Breckenridge remains the most prominent memorial of the events of October 30, 1838, and an important symbol of the work to remember these tragic events and bury the hatred surrounding them.

43. JOSEPH AND HYRUM SMITH DEATH MASKS
– Church History Museum –

News of the death of Joseph and Hyrum spread quickly after their martyrdom in Carthage Jail. Less than a day after the two prophets fell, their bodies arrived home to Nauvoo, brought in wagon by one of the survivors of the mob attack, Willard Richards (John Taylor, badly wounded, was forced to remain behind in Carthage while he recuperated). Overwhelmed by grief for the fallen Prophet and Patriarch, the citizens of Nauvoo never forgot the arrival of the bodies. Sarah M. Kimball later wrote, "The scene of the reception of those corpses in Nauvoo can be better imagined than described, for pen was never made competent to do it justice." Sarah also remembered holding the hand of Lucy Mack Smith and hearing her lament, "How could they kill my poor boys, O how could they kill them when they were so precious?"[593] With the bodies rapidly deteriorating in the summer heat, Church members moved quickly to preserve a final visage of their two slain leaders. With photography only in its infancy, the best alternative was to create a plaster mold of the martyrs' faces. In doing so, the mourning Saints created two of the most potent objects associated with the martyrdom: the death masks of Joseph and Hyrum Smith.

Death masks, common in the nineteenth century, were fashioned by covering the face with a thin layer or grease to prevent plaster of paris from adhering to the skin when it dried. Afterward a thin coat of plaster was applied to the face, followed by several layers of gauze or cloth strips dipped in plaster until a substantial mold was built up. Once the mold dried, it was removed from the face and the inside coated with grease or liquid soap, and the mask was created by pouring the mold full of plaster.[594] Although no mention is made of the creation of the death masks in contemporary histories of the martyrdom, it is likely that George Cannon, an English immigrant, created the death masks. A biography of Cannon written by his grandson records, "When the bodies of the martyrs were brought to Nauvoo, George Cannon was one of those who assisted in preparing the remains for burial. He made the coffins, and as he was one of the few in the city who had a knowledge of the process, he took plaster casts of the faces and heads of the dead leaders as they lay in state awaiting internment."[595]

David H. Cannon, the son of George Cannon, traveled west and eventually settled in St. George, Utah. Near the time of his death in 1823, he left an account of the martyrdom and the creation of the death masks: "At the time of the death of the Prophet Joseph Smith, I remember my father standing at the gate in front of the house, his arms kind of leaning on the gate. He turned, and as he did so, said, 'My God, they have killed our Prophet.' That was the time the Prophet was martyred. He made the drag on which they brought the body in. At the time the Prophet and his brother Hyrum were lying in state, my father was the one who made the death masks of the two. I remember going to my father at the time this took place. A lock of the Prophet's hair was caught in the plaster mask, and I remember Father taking some scissors and clipping the hair, then giving me the scissors to hold while he went on with this work."[596]

From 1844 to 1849 the exact location of the death masks is unknown. George Cannon died in 1844, and it is likely the masks came into possession of a "Brother Rowley" of whom we have almost no information.[597] The next time they receive mention in the historical record is in a letter from John M. Bernhisel, an eastern agent of the Church, who mentions that "the casts . . . are in possession of Brother [Philo] Dibble, who will probably take them to the valley next year." Dibble took the masks to Utah in 1850 and used them as part of a traveling exhibit on the history of the Church. In 1885 Dibble sold the masks to Harrie Brown, a sculptor in Logan, Utah. Brown's widow, in turn, sold the death masks to Wilford C. Wood of Bountiful, Utah, in 1936. These masks are now in the possession of the Museum of Church History and Art in Salt Lake City.[598]

It is not possible to determine if these masks are the originals ones cast in Nauvoo or copies, but they have become the most famous set of death masks associated with the martyrdom. The masks are also the starting point for most depictions of Joseph and Hyrum Smith. It is natural to ask, how accurate are the masks? The Prophet and Patriarch died violent deaths, and it is possible their bodies suffered disfigurement in the final moments of their lives. Evidence of this was found in bullet hole in the left side of Hyrum's face, filled with cotton before the death masks were created. Willard Richards, the only uninjured survivor of the attack, found the bodies shortly after the mob fled the scene. He was assisted by Samuel Smith, Joseph and Hyrum's younger brother, who arrived at the jail soon after the attack. Samuel had arranged for the bodies to be transported to the Hamilton House, a hotel in Carthage. The attack on the jail took place around 5 p.m., and Willard Richards began his journey to take the bodies back to Nauvoo around 8 a.m. the next morning, arriving around 3 p.m., according to Church historian Andrew Jenson. We do not know the exact time the molds of the martyrs' faces were created, but it likely occurred within twenty-four hours of their deaths.[599]

Ephraim Hatch, a scholar conducting research on the masks, asked several morticians to examine the masks and offer their opinions. They concluded it is likely the masks are genuine casts of dead persons and not sculpted imitations, and cited evidences of dehydration on Joseph's left eye. They also agreed it was possible to make masks of this quality if ice or other means were used to cool and preserve decay in the bodies. Rigor mortis can delay bacterial growth in bodies and is most pronounced in healthy individuals who die suddenly, as Joseph and Hyrum did. Ice was available in Carthage at the time. When John Taylor, who remained in Carthage recovering from his wounds, finally began the trip back to Nauvoo, he noted, "My wife rode with me, applying ice and ice-water to my wounds."[600]

An exhibition of the bodies for the public opened at 8 a.m. on Saturday, June 29, 1844, around forty-three hours after the martyrdom. According to some accounts, more than twenty thousand people filed through the Mansion House to view the bodies, some leaving behind vivid accounts of the gruesome scene. One account explains, "The scene around the bodies of the dead men was too horrible to witness. Hyrum was shot in the brain and bled none, but by noon his body was so swollen—that no one could recognize it. Joseph's blood continued to pour out of his wounds, which had been filled with cotton; the muscles relaxed and the gory fluid trickled down on the floor and formed puddles across the room. Tar, vinegar and sugar were kept burning on the stove to enable persons to stay in the apartment."[601] Given the description of the swelling of Hyrum's body, it is likely the casts for the death masks were taken before the bodies were put on display.

The masks themselves remain a poignant reminder of the untimely death of the Prophet and Patriarch. They themselves have not been spared from accident and the ravages of time. It appears that the original chin of the Hyrum Smith mask was broken off and repaired with a new, larger chin formed on the mask. At times the accuracy of Joseph's mask has been questioned, specifically, if the violent circumstances of his death made the mask appear more elongated and the chin less prominent than it was in life. Comparisons of the mask to drawings made by Nauvoo artist Sutcliffe Maudsley in life demonstrate a close correspondence between the two, suggesting the mask is an accurate representation of Joseph's face.[602]

Given the abundance of photographs of early Church leaders such as Brigham Young, Emma Smith, John Taylor, and others, there is an understandable desire to see a true-to-life representation of Joseph and Hyrum. Photography was in its infancy when the martyrdom occurred, and studios practicing the new art existed in Illinois at the time. Over the years, several claims have been made about various photographs as genuine portraits of Joseph Smith, and it is entirely possible one of them is real, though it is impossible to tell with any certainty at this time.[603] For now, the death masks remain the closest experience to gazing on the actual faces of the martyrs. The wound in Hyrum's face remains a poignant reminder of their cruel death, but both faces remain serene, as if the brothers are not gone, but in a deep sleep. The subject of innumerable paintings, drawings, and sculptures, they remain a powerful reminder that "in life they were not divided, and in death they were not separated!" (D&C 135:3).[604]

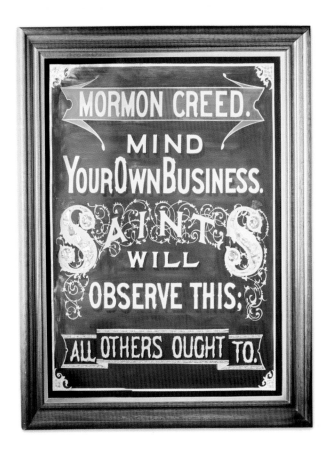

44. "MORMON CREED" MIRROR

– Church History Museum –

From the First Vision given to Joseph Smith in 1820, the faith of the Latter-day Saints was one without creeds. In the 1838 history, Joseph recorded the Savior's disapproval of Christian creeds, writing, "The Personage who addressed me said that all their Creeds were an abomination in his sight."[605] Joseph Smith avoided established creeds, instead finding joy in exploratory thoughts about religion. In an April 1843 address, he declared, "Methodists have creeds which a man must believe or be kicked out of their church. I want the liberty of thinking and believing as I please; it feels so good not to be tramelled."[606] The early Saints never accepted the creeds adopted by more orthodox Christians, nor did they form their own. However, throughout the nineteenth century, an informal, somewhat tongue-in-cheek saying began to be circulated among the Saints as the "Mormon Creed." Its status as an official Church teaching is debatable, but its popularity among the Saints was indisputable. In its simplest form, it read, "Mind Your Own Business."[607]

The Mormon Creed was born out of the political controversies that the Saints found themselves enmeshed in during the early 1840s. William Smith, brother of the Prophet, founded *The Wasp*, a newspaper with a pronounced political purpose to combat "the shafts of slander" of people opposed to the Latter-day Saints. The following was printed in the ninth issue of *The Wasp*: "Mormon Creed: To mind their own business, and let everybody else, *do likewise*. Publish this, *ye Editors,* who boast of equal rights and privileges."[608] The next appearance of the phrase came in October 1842, when the *Millennial Star,* a Church periodical in Great Britain, printed on its last page, "Mormon Creed—To mind their own business, and let everybody else do the same." The periodical vaguely attributed the saying to a Boston newspaper.[609] The phrase was reprinted again in the *Millennial Star* in June 1843, this time shortened to "Mind Your Own Business" accompanied by the explanatory note, "We think the practice of the above worthy of recommendation to many who are not over scrupulous in their statements respecting the character and religion of the Saints; also worth the notice of those Saints who forget the gospel by attacking the systems of men."[610]

The phrase was brought further into circulation among the Saints when Joseph Smith declared, "We will be in peace with all men, so long as they will mind their own business and let us along."[611] Following the martyrdom of Joseph and Hyrum Smith in 1844, the desire of the Saints to be left alone increased, and the Mormon Creed became more pronounced. In the 1845 minutes of the Council of Fifty, Brigham Young suggested to the editors of Church-sponsored newspapers "that they publish nothing more in the papers, which will tend to inflame the rage of our enemies but leave them alone and let us mind our own business."[612] By the time a new Church headquarters was established in Salt Lake Valley, the phrase was in common use. An 1852 editorial appearing in the *Deseret News* spoke of the troubles in the eastern United States and then declared, "All is peace and prosperity in Utah; men are attending 'to their own business,' as usual, according to the 'Mormon creed.'"[613]

By the 1850s, the phrase became a favorite of Brigham Young. In an 1853 address given in the Salt Lake Tabernacle, he declared, "I will repeat part of the 'Mormon Creed,' viz., 'Let every man mind his own business.' If this is observed, every man will have business sufficient on hand, so as to not afford time to trouble himself with the business of other people." He continued, "There are plenty of evils about our neighbors; this no person will pretend to deny; but there is no man or woman on earth, Saint or sinner, but what has plenty to do to watch the little evils that cling to human nature, and weed their own gardens."[614]

Within a few years, the phrase itself was attributed to Brigham Young. In 1855, Elder John Taylor made a splash when he opened the offices of *The Mormon*, a newspaper intended to defend the Saints from spurious charges, right in the heart of New York City. The masthead of the paper was its most striking feature, taking up nearly a quarter of the front page. It was an interesting fusion of American and Latter-day Saint symbols. The central image was an eagle with outstretched wings, perched on a beehive, with two unfurled American flags behind it. Above the eagle was an image of the all-seeing eye of God with rays of light emanating from it, and the words "Let there be light; and there was light" written above the eye. Written on the stripes of the flag to the left was "Truth, Intelligence, Virtue, and Faith—John Taylor," and on the right was "Truth Will Prevail—Heber C. Kimball." The Beehive was flanked by two scrolls, reading on the right, "Constitution of the United States, given by inspiration of God—Joseph Smith," and on the left, "Mormon Creed—Mind Your Own Business—Brigham Young."[615]

In areas where Church membership was relatively small, the use of the creed became even more pronounced. George Q. Cannon, writing in the *Juvenile Instructor* in 1883, remembered, "It will not be news to say to the old members of the Church who came from England, that in the earlier days of the Church the Saints kept cards posted up in their houses containing the 'Mormon' creed, 'Let every man mind his own business!'" Cannon even went so far as to make the creed a matter of salvation, writing, "We believe that Joseph Smith is credited with saying that he would give the people a key by which they could get back into the presence of God. The key was: 'Let every man mind his own business.'" Cannon does not cite the source of this quote, and a search through the public discourses of Joseph Smith fails to locate it also, though it is possible that he may have taught the phrase in private. Nevertheless, Cannon's strong advocacy of the creed as a teaching of salvation illustrates how central the teaching became in the minds of the Saints.[616]

As the conflict escalated between the United States government and the Saints over the practice of plural marriage, the Mormon Creed continued to maintain an important place as a mantra among the Saints. When the Logan Temple was dedicated in 1884, the ornate glass fixture pictured at the beginning of this chapter was placed in the temple. It read: "Mormon Creed: Mind Your Own Business. Saints will observe this, all others ought to." Finding a fixture like this in a Latter-day Saint temple is surprising to twenty-first-century Saints, though it accurately captures the frustration that the early members of the Church felt against their persecutors. The tension that the Saints faced, between in-viting all men and women to come unto Christ while also maintaining the integrity of their own beliefs, was enflamed as the Saints saw the government of the United States encroaching on the free exercise of their religion. An 1889 editorial appearing in the *Deseret News* pushed back against governmental overreach, noting, "The Latter-day Saints have the disposition to carry into practical effect one article of their creed which says, 'Mind your own business.' They have the disposition to let everybody else's business alone. If their would-be dictators will follow their example in that respect, there will be much more peace in the land . . . all classes, creeds, and parties will be free to attend and unite on such ground as they can meet upon in common."[617]

With the end of plural marriage, the Saints entered into a transitional phase where they moved closer to the mainstream of society in the United States. Persecution lessened and use of the Mormon Creed began to gradually wane. In time, only older members of the Church remembered it and often used it to admonish the young. In 1903, President Joseph F. Smith taught, "The 'Mormon' creed: 'mind your own business,' is a good motto for young people to adopt who wish to succeed, and who wish to make the best use of their time and lives. . . . Let it be remembered that nothing is quite so contemptible as idle gossip."[618] More than a century later, the Mormon Creed remains good advice, but it is not as potent now as when it became the informal creed for the Saints in the time of their persecutions.

45. Belle Spafford's 55-Cent Dress

– Church History Museum

When Belle Smith Spafford, the ninth Relief Society general president, was invited to a formal event held in her honor by the National Council of Women, many women complimented her dress. She surprised them by informing them that the expensive-looking dress was actually a homemade dress that had only cost 55 cents to make. She said, "This dress was made from a remnant of drapery fabric, clearance thread and a zipper. It is a grand example of creativity and making do with what you have."[619] Belle Spafford's "55-cent dress" demonstrates her humility throughout her lifetime of service even as she successfully led several prominent women's organizations.

When Belle S. Spafford first became Relief Society general president, she suggested that the Relief Society leave the National Council of Women (NCW), an organization in which leaders of the Relief Society had participated for more than fifty years. Every year, the NCW invited leaders of the Relief Society to their annual meeting in New York, but Spafford suggested to President George Albert Smith that they leave the council because she felt that these trips were too time-consuming and expensive. She also argued, "We really get nothing from the councils." The prophet's response changed Spafford's mindset forever:

You surprise me. Do you always think in terms of what you get? Don't you think it's well at times to think in terms of what you have to give? Now I feel that Mormon women have something to give to women of the world and I believe also that you learn from them. Rather than to terminate your membership, I suggest you take one or two of your ablest board members and attend the meetings and continue your membership in these organizations.

President Smith then told President Spafford to "attend the forthcoming meetings and make your influence felt in those organizations."[620]

Spafford clearly took this counsel to heart: she became an active member of the council and was eventually elected president of the National Council of Women, serving from 1968 to 1970.[621] The National Council of Women, which was founded in 1888, began as a women's suffrage group and served to represent the voice of women while informing women on issues related to women's rights, welfare, and more. On the role of the NCW, Spafford said, "We regard the council as the voice of the American woman."[622] While serving in many prominent positions in the NCW, she traveled the world giving speeches and addressing women.

She managed this responsibility all while serving as the Relief Society general president for the Church. She was president of the Relief Society for twenty-nine years and served under the direction of six different prophets. She was sustained as president in April 1945 and served until October 1974.[623] She was a strong advocate of the importance of the Relief Society and its role in helping women across the world. Spafford said:

> Tremendous changes. . . have taken place in the social, economic, industrial, and educational life of most countries in the world since Relief Society was founded. And I don't think any change in the world has been more significant than the change in the status of women. . . . Yet, in the midst of all this change. . . Relief Society has been just as constant in its purpose as truth is constant. The purposes that were important for the handful of women in Nauvoo are still important to women world-wide.[624]

Belle Spafford devoted most of her life to Church service, all while championing the role of women as she served as president of two major women's organizations.

A blessing, given to Joseph Smith, 3rd, by his father, Joseph Smith, Senr, on Jan.y 17, 1844.

Blessed of the Lord is my son Joseph, who is called the third,— for the Lord knows the integrity of his heart, and loves him, because of his faith, and righteous desires. And, for this cause, has the Lord raised him up;— that the promises made to the fathers might be fulfilled, even that the anointing of the progenitor shall be upon the head of my son, and his seed after him, from generation to generation. For he shall be my successor to the Presidency of the High Priesthood: a Seer, and a Revelator, and a Prophet, unto the Church; which appointment belongeth to him by blessing, and also by right.

Verily, thus saith the Lord: if he abides in me, his days shall be lengthened upon the earth, but if he abides not in me, I, the Lord, will receive him, in an instant, unto myself.

When he is grown, he shall be a strength to his brethren, and a comfort to his mother. Angels will minister unto him, and he will be wafted as on eagle's wings, and be as wise as serpents, even a multiplicity of blessings shall be his. Amen.

46. MARK HOFMANN FORGERY OF JOSEPH SMITH III BLESSING

– Community of Christ Library –

On March 2, 1981, Mark William Hofmann sold a document to the Church Historical Department that he claimed was a transcription of a father's blessing given to Joseph Smith III by his father, Joseph Smith Jr.[625] This document, dated January 17, 1844, caused a stir in the media and among members of The Church of Jesus Christ of Latter-day Saints because, as the *Deseret News* reported on March 19, 1981, it included "the possibility of Joseph Smith III succeeding his father as prophet and church leader."[626]

In this document, supposedly transcribed by Joseph Smith's clerk at the time, Thomas Bullock, Joseph Smith pronounces a blessing on his eleven-year-old son, stating that Joseph Smith III "shall be my successor to the Presidency of the High Priesthood: a Seer, and a Revelator, and a Prophet, unto the Church; which appointment belongeth to him by blessing, and also by right."[627] Hoffman, knowing that this passage of the document would bring up doubts about the line of Church authority and claiming that he had obtained this controversial document from a descendant of Thomas Bullock, offered to sell it to the Church. When the director of the Church's archives did not agree to purchase the document, Hofmann let the Church Historical Department know that the Reorganized Church of Jesus Christ of Latter-day Saints (RLDS: now the Community of Christ) was interested in purchasing it. The Historical Department then, with (First Counselor in the First Presidency) President Gordon B. Hinckley's approval and after having the document's handwriting authenticated, purchased the document "for about $20,000 in trade."[628] Soon after, the First Presidency decided to offer the document to the RLDS church, which gave the First Presidency a copy of *A Book of Commandments* in exchange for the document.[629]

Less than a month later, in a general conference address on the subject, President Hinckley affirmed that the document, partly due to it being a father's blessing and not an ordination, "[did] not seriously raise any question concerning the validity of succession in the presidency through the Council of the Twelve Apostles as that body was established by the Prophet and as it has functioned under the revelations of God."[630]

Four years later, it was revealed that Hofmann had forged the document, and many others, with the intention to extort money as well as embarrass the Church. Hofmann's deception was discovered only after the police arrested Hofmann for murdering two people with homemade bombs in order to protect himself from document dealers who were beginning to suspect him of fraud. Hofmann was put at the forefront of the murder investigation on October 16, 1985, when a third bomb accidentally went off in his car and injured him.[631] It was then that Hofmann admitted to forging famous documents such as the Anthon Transcript (a transcription of hieroglyphics copied from the gold plates, which Martin Harris was known to have shown to Charles Anthon in New York) and the Salamander Letter (which recounts Joseph Smith dealing with folk magic and money-digging, and which claims that he was visited by a spirit in the shape of a white salamander).[632]

Mark Hofmann's forgeries of Church documents—which fooled even forgery experts, historical scholars, and the FBI—ended when he pleaded guilty to murder and fraud in January of 1987 and was subsequently sentenced to serve life in prison.[633]

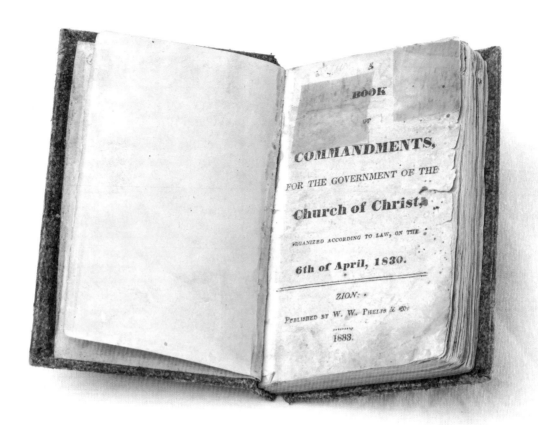

47. Book of Commandments

— Community of Christ Library —

By 1831, Joseph Smith was leading a fledgling religious movement and played an instrumental role in bringing forth a new book of scripture. The flood of revelation did not cease with the end of the inspired translation of the Book of Mormon. The young prophet continued to receive revelations providing divine counsel to his associates and vital instructions for governing the Church. John Whitmer, the Church historian (see D&C 47), copied down the revelations into the records known today as the manuscript revelation books.[634] Many revelations first came to public view after publication in the Church newspaper, the *Evening and Morning Star,* during the summers of June 1832 and 33.[635] During this time Church members began to investigate the possibility of compiling the revelations given to their Prophet in a new book of scripture. These efforts yielded the creation of a new and unique volume of God's word; the book was not a translation of a text given to an ancient people. The new volume was made of modern revelation given to the Lord's people in the latter days. It was not a record of a saga from antiquity, but an acknowledgment of the word of God given to His servants in contemporary times.

The first record of an effort to produce this new book of scripture is found in the minutes of a conference held in Hiram, Ohio, on November 1, 1831.

The Lord signaled his sanction for the new venture by providing an inspired preface to the book, saying, "Hearken O ye People of my Church saith the voice of him who dwells on high & whose eyes are upon all men yea verily I say hearken ye People from afar. . . . Behold this is mine authority & the authority of my servants & my preface unto the Book of my Commandments which I have given them to Publish unto you" (D&C 1:1, 6).[636] A revelation given the same day provided an appendix for the book with a listing of the signs of the times (see D&C 133).[637] Another revelation given ten days later commanded Oliver Cowdery and John Whitmer to take the revelations to Missouri and begin work on printing the book (see D&C 69).[638] A few months later, with the preparations now well underway, Joseph Smith and other Church leaders appointed a committee of three—William W. Phelps, Oliver Cowdery, and John Whitmer—to "review the Book of Commandmants & select for printing such as shall be deemed by them proper, as dictated by the Spirit & make all the necessary verbal corrections."[639]

The Book of Commandments was never fully completed, but when printed it contained most of the revelations given to Joseph Smith before September 1831. There are seven items found in earlier manuscript revelation books not found published in the Book of Commandments. The committee made the decisions concerning what was left out of the book, but they gave no record explaining why these items were left out. Some of the missing revelations, including D&C 17, 51, 57, and 74, appeared in the Doctrine and Covenants when it was published in 1835.[640]

The effort to print the Book of Commandments came to an abrupt end on July 20, 1833, when a mob of four to five hundred Missouri vigilantes attacked the printing office, destroying many of the printed copies of the Book of Commandments before they were completed. Several Church members witnessed the destruction of the printing office and attempted to rescue the printings from the mob. The most well known of the accounts from the Saints who rescued the manuscript comes from Mary and Caroline Rollins. Mary later recalled, "When the mob was tearing down the printing office, a two story building, driving Brother Phelps' family out of the lower part of the house, they (the mob) brought out some large sheets of paper, saying 'Here are the Mormon commandments.'" Viewing the destruction, Mary and Caroline felt compelled to take action. Mary continues, "My sister, 12 years old (I was then 14) and myself were in a corner of a fence watching them. When they spoke about them being the commandments, I was determined to have some of them. So while their backs were turned, prying out the gable end of the house, we ran and gathered up all we could carry in our arms." Mary and Caroline quickly escaped, pursued by two members of the mob. The two young girls escaped into a corn field by laying down and hiding as the mobbers ran past them. They escaped to the home of a nearby member, who hid the manuscripts away for safekeeping. Mary later recalled, that "Oliver Cowdery bound them in small books and gave me one."[641]

Another Saint who risked life and limb to save the manuscript was John Taylor of Kentucky, a twenty-year-old convert of just seven months. He recalled: "I asked [Bishop] Partridge if I might go and get out some copies of the Book of Commandments. He said it would most likely cost me my life if I attempted it. I told him I did not mind hazarding my life to secure some copies of the commandments. He then said I might go." Taylor crept up to the print shop and reached through the cracks between the logs, pulling out as many copies of the manuscript as possible until he was discovered by the mob. Recalling the terrifying encounter he recalled, "A dozen men surrounded me and commenced throwing stones at me and I shouted out 'Oh my God must I be stoned to death like Stephen for the sake of the word of the Lord.' The Lord gave me strength and skill to elude them and make my escape without being hit by a stone." John ends his account by saying, "I delivered the copies to [Bishop] Partridge who said I had done a good work and my escape was a miracle. These I believe are the only copies of that edition of the Book of Commandments preserved from destruction."[642]

Because the Book of Commandments was never officially published, the surviving sheets were gathered up and bound together by individual Church members. The surviving copies of the book exist in a wide variety of bindings.[643] In the aftermath of the mobbing, Joseph Smith and other Church leaders chose to start work on an expanded edition of the revelations, producing a new volume named the Doctrine & Covenants in 1835. The copies of the Book of Commandments that survived the mob attack in Jackson County became increasingly rare as time went on. Today fewer than thirty copies of the book are known to exist, and the small volume regularly tops lists of the most expensive Latter-day Saint books.[644] The original printers planned to offer the Book of Commandments "from 25, to 50 cents a copy," but today an original copy of the book is valued at more than a million United States dollars.[645] One collector emphasized that the book "could be on almost any list of the 'most expensive books.'"[646]

Because the Book of Commandments was never finished, it ends abruptly with the phrase, "For verily I say that the rebellious are not of the blood of Ephraim," a passage now found in section 64, verse 36 of the current edition of the Doctrine and Covenants. In his copy of the Book of Commandments, now in custody of the Church History Department, Wilford Woodruff chose to continue writing the revelation, along with the revelation known as the Word of Wisdom, in the blank pages found in the back of the book.[647] The additional copy featured in this book is a rarity even in this most rare of Latter-day Saint books. Underneath two pieces of masking tape placed on the front cover, written in light pencil the name "Joseph Smith" is found. Provenance documents in the Community of Christ archives indicate this copy of the Book of Commandments was donated by Frederick Madison Smith's family and was likely owned by Joseph Smith Jr. during his lifetime.[648]

Regardless of its monetary value, the Book of Commandments is unique as the first truly modern volume of scripture produced by the Latter-day Saints. The intense persecutions surrounding its creation also attest to the rising level of animosity against the work of the Restoration. The limited distribution of the book was likely a disappointment to many Church members in the period, though the revelations gained wider circulation with the publication of the Doctrine and Covenants two years later. Nevertheless, a book now existed where revelations given to a modern prophet joined the voices of ancient prophets found in the Bible and the Book of Mormon. Forged in fire, the word of God in the latter days was now going forth.

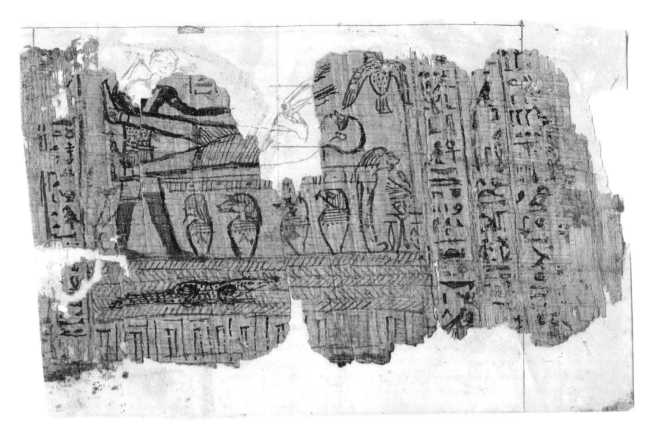

48. JOSEPH SMITH PAPYRI

– Church History Library –

Of the books in the Latter-day Saint canon of scripture, perhaps the most controversial in terms of its origins is the book of Abraham. The origins of the record are announced in just a few simple sentences preceding the text of the book: "A translation of some ancient Records that have fallen into our hands from the catacombs of Egypt. The writings of Abraham while he was in Egypt, called the Book of Abraham, written by his own hand, upon papyrus."[649] Those few words underline a debate over the origin of the book spanning two centuries, taking place on several continents, diving into the earliest ages of antiquity and even involving the Emperor Napoleon. Even more tantalizing, fragmentary pieces of the source papyri were discovered in the 1960s, igniting a whole new series of debates about the origins of the book.

The Joseph Smith Papyri, as they are commonly called by scholars of the subject, have been in the hands of the Church since the 1960s. It is clear that these fragments are not the source of the text of the book of Abraham, though they clearly contain a version of the facsimiles traditionally accompanying the book in its printing. How did these rare fragments come into the possession of Joseph Smith? They most likely came from tombs exhumed near the ancient Egyptian city of Thebes in the early decades of the nineteenth century by an Italian antiquities dealer named Antonio Lebolo. Lebolo's expeditions to Egypt came as part of a general excitement over Egyptian antiquities caused by the expeditions of Napoleon Bonaparte into the region in the late eighteenth and early nineteenth centuries. Sometime between 1817 and 1821, Lebolo unearthed a tomb holding a large collection of mummies and papyri.[650] After Lebolo's death in 1830, his estate and his Egyptian collection made its way to the United States, where it became part of a traveling exhibition shown in nearly a dozen cities throughout the United States.[651]

When the display came to Kirtland, several Church members met with an antiquities dealer named Michael Chandler. Chandler's exact relationship to Lebolo and the collection are not fully known, but he had been referred to Joseph Smith as a person who could perhaps translate the ancient characters on the papyri. A letter from W. W. Phelps, one of Joseph's close associates, captures the excitement in Kirtland surrounding the papyri: "On the last of June four Egyptian mummies were brought here. With them were two papyrus rolls, besides some other ancient Egyptian writings. . . . They were presented to President Smith. He soon knew what they were and said that the rolls of papyrus contained a sacred record kept by Joseph in Pharaoh's court in Egypt and the teachings of Father Abraham. . . . These records of old times when we translate and print them in a book will make a good witness for the Book of Mormon."[652] Shortly after his meeting with Chandler in June or July 1835, Joseph and several Church members purchased four mummies from Chandler, along with most, if not all, of the papyri in the collection.[653]

Shortly after, Joseph began the work of translating the records. His journal from October to December 1835 contains nine entries related to the translation work carried out on the ancient Egyptian materials. A typical entry from November 19, 1835, reads, "I returned home and spent the day in translating the Egyptian records."[654] The text produced by the Prophet during this period is a remarkable account of the early life of the biblical patriarch Abraham. The work recontextualizes Abraham as an early witness of Jesus Christ. It provides some of the most valuable teachings known on the premortal nature of humanity and the selection of Christ as the Savior of God's children. It also includes a new account of the creation of the earth, detailing how the Creation was planned before it was carried out.[655] Perhaps most poignantly, the account explains how Abraham—a man most known for having his faith tested by God asking him to sacrifice his son—was nearly sacrificed himself as a young man by his wicked father.

The book of Abraham was first published in three installments of the *Times and Seasons* in Nauvoo. Elder John Taylor, the editor of the paper, wrote in the February 1, 1843, issue of the paper about Joseph Smith's plans to publish more of the translation. However, the Prophet's martyrdom in June 1844 prevented any more of the record coming to light. Following Joseph's death, the mummies and the papyri remained in the hands of Lucy Mack Smith, the Prophet's mother. She retained them until her death in 1856, whereupon Emma Smith and her second husband, Lewis Bidamon, sold the materials to a man named Abel Combs. Shortly thereafter, Combs sold at least two of the mummies and most of the papyri to the St. Louis Museum. In 1863, the collection was moved to Chicago, Illinois. There, two of the mummies and parts of the papyri remained on display until the museum was incinerated in the Chicago fire of 1871.[656]

After the Chicago fire, it was generally assumed that all of the materials associated with the book of Abraham were destroyed. The entire debate on the matter was upturned in 1967, when eleven fragments of the Joseph Smith Papyri were discovered in the collection of the New York Metropolitan Museum of Art. The fragments came to light through the efforts of Dr. Aziz Atiya, a distinguished professor of history at the University of Utah. Research into the provenance of the fragments revealed that Abel Combs had not sold all of the papyri to the St. Louis museum but had retained some of the pieces. These fragments appear to have broken off the main rolls and were attached to several pieces of paper before being placed in large glass picture frames. In his will Combs gave the fragments to Charlotte Benecke Weaver, who nursed him through his final illness. When she died, her daughter, Alice Heusser, inherited the fragments. After Alice's death, her husband sold the fragments to the New York Metropolitan Museum of Art in 1946. When the true nature of the fragments came to light, they were returned to the Church, and they have remained in the Church's ownership ever since.[657]

Scholarly analysis after the papyri came into Church possession revealed that the fragments are part of an ancient Egyptian religious text known as the Book of Breathings. The text on the fragments is not the book of Abraham, and the fragments date to a period nearly two thousand years after the time of Abraham.[658] What then, is their connection to the book of Abraham?

There are several prominent theories to explain the connection between the papyri and the book of Abraham. One of the most prominent is that the text of the book of Abraham was written on the papyri scrolls, but we do not have the portion of the scrolls containing the text. Accounts from those who saw the papyri Joseph Smith worked with described "a long roll" or several roles of papyri.[659] Scholars estimate that the fragments currently available only represent about thirteen percent of the original scrolls and are unsure of the size of the original collection. Another prominent theory is that the study of the papyri may have led to a revelation about the life of Abraham, resulting in a text given through pure inspiration. Throughout his life Joseph Smith used the term "translation" broadly to describe working with an original document (as in the Book of Mormon translation) or receiving text through divine inspiration (such as the New Translation of the Old and New Testaments). All forms of translation carried out by the Prophet during his lifetime involved some kind of divine power. Whether he translated from a lost portion of the papyri or received the text directly from inspiration, the power of God was involved.[660]

As for the facsimiles found on the Joseph Smith Papyri, it is possible that illustrations once connected to Abraham and his story were removed from their original context and reinterpreted in terms of Egyptian burial practices. Though its exact origins remained steeped in mystery, an examination of the text of the book of Abraham itself provides several compelling evidences of the ancient genesis of the book. The descriptions of human sacrifices in the book align well with recent scholarly discoveries of similar punishments dating back to Abraham's time. The description of "the plain of Olishem" (Abraham 1:10), a name not mentioned in the Bible, match up with an ancient inscription was discovered and translated in the twentieth century which mentions a town named Ulisum in northwestern Syria.[661] Abraham 3:22–23 is written in a poetic form common in Near Eastern languages but unknown in the period Joseph Smith produced the text.[662] In addition to these and other textual evidences, there are a number of intriguing parallels to apocryphal traditions surrounding Abraham found within the book. Some of these include the idolatry of Terah, Abraham's father, the famine in Abraham's homeland, Abraham's knowledge of Egyptian idols, and Abraham's knowledge of astronomy. Some of these apocryphal stories may have been available in Joseph Smith's lifetime, but others only emerged after his death.[663] One scholar, writing of Joseph Smith's interpretation of the facsimiles in the book concluded, "If Joseph had simply been guessing, his probability of being correct would be enormously smaller than that of being wrong. If we were to find that the Prophet had explained only one or two things in the facsimiles correctly, this could be attributed to chance. But when we find many examples of his explanations being correct, this kind of accuracy for all practical purposes eliminates chance or 'good guessing.'"[664]

Ultimately the Joseph Smith Papyri provide an interesting historical puzzle, but one that is currently unsolvable through scholarly means. Their existence means Joseph Smith did have actual ancient records in his hands, though the debate over the origin of the scriptural text of Abraham will continue. An official statement published by the Church on the subject concludes, "The veracity and value of the book of Abraham cannot be settled by scholarly debate concerning the book's translation and historicity. The book's status as scripture lies in the eternal truths it teaches and the powerful spirit it conveys. . . . The truth of the book of Abraham is ultimately found through careful study of its teachings, sincere prayer, and the confirmation of the Spirit."[665]

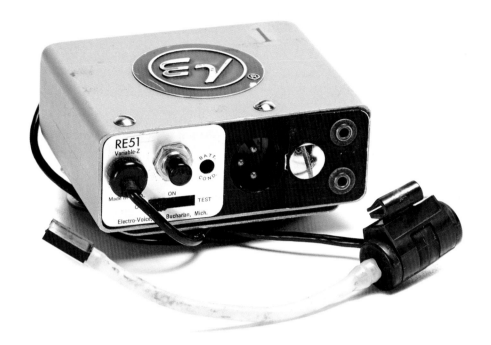

49. President Spencer W. Kimball's Microphone

– Church History Museum –

Spencer W. Kimball was a man of faith and action. It would seem, from many accounts, that the hardest thing for him to do was rest. Plagued throughout his life with "boils, ulcers, several heart attacks, open heart surgery, impaired hearing, and cancer of the larynx," President Kimball gave all that he had to the Church.[666] "If the Lord sees He can use us and needs us, He will heal us," he said on one occasion.[667] Though he was certainly used as an instrument in the hands of the Lord, he was never completely relieved from the repercussions of his many ailments. For much of his time as an apostle and throughout the duration of his time as a prophet, President Kimball's voice was soft, hoarse, and gravelly as a result of his many throat operations. However, even in his weakness, he was made strong.

In 1948 Spencer Kimball's sister Helen Farr, who had been sick with cancer for many months, passed away. Thus began a fear of cancer that never left President Kimball. He had been astonished at how the cancer had so "terribly devastated her face," but even more heart-wrenching was the sparse attendance at her funeral; aside from Spencer, no relatives from the Kimball side of the family attended. It hurt and devastated Spencer to watch his sister die so young "and so little noticed. From that winter on, Spencer felt personal fear of the black angel of cancer."[668]

In the spring of 1950, when Spencer began to experience a consistent hoarseness in his throat, his fears of cancer were heightened: "Cancer! Cancer of the throat would render me useless from now on for the Church," he expressed in his journal after his first doctor's visit. A biopsy confirmed that it was an infection that would need to be cauterized, but, to Spencer's relief, it was not cancer. From that point on, "every few months he had his throat checked for cancer. The fear never totally left."[669]

Six years later, around Christmastime of 1956, Spencer woke one morning with blood in the back of his throat. He consulted a throat cancer specialist in New York by the name of Dr. Martin, who recommended immediate biopsy. Spencer, who earlier had such fears of cancer, found himself surprisingly calm. He wrote in his journal before the operation, "I pray only Thy will be done. If my work justifies my continuance of it, I pray my life and my voice may be extended and strengthened. If my work is done. . . . I am resigned to do whatever He wills."[670] Spencer went forward with the biopsy.

"By June 1957 Spencer's physician, Dr. Cowan, was worried that Spencer's raw throat was not healing. He urged a second consultation with Dr. Martin in New York." Before going to New York, Spencer wrote a letter to President McKay, apologizing for going through with previous surgery without his permission and asked him what he should do.[671] When Dr. Martin recommended immediate surgery to remove one of the vocal cords, President McKay stated that "even should [Spencer Kimball] lose his voice entirely, he could still serve effectively in other ways" and advised him to go forward with the procedure.[672] The surgery removed one of Kimball's vocal cords and half of the other, leaving him barely able to speak above a hoarse whisper.[673]

Finally, six months after the operation, Dr. Cowan declared Elder Kimball's throat healed, but as the hoarseness persisted, President Kimball was worried about using his voice again to address the Saints. The opportunity came at a stake conference in the Gila Valley where President Kimball had previously served as a stake president. "There would be no more sympathetic group in the whole church than this one," he thought.[674] Elder Kimball used his characteristic humor to introduce his audience to his new voice: "I must tell you what has happened to me," said Elder Kimball. "I went away to the East, and while there I fell among cutthroats!" Elder Boyd K. Packer, who was present at the conference, later remarked, "After that it didn't matter what he said. Elder Kimball was back!"[675]

Elder Kimball was back, indeed, but his challenges were not over. For President Kimball, the problems with his throat did not merely impact him physically but took a toll emotionally as well. Following his last operation and the many months of silence, President Kimball had refrained from setting apart missionaries "for fear that his whispering might detract from the occasion for them." He wrote, "I seem so useless. I find myself withdrawing, becoming almost anti-social, quite opposite to my normal nature."[676] Sometime later, following his address at the Gila Valley Stake conference, President Kimball had another discouraging experience when President Lee announced him as the next speaker at a stake conference in Dallas, Texas. "He stood and opened his mouth, but only an ugly grating noise came out. He swallowed and gulped and tried again, with the same sickening feeling. The thought came: 'Better quit—you can't do it—you can't impose on the people like this.'"[677] But he tried again, this time found his voice, and delivered his short sermon. The next day there was another meeting in Houston. President Kimball said to Elder Lee, "I hope you won't embarrass me again." To which President Lee responded, "Oh I'm sure we'll call on you again. I think it's important for the people to hear your witness."[678]

And indeed it was. A short time later, in 1970, President Kimball's opportunities to bear witness expanded as he was set apart as Acting President of the Quorum of the Twelve Apostles. The Lord was preparing him to lead His church. In the meantime, the struggles with his health continued. One year later, in 1971, his cancer returned and President Kimball submitted to radiation treatment. His doctors urged him to undergo another operation rather than radiation, but President Kimball, fearing that another operation would "probably destroy what voice remained," explained that "since he needed a voice for his work, his voice was almost of the same importance as his life."[679]

Only two years later, upon President Harold B. Lee's sudden and unexpected death, Spencer W. Kimball's voice became of even greater importance when he was called as the twelfth President of The Church of Jesus Christ of Latter-day Saints. His diminished voice had often made him feel inadequate, and he feared that others merely tolerated it. But, as Elder Lee had once observed, "When [President Kimball] spoke, people leaned forward and listened with special intentness." [680] Part of that intentness came from his need to whisper, part came from the conviction of his words, and part from the voice that uttered them. His new voice was soft, deep, and gravelly. It was, in Elder Packer's words, "a quiet, persuasive, mellow voice, an acquired voice, an appealing voice, a voice . . . loved by the Latter-day Saints."[681]

It was this beloved voice that called the Saints to lengthen their stride and that declared powerfully that he wanted an army of missionaries. When asked if every young man should go on a mission, he firmly responded, "The answer has been given by the Lord. It is 'Yes.'"[682] As a result, the missionary force doubled, and fifty-one new missions were created. It was this voice, too, that announced that

the priesthood would be extended to all worthy males.[683] The Saints heard because of a microphone. They hearkened to the voice of a prophet of God.

The weakness of his voice had given President Kimball many opportunities to strengthen his faith. One Sunday in 1952, two years after his first throat biopsy, Spencer stood to speak to a congregation in Moore, Idaho, when suddenly "the public address system went out." He knew that to raise his voice "might damage the throat he had carefully nursed for two years." But he could not disappoint the faithful saints who had come to hear him. "A week later, his voice still hoarse and broken from the terrific pressure of that experience, Spencer fasted three full days for faith to heal his throat. On the third day, though his voice remained hoarse, he broke his fast with a calm assurance that the Lord would bless his life."[684]

On that occasion, the power of his faith and conviction magnified his voice for a waiting audience of Saints. In his later years, it was magnified by the aid of a small microphone that hid on his glasses frame, connecting to a small apparatus that was hidden under his shirt. But then, too, it resonated from the many years that had humbled and strengthened him. At the opening of a display in Rexburg, Idaho, honoring the life and ministry of President Spencer W. Kimball, Sister Bednar remarked, "I think the fact that he had so much adversity with his health is significant. . . . It's incredible he was able to retrain his voice, even though it was a whisper." Among the items in the display were a pair of old shoes, and the caption beside them read, "My life is like my shoes—meant to be worn out in the service of God."[685] Also on display was the microphone that President Kimball used when he lost his voice from cancer, beside which a caption might have read, "My voice is like this microphone—small, but magnified."

50. MANTI TEMPLE HAIR WREATH

– Church History Museum –

The Manti Temple in the Sanpete Valley of Southern Utah, the fifth temple constructed in this dispensation and the third in the Rocky Mountains, was announced by Brigham Young on December 4, 1873.[686] The construction and design of the temple was a result of the coordinated efforts and sacrifice of Latter-day Saints living in the Sanpete Valley, who took great pride and joy in their temple, which was created by their own hands. One example of this personal pride and ownership in the temple is a wreath of hair that the members of the Relief Society created and donated to be hung in the Manti Temple. The hair wreath represents the unity of the members of the Church, and more particularly of the sisters who contributed in the work of constructing the temple.

Early on at the settlement of the Sanpete Valley, Heber C. Kimball prophesied that a temple would be built on a hill in Manti and "more than that, the rock will be quarried from that hill to build it with, and some of the stone from that quarry will be taken to help complete the Salt Lake Temple." Years later, Brigham Young reinforced President Kimball's prophecy by stating, "The temple should be built on Manti Stone Quarry."[687]

On April 25, 1877, Brigham Young, accompanied by Elder Warren S. Snow, dedicated the temple site at Manti. Elder Snow remembered:

> We two were alone, President Young took me to the spot where the Temple was to stand, we went to the southeast corner, and President Young said: "Here is the spot where the Prophet Moroni stood and dedicated this piece of land for a Temple site, and that is the reason why the location is made here, and we can't move it from this spot; and if you and I are the only persons that come here at high noon today, we will dedicate this ground."[688]

At the appointed time, several hundred Latter-day Saints came to the Temple Hill site to hear President Brigham Young give the dedicatory prayer and instructions on the Manti Temple construction.[689]

He instructed the Saints in Manti to "rear this Temple with clean hands and pure hearts." He also stated, "We now call upon the people, through the several Bishops who preside in this and the neighboring settlement for men to come here with teams and wagons, plows and scrapers, picks and shovels to prepare this ground for the mason-work." President Young called upon "the sisters also to render what assistance they can in this matter."[690]

Five days later, a hundred men gathered at the stone quarry to begin the work of excavating and leveling the site. Though the members' response to the call to work on the temple was quick, the work of construction was slow—it would take eleven years to complete, almost two of which were spent digging and blasting holes and tunnels in order to provide a level foundation for the site.[691] The cornerstones were placed on April 14, 1879, and construction on the exterior of the temple began. The construction of the temple was significant because it was done through the efforts of the members themselves. As Church historian Richard O. Cowan points out, "Almost all the materials needed for the temple were donated or produced locally." Local members of the Church raised funds to pay for the materials needed for the building and the resources for the workmen; members contributed clothing, food, quilts, and many other necessities for the men. Women donated food and made bread for those working on the construction site.[692] Handymen also contributed their time and skills to create the interior woodworking, most notably the two large spiral staircases. These staircases are famous for their exquisite workmanship and impressive size. As former Church architect James McCrea stated, "There are only three stairways in the United States constructed with no central support and of a large size. Two are in the Manti Temple, and the other is located in the Octagon, headquarters for the American Institute of Architects, in Washington D.C."[693]

The temple was completed during a time of great persecution for the leaders of the Church due to laws prohibiting plural marriage. Many Church leaders went undercover to avoid federal authorities, including President Wilford Woodruff. Because of this, a private dedication of the Manti Temple was held on May 17, 1888. President Lorenzo Snow then led the three public dedications held from May 21–23, 1888.[694] At the temple's first public dedication, Elder Franklin D. Richards of the Quorum of the Twelve Apostles summarized the importance of the temple to the Saints living and dead: "The erecting of the Temple was a matter of as much interest and concern to those who had passed behind the veil as to the living. For years, ever since the site had been selected for it, they had watched with anxiety for its completion."[695]

Members of the Manti South Ward Relief Society also invested their time and efforts in the completion of the temple, which is why in 1888, they designed and created a hair wreath to hang inside the Manti Temple. Artwork, jewelry, and decorations created from hair became popular in the Victorian Era, and hair work became a common pastime for women and a skill they passed on to their daughters. Women's magazines in the mid-nineteenth century included instructions on how to weave hair into flowers or wreaths. Many Latter-day Saint women also participated in this tradition, creating family hair wreaths or even watch chains to send to their fiancés who were serving missions.[696] Often, Latter-day Saint women created hair work as a reminder of the resurrection of the dead. For example, in 1844, thirteen-year-old Mary Ann Broomhead created an embroidery sampler using her hair to honor Joseph and Hyrum Smith following their martyrdom. Using her hair as stitching, she embroidered the words, "When the earth shall be restored/ They will come with Christ the Lord." Because many Latter-day Saint women who participated in the tradition of hair work used the hair to represent the resurrection of the dead, it is no surprise that hair wreaths were sometimes hung in temples of The Church of Jesus Christ of Latter-day Saints. For instance, a hair wreath containing the hair of Joseph Smith, twenty-eight other General Authorities, and eight Relief Society leaders hung in the Salt Lake Temple until 1967.[697]

The hair wreath that hung in the Manti Temple was designed by Mary W. Wintch, a member of the Manti South Ward, who wove together strands of hair from members of the Relief Society. In the center of the wreath is a painted wood piece created by Janne Sjodhal, which he cut into the shape of a baptismal font on the back of oxen. Hair flowers bloom out of the font and surround the central image in a wreath, emphasizing the connection between the Resurrection and the members' hair. Inscribed on the artwork is the phrase, "These locks of hair, O Lord, thou hast seen us wear, so now we commit them to Thy Holy Temple's care."[698] The inscription demonstrates that, for the woman whose hair decorated the temple, the wreath represented their dedication and obedience to the Lord and the sacrifices they made in order to obey the commandment to build a temple. Additionally, the fact that the hair of many individual members was woven together to create the wreath represents the unity of these Latter-day Saints and their collective efforts to build the Manti Temple. According to Church historian Mark L. Staker, "The hair from these individuals was brought together in one common image to create unity from individuality."[699]

Though this hair wreath no longer hangs in the Manti Temple—it is currently housed in the Museum of Church History and Art in Salt Lake City, Utah—it is still an important symbol of the Resurrection and work performed for the dead in the Manti Temple. The artwork is also a historical reminder of the importance of the Manti Temple to these Latter-day Saints who sacrificed and contributed much to the construction of this sacred building.

"WE ARE *proud* OF THE *artistic heritage* THAT THE CHURCH HAS BROUGHT TO US FROM ITS EARLIEST *beginnings...*"

—SPENCER W. KIMBALL

"THE GOSPEL VISION OF THE ARTS," *ENSIGN*, JULY 1977.

1   LeRoy S. Wirthlin, "Nathan Smith (1762–1828) Surgical Consultant to Joseph Smith," *BYU Studies* 17, no. 3 (1977): 2.

2   John W. Jordan, ed., *Colonial and Revolutionary Families of Pennsylvania* (New York: Lewis Publishing Company, 1911), Vol. 2, p. 1014.

3   Wirthlin, "Nathan Smith," 4.

4   Nathan Smith to Professor Benjamin Silliman, 31 March 1812, as cited in Emily A. Smith, *The Letters of Nathan Smith, M.R., M.D.* (New Haven, CT: Yale University Press, 1914), 85–86.

5   "Lucy Mack Smith, History, 1844–1845, Page [11], bk. 2," p. [11], bk. 2, *The Joseph Smith Papers*, http://www.josephsmithpapers.org/paper-summary/lucy-mack-smith-history-1844-1845/29. All quotations from this source corrected for spelling and grammar.

6   Wirthlin, "Nathan Smith," 6–7.

7   "Lucy Mack Smith, History, 1844–1845, Page [11], bk. 2," p. [12], bk. 2, *The Joseph Smith Papers*, http://www.josephsmithpapers.org/paper-summary/lucy-mack-smith-history-1844-1845/30.

8   "Lucy Mack Smith, History, 1844–1845, Page [11], bk. 2," p. [12], bk. 2, *The Joseph Smith Papers*, http://www.josephsmithpapers.org/paper-summary/lucy-mack-smith-history-1844-1845/30.

9   "Lucy Mack Smith, History, 1844–1845, Page [11], bk. 2," p. [12], bk. 2, *The Joseph Smith Papers*, http://www.josephsmithpapers.org/paper-summary/lucy-mack-smith-history-1844-1845/30.

10   Wirthlin, "Nathan Smith," 7.

11   Richard Bushman, *Joseph Smith: Rough Stone Rolling* (New York: Alfred K. Knopf, 2005), 21.

12   "Lucy Mack Smith, History, 1844–1845, Page [11], bk. 2," p. [1], bk. 3, *The Joseph Smith Papers*, http://www.josephsmithpapers.org/paper-summary/lucy-mack-smith-history-1844-1845/31.

13   "Lucy Mack Smith, History, 1844–1845, Page [11], bk. 2," p. [2], bk. 3, *The Joseph Smith Papers*, http://www.josephsmithpapers.org/paper-summary/lucy-mack-smith-history-1844-1845/32.

14   "History, 1838–1856, volume A-1 [23 December 1805–30 August 1834]," p. 131, *The Joseph Smith Papers*, http://www.josephsmithpapers.org/paper-summary/history-1838-1856-volume-a-1-23-december-1805-30-august-1834/137.

15   "History, 1838–1856, volume A-1 [23 December 1805–30 August 1834]," p. 131, *The Joseph Smith Papers*, http://www.josephsmithpapers.org/paper-summary/history-1838-1856-volume-a-1-23-december-1805-30-august-1834/137.

16   Oliver S. Hayward, MD and Constance E. Putnam, Dr. Nathan Smith and Early American Medical Education (Hanover, NH: University Press of New England, 1998), 182–84.

17   "Book of Mormon, 1830," iii, *The Joseph Smith Papers*, http://www.josephsmithpapers.org/paper-summary/book-of-mormon-1830/9

18   For a concise explanation of what we know about the translation process, see "Book of Mormon Translation," https://www.lds.org/topics/book-of-mormon-translation?lang=eng; see also Dirkmaat, Gerrit, and Michael, *From darkness unto light: Joseph Smith's translation and publication of the Book of Mormon* (Provo, UT: Salt Lake City, UT: Religious Studies Center; Deseret Book, 2015).

19   "Mormon Relics," Weekly Inter Ocean [Chicago], October 26, 1886, 9; cited in *The Joseph Smith Papers*, Revelations and Translations, vol. 3, pt. 1, xx.

20   "Notes on Seer Stone Images," *The Joseph Smith Papers*, http://www.josephsmithpapers.org/site/note-on-seer-stone-images?p=1&highlight=oval-shaped,%20chocolate%20colored%20stone.

21   "Mormonism—No. II," *Tiffany's Monthly*, August 1859, 165–66; Lucy Mack Smith, History, 1844–1845, bk. 5, 7–8, cited in *The Joseph Smith Papers*, Introduction to Revelations and Translations, vol. 3 (Salt Lake City, UT: Church Historians Press, 2015), xix.

22   Emma Smith Bidamon, Nauvoo, IL, to Emma Pilgrim, March 27, 1870, in John Clark, "Translation of Nephite Records," *Return*, July 15, 1895, 2; italics in original, cited in *The Joseph Smith Papers*, Revelations and Translations, 3: xix.

23   *The Joseph Smith Papers*, Revelations and Translations, 3:xix.

24   JS History, vol. A-1, 7–8, in *The Joseph Smith Papers*, H1:234-236 (Draft 2), see *The Joseph Smith Papers*, Revelations and Translations, 3:xv.

25   Michael Hubbard MacKay and Nicholas J. Frederick, *Joseph Smith's Seer Stones* (Provo, UT; Salt Lake City, UT: Religious Studies Center, Deseret Book, 2016), 7–8.

26   Cited in MacKay and Frederick, *Joseph Smith's Seer Stones*, 38, spelling and punctuation corrected.

27   "Elders' Journal, July 1838," 43, *The Joseph Smith Papers*, http://www.josephsmithpapers.org/paper-summary/elders-journal-july-1838/11.

28   "Last Testimony of Sister Emma," *Saints' Herald* 26 (Oct. 1, 1879), 289–90, cited in "Book of Mormon Translation," https://www.lds.org/topics/book-of-mormon-translation?lang=eng#overview.

29   "Book of Mormon, 1830," 589, *The Joseph Smith Papers*, = http://www.josephsmithpapers.org/paper-summary/book-of-mormon-1830/595.

30   *Latter-day Saints Messenger and Advocate*, 1, no. 5 (1835): 7.

31   *Latter-day Saints Messenger and Advocate*, 2, no. 1 (1835): 195–6.

32   "Lucy Mack Smith, History, 1844–1845, Page [12], bk. 3," p. [12], bk. 3, *The Joseph Smith Papers*, accessed July 9, 2019, https://www.josephsmithpapers.org/paper-summary/lucy-mack-smith-history-1844-1845/42, spelling and punctuation corrected.

33   Andrew H. Hedges, "'All My Endeavors to Preserve Them': Protecting the Plates in Palmyra, 22 September–December 1827," *Journal of Book of Mormon Studies*, 8, no. 2 (1999): 17.

34   Dean C. Jesse, "Joseph Knight's Recollection of Early Mormon History," BYU Studies 12, no. 1 (1976): 32.

35   Hedges, "Protecting the Plates," 17.

36   "Lucy Mack Smith, History, 1845," p. 111, *The Joseph Smith Papers*, accessed July 9, 2019, https://www.josephsmithpapers.org/paper-summary/lucy-mack-smith-history-1845/118.

37   "Lucy Mack Smith, History, 1844–1845, Page [1], bk. 6," p. [1], bk. 6, *The Joseph Smith Papers*, accessed July 9, 2019, https://www.josephsmithpapers.org/paper-summary/lucy-mack-smith-history-1844-1845/69.

38   "Lucy Mack Smith, History, 1845," p. 111, *The Joseph Smith Papers*, accessed July 9, 2019, https://www.josephsmithpapers.org/paper-summary/lucy-mack-smith-history-1845/118.

39   Hedges, "Protecting the Plates," 20–21.

40   Proctor and Proctor, History of Joseph Smith, 141.

41   Hedges, "Protecting the Plates," 20, and William Smith identified this garment as a "tow frock" and said that Joseph had not brought it "especially to wrap the plates in" but that it was "his every day frock such as young men used to wear then." William Smith, "The Old Soldier's Testimony," *The Saints' Herald* 31, no. 40 (1884): 643; "Another Testimony: Statement of William Smith Concerning Joseph, the Prophet," *Deseret Evening News*, January 20, 1894.

42   Hedges, "Protecting the Plates," 21; Proctor and Proctor, *History of Joseph Smith*, 144; Orson Pratt, "An Interesting Account of Several Remarkable Visions, and of the Late Discovery of Ancient American Records," in *The Papers of Joseph Smith, vol. 1, Autobiographical and Historical Writings*, ed. Dean C. Jessee (Salt Lake City: Deseret Book, 1999), 400; and Dan Vogel, ed. and comp., *Early Mormon Documents* (Salt Lake City: Signature Books, 1996), 1:526

43   Proctor and Proctor, *History of Joseph Smith*, 144.

44   Hedges, "Protecting the Plates," 21, and Proctor and Proctor, *History of Joseph Smith*, 144.

45   Proctor and Proctor, *History of Joseph Smith*, 144.

46   *Church History in the Fulness of Times* (Salt Lake City: The Church of Jesus Christ of Latter-day Saints, 1993), 44.

47   Kirk B. Henrichsen, comp., "How Witnesses Described the 'Gold Plates,'" Journal of Book of Mormon Studies 10, no. 1 (2001): 16–21, 78.

48   Read H. Putnam, "Were the Gold Plates Made of Tumbaga?" *The Improvement Era* 69, no. 9 (September 1966): 788.

49   "The Testimony of Eight Witnesses," Book of Mormon; Joseph Smith Jr., "Church History," *Times and Seasons*, March 1, 1842.

50   David M. Pendergast, "Tumbaga Object from the Early Classic Period, Found at Altun Ha, British Honduras (Belize)," *Science* 168 (April 3, 1970): 117.

51   "Times and Seasons, 2 May 1842," p. 773, *The Joseph Smith Papers*, accessed July 22, 2019, https://www.josephsmithpapers.org/paper-summary/times-and-seasons-2-may-1842/7

52   "Visit of E. C. Brand to John Whitmer," 18 February 1875, copied onto a letter from John Whitmer to Mark H. Forscutt, 5 March 1876, Whitmer Papers, Community of Christ Library Archives, Independence, Missouri. Quoted in Michael Hubbard MacKay, Gerrit J. Dirkmaat, and Robin Scott Jensen, "The 'Caractors' Document: New Light on an Early Transcription of the Book of Mormon Characters," *Mormon Historical Studies*, 14, no. 1 (Spring 2014), 131–52.

53   George Q. Cannon Journal, February 27, 1884, Church History Library, Salt Lake City, UT, quoted in MacKay et al., 131–32.

54   Richard E. Bennett, "Martin Harris's 1828 Visit to Luther Bradish, Charles Anthon, and Samuel Mitchill," in *The Coming Forth of the Book of Mormon: A Marvelous Work and Wonder*, ed. Dennis L. Largey, Andrew H. Hedges, John Hilton III, and Kerry Hull (Salt Lake City and Provo, UT: Deseret Book and Religious Studies Center, 2015), 106.

55   MacKay et al., 137–38.

56   Ibid., 134–35.

57   Ibid., 134–35.

58   "Lucy Mack Smith, History," 1844–1845, page [10], book 3, *The Joseph Smith Papers*, https://www.josephsmithpapers.org/paper-summary/lucy-mack-smith-history-1844-1845/40, spelling and punctuation added. Lucy's history was written in 1845 at the request of the Quorum of the Twelve. She was assisted by Martha Jane Knowlton Coray, who acted as her scribe in preparing the manuscript. Coray wrote two manuscripts, one of which stayed with Lucy Mack Smith when the majority of the Saints began their westward exodus, and the other retained by the Church. Both manuscripts are available on *The Joseph Smith Papers* website. "Lucy Mack Smith, History, 1845," Historical Introduction, *The Joseph Smith Papers*, https://www.josephsmithpapers.org/paper-summary/lucy-mack-smith-history-1845/2.

59   Wandle Mace Reminscence, circa 1890, in *Early Mormon Documents*, 4 vols., ed. Dan Vogel (Salt Lake City, UT: Signature Books, 1996), 1:452.

60   "Lucy Mack Smith, History, 1844–1845, Page [7], bk. 5," page [8], book 5, *The Joseph Smith Papers*, https://www.josephsmithpapers.org/paper-summary/lucy-mack-smith-history-1844-1845/62, spelling and punctuation added.

61   "Lucy Mack Smith, History, 1845," pages 114–15, *The Joseph Smith Papers*, https://www.josephsmithpapers.org/paper-summary/lucy-mack-smith-history-1845/121, spelling and punctuation added.

62   "Revelation, June 1829–E [D&C 17]," page 119, *The Joseph Smith Papers*, https://www.josephsmithpapers.org/paper-summary/revelation-june-1829-e-dc-17/1

63   "Lucy Mack Smith, History, 1844–1845," page [5], book 7, *The Joseph Smith Papers*, https://www.josephsmithpapers.org/paper-summary/lucy-mack-smith-history-1844-1845/85, spelling and punctuation added.

64   "Lucy Mack Smith, History, 1844–1845," pages [5–6], book 7, *The Joseph Smith Papers*, https://www.josephsmithpapers.org/paper-summary/lucy-mack-smith-history-1844-1845/86, spelling and punctuation added.

65   "Lucy Mack Smith, History, 1845," pages 131–32, *The Joseph Smith Papers*, https://www.josephsmithpapers.org/paper-summary/lucy-mack-smith-history-1845/138, spelling and punctuation added.

66   Jeffrey R. Holland, "A Standard unto My People," Church Educational Symposium, Brigham Young University, August 9, 1994, Provo, Utah.

67   "Lucy Mack Smith, History, 1845," page 136, *The Joseph Smith Papers*, accessed https://www.josephsmithpapers.org/paper-summary/lucy-mack-smith-history-1845/143.

68   "Lucy Mack Smith, History, 1844–1845, page [11], bk. 8," page [11], book 8, *The Joseph Smith Papers*, https://www.josephsmithpapers.org/paper-summary/lucy-mack-smith-history-1844-1845/103, spelling and punctuation added.

69   "Lucy Mack Smith, History, 1844–1845, page [4], bk. 9," page [7], book 9, *The Joseph Smith Papers*, https://www.josephsmithpapers.org/paper-summary/lucy-mack-smith-history-1844-1845/111, spelling and punctuation added.

70   "Lucy Mack Smith, History, 1844–1845, page [4], bk. 9," page [7], book 9, *The Joseph Smith Papers*, https://www.josephsmithpapers.org/paper-summary/lucy-mack-smith-history-1844-1845/111.

71   "Lucy Mack Smith, History, 1844–1845, page [4], book 9," page [8], book 9, *The Joseph Smith Papers*, https://www.josephsmithpapers.org/paper-summary/lucy-mack-smith-history-1844-1845/112, spelling and punctuation added.

72   "Lucy Mack Smith, History, 1845," pages 208–9, 212–13, *The Joseph Smith Papers*, https://www.josephsmithpapers.org/paper-summary/lucy-mack-smith-history-1845/216.

73   "Letter to the Church, circa March 1834," p. 142, *The Joseph Smith Papers*, accessed April 5, 2018, http://www.josephsmithpapers.org/paper-summary/letter-to-the-church-circa-march-1834/1

74   "History, 1838–1856, volume E-1 [1 July 1843–30 April 1844]," p. 1755, *The Joseph Smith Papers*, accessed April 5, 2018, http://www.josephsmithpapers.org/paper-summary/history-1838-1856-volume-e-1-1-july-1843-30-april-1844/127

75   "Bible Used for Bible Revision," *The Joseph Smith Papers*, accessed April 5, 2018, http://www.josephsmithpapers.org/paper-summary/bible-used-for-bible-revision/3

76   Kent Jackson, "Joseph Smith's New Translation of the Bible," in *Joseph Smith, the Prophet and Seer* (2010), 51-76.

77   *Doctrines of the Restoration: Sermons and Writings of Bruce R. McConkie*, ed. Mark L. McConkie (Salt Lake City: Bookcraft, 1989), 269.

78   We indebted for this concise explanatory list of the JST categories to Scott H. Faulring, Kent P. Jackson, and Robert J. Matthews. Please see *Joseph Smith's New Translation of the Bible: Original Manuscripts*, ed. Scott H. Faulring, Kent P. Jackson, and Robert J. Matthews (Provo, UT: Religious Studies Center, 2004), 8-10.

79   Robert J. Matthews, *A Plainer Translation: Joseph Smith's Translation of the Bible: A History and Commentary* (Provo, UT: Brigham Young University Press, 1985), 60.

80   Ibid., 56-60.

81   "Letter to Church Leaders in Jackson County, Missouri, 2 July 1833," p. 51, *The Joseph Smith Papers*, accessed April 30, 2018, http://www.josephsmithpapers.org/paper-summary/letter-to-church-leaders-in-jackson-county-missouri-2-july-1833/1

82   "History, 1838–1856, volume C-1 [2 November 1838–31 July 1842]," p. 1014, *The Joseph Smith Papers*, accessed April 30, 2018, http://www.josephsmithpapers.org/paper-summary/history-1838-1856-volume-c-1-2-november-1838-31-july-1842/186

83   Grant Underwood, "Book of Mormon Usage in Early LDS Theology," *Dialogue* 17, no. 3 (Autumn 1984): 39.

84   "Old Testament Revision 1," page 16, *The Joseph Smith Papers*, http://www.josephsmithpapers.org/paper-summary/old-testament-revision-1/18.

85   Emer Harris, Statement, April 6, 1856, Utah Stake General Minutes, 1855–56, LR 9629, series 11, vol. 10, Church History Library, The Church of Jesus Christ of Latter-day Saints, Salt Lake City, UT.

86   "Revelation, September 1830-B [D&C 28]," page 40, *The Joseph Smith Papers*, http://www.josephsmithpapers.org/paper-summary/revelation-september-1830-b-dc-28/1.

87   "Revelation, 6 June 1831 [D&C 52]," page 87, *The Joseph Smith Papers*, http://www.josephsmithpapers.org/paper-summary/revelation-6-june-1831-dc-52/1.

88   "Revelation, 20 July 1831 [D&C 57]," page 93, *The Joseph Smith Papers*, http://www.josephsmithpapers.org/paper-summary/revelation-20-july-1831-dc-57/1.

89   Richard Francaviglia, *The New Mapmakers of Zion* (Salt Lake City: University of Utah Press, 2015), 31.

90   "Plat of the City of Zion, circa Early June–25 June 1833," page [2], *The Joseph Smith Papers*, http://www.josephsmithpapers.org/paper-summary/plat-of-the-city-of-zion-circa-early-june-25-june-1833/2.

91   "Plat of the City of Zion, circa Early June–25 June 1833," page [1], *The Joseph Smith Papers*, http://www.josephsmithpapers.org/paper-summary/plat-of-the-city-of-zion-circa-early-june-25-june-1833/1.

92   Parley P. Pratt, "One Hundred Years Hence, 1945," in *The Essential Parley P. Pratt* (Salt Lake City, UT: Signature Books, 1990), 142.

93   "Revelation, 2 August 1833-A [D&C 97]," page 64, *The Joseph Smith Papers*, http://www.josephsmithpapers.org/paper-summary/revelation-2-august-1833-a-dc-97/4, emphasis in original.

94   "Revelation, 2 August 1833-A [D&C 97]," page 63, *The Joseph Smith Papers*, http://www.josephsmithpapers.org/paper-summary/revelation-2-august-1833-a-dc-97/3.

95   "Revised Plat of the City of Zion, circa Early August 1833," page [1], *The Joseph Smith Papers*, http://www.josephsmithpapers.org/paper-summary/revised-plat-of-the-city-of-zion-circa-early-august-1833/1.

96   "Revised Plan of the House of the Lord, circa 10 August–circa 4 September 1833," page [1], *The Joseph Smith Papers*, http://www.josephsmithpapers.org/paper-summary/revised-plan-of-the-house-of-the-lord-circa-10-august-circa-4-september-1833/1.

97   "Proposal for Zion's City Center from Edward Partridge, circa Late September 1833," page [1], *The Joseph Smith Papers*, http://www.josephsmithpapers.org/paper-summary/proposal-for-zions-city-center-from-edward-partridge-circa-late-september-1833/1.

98   John Hamer, "The Temple Lot: Visions and Realities," https://bycommonconsent.com/2009/01/19/the-temple-lot/.

99   Orson F. Whitney, *The Life of Heber C. Kimball* (Salt Lake City, UT: Deseret Book, 2001), 65.

100 Reid N. Moon, "Gospel Insights from the Never-Before-Published Farewell Letter of Phebe W. Carter [Woodruff]," *Meridian Magazine*, July 28, 2015. https://ldsmag.com/gospel-insights-from-the-never-before-published-farewell-letter-of-phebe-w-carter-woodruff/

101 Ibid.

102 Edward W. Tullidge, *The Women of Mormondom* (New York: self-published, 1877), 412.

103 Ibid., 412.

104 Phoebe C. Woodruff to Family. 1835, transcription in author's possession.

105 Tullidge, *The Women of Mormondom*, 412.

106 Jas. T. Jakeman, "Phoebe Whittemore Carter Woodruff," in *Daughters of the Utah Pioneers and Their Mothers* (Western Album Publishing Company inc., n.d).

107 Andrew Jensen, "Wilford Woodruff," in *Latter-day Saint Biographical Encyclopedia Volume 1* (Salt Lake City, UT: Andrew Jensen History Company, 1901), 21–22.

108 Linda Madsen Sheffield, "A Letter from Phoebe Carter Woodruff to Mama," *BYU Studies Quarterly* 19, no. 2 (1979): 200.

109 Phoebe C. Woodruff to Family, 1835, transcription in author's possession.

110 Wilford Woodruff, *Leaves from My Journal* (American Fork, UT: Covenant Communications Inc., 2005), 94–98.

111 Ibid., 94–98.

112 Linda Madsen Sheffield, "A Letter from Phoebe Carter Woodruff to Mama," *BYU Studies Quarterly* 19, no. 2 (1979), 200.

113 Tullidge, *The Women of Mormondom*, 399–400.

114 Matthias F. Cowley, *Wilford Woodruff: History of his Life and Labors* (Salt Lake City, UT: Bookcraft, 1964), 95.

115 Reid N. Moon, "Tales of a [Mormon] Treasure Hunter," *New Meridian Magazine*, April 8, 2015, https://ldsmag.com/new-meridian-column-tales-of-a-mormontreasure-hunter.

116 Orson F. Whitney, *Life of Heber C. Kimball: An Apostle, the Father and Founder of the British Mission* (Salt Lake City, UT: The Kimball Family, 1888), 116.

117 "History, 1838–1856, volume B-1 [1 September 1834–2 November 1838]," page 761, *The Joseph Smith Papers*, https://www.josephsmithpapers.org/paper-summary/history-1838-1856-volume-b-1-1-september-1834-2-november-1838/215

118 "Introduction of the Gospel in Great Britain," *The Latter-day Saints' Millennial Star*, 59, no. 28, July 15, 1897, 433, 436.

119 Whitney, *Life of Heber C. Kimball*, 137.

120 Ibid.

121 "Introduction of the Gospel in Great Britain," *Millennial Star*, 438.

122 James R. Moss, "The Kingdom Builders," *Ensign*, December 1979, 27–28.

123 Brigham Young, et al. "Communications," *Times and Seasons* 1, no. 5, 70.

124 Moon, "Mormon Treasure Hunter."

125 See Ronald K. Esplin, "Joseph Smith and the Kirtland Crisis," in *Joseph Smith, the Prophet and Seer*, eds. Richard Neitzel Holzapfel and Kent P. Jackson (Provo, UT: Religious Studies Center, Brigham Young University; Salt Lake City, UT: Deseret Book, 2010), 261–90, https://rsc.byu.edu/archived/joseph-smith-prophet-and-seer/joseph-smith-and-kirtland-crisis-1837.

126 "Minutes, 22 December 1836," *The Joseph Smith Papers*, 443, http://www.josephsmithpapers.org/paper-summary/minutes-22-december-1836/1.

127 "Revelation, 16–17 December 1833 [D&C 101]," *The Joseph Smith Papers*, 80, http://www.josephsmithpapers.org/paper-summary/revelation-16-17-december-1833-dc-101/8.

128 Brigham Young, discourse, October 9, 1852, in *The Complete Discourses of Brigham Young 1*, ed. Richard S. Van Wagoner (Salt Lake City, UT: Smith-Petit Foundation, 2009), 601.

129 See Jeffrey N. Walker, "The Kirtland Safety Society and Grandison Newell," *BYU Studies* 54, no. 3, 43.

130 "Kirtland Safety Society Notes, 4 January–9 March 1837," *The Joseph Smith Papers*, accessed July 15, 2019, https://www.josephsmithpapers.org/paper-summary/kirtland-safety-society-notes-4-january-9-march-1837/1.

131 "Kirtland Safety Society," http://www.josephsmithpapers.org/topic/kirtland-safety-society?highlight=Grandison%20Newell,

132 Walker, "Kirtland Safety Society," 54.

133 Mark Staker, Hearken, *O Ye People: The Historical Setting of Joseph Smith's Ohio Revelations* (Salt Lake City, UT: Greg Kofford Books, 2009), 484.

134 Walker, "Kirtland Safety Society," 56–57; see also D. Paul Sampson and Larry T. Wimmer, "The Kirtland Safety Society: The Stock Ledger Book and

the Bank Failure," *BYU Studies* 12, no. 4, 427–36.

135 Staker, Hearken, O Ye People, 528.

136 "Minutes, 3 September 1837," p. 236, *The Joseph Smith Papers*, accessed July 15, 2019, https://www.josephsmithpapers.org/paper-summary/minutes-3-september-1837/3

137 Wilford Woodruff Journal, 6 January 1837, cited in Historical Introduction, "Minutes, 3 September 1837," p. 236, *The Joseph Smith Papers*, accessed July 15, 2019, https://www.josephsmithpapers.org/paper-summary/minutes-3-september-1837/3

138 *Teachings of Presidents of the Church: Joseph Smith* (Salt Lake City, UT: The Church of Jesus Christ of Latter-day Saints, 1998), p. 317.

139 Watson, *Brigham Young History*, 1801-44, p. 16-17

140 "Revelation, 20 July 1831 [D&C 57]," 93, *The Joseph Smith Papers*, http://www.josephsmithpapers.org/paper-summary/revelation-20-july-1831-dc-57/1

141 Max H. Parkin, "Mormonism on Missouri's Western Frontier, 1830–1838," in *History of the Saints: Tragedy and Truth: What Happened at Hawn's Mill*, ed. Alexander L. Baugh (American Fork, UT: Covenant Communications, 2014), 20.

142 Alma R. Blair, "The Haun's Mill Massacre," *BYU Studies* 13, no. 1 (1972), 1.

143 Gerrit Dirkmaat, "The 1838 Mormon-Missouri War: Historical Setting to the Hawn's Mill Tragedy," in *History of the Saints: Tragedy and Truth: What Happened at Hawn's Mill*, ed. Alexander L. Baugh, Glenn Rawson, and Dennis Lyman (American Fork, UT: Covenant Communications), 32–33.

144 Dirkmaat, "The 1838 Mormon-Missouri War," 35–36.

145 Alexander L. Baugh, "The Battle Between Mormon and Missouri Militia at Crooked River," in *Regional Studies in Latter-day Saint History: Missouri*, ed. Arnold K. Garr and Clark V. Johnson (Provo, UT: Department of Church History and Doctrine, 1994), 85–88.

146 "Patten, David Lyman," *The Joseph Smith Papers*, http://www.josephsmithpapers.org/person/david-wyman-patten

147 Lycurgus A. Wilson, *The Life of David W. Patten: The First Apostolic Martyr* (Salt Lake City, UT: The Deseret News, 1904), 6.

148 Ibid., 7.

149 Lorenzo Snow, preface to *The Life of David W. Patten: The First Apostolic Martyr*, by Lycurgus A. Wilson (Salt Lake City, UT: The Deseret News, 1900).

150 "Minutes and Discourse, 2 May 1835, as Reported by William E. McLellin–A," 187, *The Joseph Smith Papers*, http://www.josephsmithpapers.org/paper-summary/minutes-and-discourse-2-may-1835-as-reported-by-william-e-mclellin-a/1 (see note 3)

151 "Revelation, 3 November 1835," 18, *The Joseph Smith Papers*, http://www.josephsmithpapers.org/paper-summary/revelation-3-november-1835/2

152 L. Todd Dudley, "All But Two: The Disaffection of Ten of the Original Twelve Modern Apostles" (honor's thesis, Brigham Young University, 1994), 28–29.

153 Wilford Woodruff Journal, 5:63, June 25, 1857, cited in Dudley, "All But Two," 31.

154 "Letter to the Presidency in Kirtland, 29 March 1838," 24, *The Joseph Smith Papers*, http://www.josephsmithpapers.org/paper-summary/letter-to-the-presidency-in-kirtland-29-march-1838/2

155 "History, 1838–1856, volume B-1 [1 September 1834–2 November 1838]," 790, *The Joseph Smith Papers*, http://www.josephsmithpapers.org/paper-summary/history-1838-1856-volume-b-1-1-september-1834-2-november-1838/244

156 Wilson, *The Life of David W. Patten*, 53.

157 Alexander L. Baugh, *A Call to Arms: The 1838 Mormon Defense of Northern Missouri* (Provo, UT: BYU Studies, 2000), 104.

158 Dirkmaat, "The 1838 Mormon-Missouri War," 51–52.

159 Baugh, A Call to Arms, 107–108.

160 Wilson, The Life of David W. Patten,70–71.

161 "The Heavens are Opened Exhibit at the Church History Museum," *Pioneer* 16, nos. 2–4 (2016), 138–39.

162 Baugh, *A Call to Arms*, 104.

163 Mark Ashurst-McGee, David W. Grua, Elizabeth A. Kuehn, Brenden W. Resink, and Alexander L. Baugh, eds., Documents, Volume 6: February 1838–August 1839, Documents 6, *The Joseph Smith Papers* (Salt Lake City, UT: Church Historians' Press, 2008), 270.

164 Alexander L. Baugh, *A Call to Arms: The 1838 Mormon Defense of Northern Missouri* (Provo, UT: BYU Studies, 2000), 149.

165 Stephen C. LeSuer, *The 1838 Mormon War in Missouri* (Columbia, MO: University of Missouri Press, 1987), 182–83.

166 Mark-Ashurst-McGee et al., Documents 6, *The Joseph Smith Papers*, 270–72.

167 "'Extract, from the Private Journal of Joseph Smith Jr.,' July 1839," 6, *The Joseph Smith Papers*, http://www.josephsmithpapers.org/paper-summary/extract-from-the-private-journal-of-joseph-smith-jr-july-1839/5.

168 "Lucy Mack Smith, History, 1844–1845, Page [1], bk. 16," 4, *The Joseph Smith Papers*, http://www.josephsmithpapers.org/paper-summary/lucy-mack-smith-history-1844-1845/194.

169 Parley P. Pratt, *The Autobiography of Parley P. Pratt*, eds. Scot Facer Proctor and Maurine Jensen Proctor (Salt Lake City, UT: Deseret Book, 2000), 262–63.

170 Andrew Jenson, ed., *The Historical Record* (Salt Lake City, UT, 1888), vols. 7–8, 667, https://babel.hathitrust.org/cgi/pt?id=hvd.32044050836022;view=1up;seq=691.

171 Reid L. Neilson, Justin R. Bray, and Alan D. Johnson, eds., *Rediscovering the Sites of the Restoration: The 1888 Travel Writings of Mormon Historian Andrew Jenson, Edward Stevenson, and Joseph S. Black* (Provo, UT: Religious Studies Center, 2015), 153, also Mark-Ashurst-McGee et al., Documents 6, *The Joseph Smith Papers*, 274–75.

172 "History, 1838–1856, volume C-1 [2 November 1838–31 July 1842]," 952, *The Joseph Smith Papers*, http://www.josephsmithpapers.org/paper-summary/history-1838-1856-volume-c-1-2-november-1838-31-july-1842/134.

173 Mark-Ashurst-McGee et al., Documents 6, *The Joseph Smith Papers*, 274–75.

174 Alexander McRae, "Incidents in the History of Joseph Smith," Deseret News, November 9, 1854, https://newspapers.lib.utah.edu/details?id=2581216.

175 Edward W. Tullidge, *Women of Mormondom* (New York: Tullidge & Crandall, 1877), 253.

176 Neilson, Bray, and Johnson, *Rediscovering the Sites of the Restoration*, 156, also Mark-Ashurst-McGee et al., Documents 6, *The Joseph Smith Papers*, 277.

177 Mark-Ashurst-McGee et al., Documents 6, *The Joseph Smith Papers*, 277.

178 "Letter to Isaac Galland, 22 March 1839," *The Joseph Smith Papers*, 52, http://www.josephsmithpapers.org/paper-summary/letter-to-isaac-galland-22-march-1839/2.

179 "Letter to Emma Smith, 21 March 1839," *The Joseph Smith Papers*, 1, http://www.josephsmithpapers.org/paper-summary/letter-to-emma-smith-21-march-1839/1, spelling and punctuation corrected.

180 Neilson et al., *Rediscovering the Sites of the Restoration*, 154.

181 *Joseph Smith III, The Memoirs of Joseph Smith III, 1832–1914* (Independence, MO: Herald Publishing House, 2010), 721.

182   Private measurements taken by Casey Paul Griffiths, October 20, 2017. Photographs in author's possession.

183   Alvin R. Dyer, *The Refiner's Fire* (Salt Lake City, UT: Deseret Book, 1969), 300–1.

184   Jeffrey R. Holland, "Lessons From Liberty Jail," BYU Devotional, September 7, 2008, https://speeches.byu.edu/talks/jeffrey-r-holland_lessons-liberty-jail/.

185   See "Revelation, July 1830–A [D&C 24]," 33, *The Joseph Smith Papers*, http://www.josephsmithpapers.org/paper-summary/revelation-july-1830-a-dc-24/2

186   See "Revelation, 22–23 September 1832 [D&C 84]," 3, *The Joseph Smith Papers*, http://www.josephsmithpapers.org/paper-summary/revelation-22-23-september-1832-dc-84/3

187   See Heidi Bennett, "July 22, 1839: A Day of God's Power," https://history.lds.org/article/museum-treasure-a-day-of-gods-power?lang=eng.

188   *Teachings of Presidents of the Church: Wilford Woodruff* (Salt Lake City, UT: The Church of Jesus Christ of Latter-day Saints, 2004), 142.

189   "History, 1838–1856, volume C-1 [2 November 1838–31 July 1842]," 964, *The Joseph Smith Papers*, http://www.josephsmithpapers.org/paper-summary/history-1838-1856-volume-c-1-2-november-1838-31-july-1842/146

190   Wilford Woodruff, "Leaves from my Journal," *Millennial Star*, no. 42, October 17, 1881, https://contentdm.lib.byu.edu/digital/collection/MStar/id/4917/rec/43

191   Ibid.

192   Ibid.

193   "History, 1838–1856, volume C-1 [2 November 1838–31 July 1842]," 964, *The Joseph Smith Papers*, http://www.josephsmithpapers.org/paper-summary/history-1838-1856-volume-c-1-2-november-1838-31-july-1842/146

194   "Wilford Woodruff Journal, July 22, 1839," *Wilford Woodruff Journals and Papers, 1828-1898*, Church History Library, https://dcms.lds.org/delivery/DeliveryManagerServlet?dps_pid=IE15013159, some spelling and punctuation added; see also "History of Brigham Young," Millennial Star 27, no. 1 (May 27, 1865): 326. https://contentdm.lib.byu.edu/digital/collection/MStar/id/8239/rec/27

195   "Wilford Woodruff Journal, May 25, 1857," *Wilford Woodruff Journals and Papers, 1828-1898*, Church History Library, https://dcms.lds.org/delivery/DeliveryManagerServlet?dps_pid=IE15066862

196   Michael W. Homer, *Joseph's Temple: The Dynamic Relationship Between Freemasonry and Mormonism* (Salt Lake City, UT: University of Utah Press, 2014), 145, see also Matthew B. Brown, Exploring the Connection Between Mormons and Masons (American Fork, UT: Covenant Communications, 2009), 69.

197   Jasper Ridley, *The Freemasons: A History of the World's Most Powerful Secret Society* (New York: Arcade Publishing, 1999, 2001), 176, 186.

198   See Paul Moritsen, "Secret Combinations and Flaxen Cords: Anti-Masonic Rhetoric and the Book of Mormon," *Journal of Book of Mormon Studies* 12, no. 1 (2003): 64–77, 116–118.

199   Steven C. Harper, "Freemasonry and the Latter-day Saint Temple Endowment Ceremony," *A Reason for Faith: Navigating LDS History and Church History* (Provo, UT: Religious Studies Center, 2016), 144–46.

200   See Brown, *Exploring the Connection*, 45–55.

201   Glen M. Leonard, *Nauvoo: A Place of Peace, A People of Promise* (Salt Lake City, UT: Deseret Book, 2002), 314–15.

202   Leonard, *Nauvoo*, 314.

203   Homer, *The Dynamic Relationship*, 148–149.

204   Harper, "Freemasonry," 148.

205   "History, 1838–1856, volume C-1 [2 November 1838–31 July 1842]," *The Joseph Smith Papers*, 1328, http://www.josephsmithpapers.org/paper-summary/history-1838-1856-volume-c-1-2-november-1838-31-july-1842/502.

206   The nine men who received this first endowment were James Adams, Hyrum Smith, Newel K. Whitney, George Miller, Brigham Young, Heber C. Kimball, Willard Richards, William Marks, and William Law. See "History, 1838–1856, volume C-1," *The Joseph Smith Papers*, 1328, and "Journal, December 1841–December 1842," *The Joseph Smith Papers*, 94, http://www.josephsmithpapers.org/paper-summary/journal-december-1841-december-1842/25.

207   Benjamin F. Johnson, *My Life's Review* (Independence, MO: Zion's Printing, 1947), 94–97, https://archive.org/stream/BenjaminFJohnsonMyLifesReview/Benjamin%20F%20Johnson%20My%20Lifes%20Review_djvu.txt.

208   Heber C. Kimball to Parley P. Pratt, June 17, 1842, quoted in Harper, "Freemasonry," 149, spelling and grammar corrected.

209   Ibid., 149–150.

210   "History, 1838–1856, volume C-1 [2 November 1838–31 July 1842]," 1328, *The Joseph Smith Papers*, http://www.josephsmithpapers.org/paper-summary/history-1838-1856-volume-c-1-2-november-1838-31-july-1842/502.

211   Harper, "Freemasonry," 153.

212   Leonard, *Nauvoo*, 319–20.

213   Joseph F. Morcombe, "Masonry and Mormonism," *Masonic Standard* (Sept. 1, 1906): 11, quoted in Homer, The Dynamic Relationship, 167.

214   Leonard, *Nauvoo*, 320.

215   "History, 1838–1856, volume F-1 [1 May 1844–8 August 1844]," *The Joseph Smith Papers*, 269, accessed October 26, 2018, https://www.josephsmithpapers.org/paper-summary/history-1838-1856-volume-f-1-1-may-1844-8-august-1844/276.

216   See Homer, *The Dynamic Relationship*, 170–74.

217   Leonard, *Nauvoo*, 321.

218   *Teachings of the Presidents of the Church: Joseph Smith* (Salt Lake City: The Church of Jesus Christ of Latter-day Saints, 2011), 528–30.

219   Gordon B. Hinckley, "Joseph, the Seer," *Ensign*, September 1994, 70–71.

220   "Hyrum Smith: A Man of Mildness and Integrity," *Museum Treasures*, https://history.lds.org/article/hyrum-smith-clothing?lang=eng.

221   Eldred G. Smith and Hortense Smith, "Witness the Restoration: The Smith Family Artifacts and Their Story" (Salt Lake City: Church History Library, 2004), video recording.

222   Shannon M. Tracy, *In Search of Joseph* (Orem, UT: Kenning House, 1995), 78.

223   Smith and Smith, "Witness the Restoration."

224   Willard Richards, "Two Minutes in Jail," Times and Seasons 5 (August 1, 1844): 598–99; Joseph L. Lyon and David W. Lyon, "Physical Evidence at Carthage Jail and What It Reveals about the Assassination of Joseph and Hyrum Smith," *BYU Studies Quarterly* 47, no. 4 (2008): 41.

225   Smith and Smith, "Witness the Restoration."

226   Lyon and Lyon, "Physical Evidence at Carthage Jail," 43.

227   Richards, "Two Minutes in Jail," 536.

228   Lyon and Lyon, "Physical Evidence at Carthage Jail," 43–44.

229   Smith and Smith, "Witness the Restoration."

230   John Taylor, 536, 538.

231   Lyon and Lyon, "Physical Evidence at Carthage Jail," 45, 48.

232   Ibid., 48.

233   "Willard Richards's Eyewitness Account from Carthage Jail," in *Cultures in Conflict: A Documentary History of the Mormon War in Illinois*, ed. John E. Hallwas, Roger D. Launius (Logan, UT: Utah State University Press, 1995), 211.

234   John Taylor, "An Account of the Martyrdom of Joseph Smith," in *Fate of Persecutors of the Prophet Joseph Smith*, comp. N. B. Lundwall (Salt Lake City, UT: Bookcraft, 1952), 199.

235　William R. Hamilton, "A Youth's Recollection of the Smith Murders," in *Cultures in Conflict*, 230.

236　John Taylor, "An Account of the Martyrdom of Joseph Smith," in *Fate of Persecutors of the Prophet Joseph Smith*, comp. N.B. Lundwall (Salt Lake City, UT: Bookcraft, 1952), 199.

237　John Hay, "The Mormon Prophet's Tragedy," *Atlantic Monthly* (December 1869), 671–78, in Hamilton, *Cultures in Conflict*, 259–60.

238　See B. H. Roberts, *A Comprehensive History of The Church of Jesus Christ of Latter-day Saints*, 6 vols. (Salt Lake City, UT: The Church of Jesus Christ of Latter-day Saints, 1930), 2:285n19; see also Joseph L. Lyon and David W. Lyon, "Physical Evidence at Carthage Jail and What It Reveals about the Assassination of Joseph and Hyrum Smith," *BYU Studies* 47, no. 4 (2008): 34.

239　John Taylor, "An Account of the Martyrdom of Joseph Smith," in *Fate of Persecutors of the Prophet Joseph Smith*, comp. N. B. Lundwall (Salt Lake City, UT: Bookcraft, 1952), 196.

240　Joseph Johnstun, "Weapons Related to the Murder of Joseph and Hyrum Smith," *John Whitmer Historical Association Journal* 35 (Fall/Winter 2015):2, 45.

241　Johnstun, "Weapons Related," 49–51.

242　John Taylor, "An Account of the Martyrdom of Joseph Smith," in *Fate of Persecutors of the Prophet Joseph Smith*, comp. N. B. Lundwall (Salt Lake City, UT: Bookcraft, 1952), 196.

243　Johnstun, "Weapons Related," 51–52; interview with Alan Morrell, July 10, 2017, notes in author's possession.

244　Johnstun, "Weapons Related," 52–53.

245　Linda King Newell and Valeen Tippetts Avery, *Mormon Enigma: Emma Hale* (Garden City, NY: Doubleday and Company, 1984), 189.

246　Ibid., 188–89.

247　Ibid., 190.

248　Dean C. Jessee, ed. *Personal Writings of Joseph Smith* (Salt Lake City, UT: Deseret Book, 1984), 597–98.

249　Newell and Avery, *Mormon Enigma*, 188.

250　George Q. Cannon, *Life of Joseph Smith the Prophet* (Provo, UT: Stratford Books, 2005), 555.

251　Newell and Avery, *Mormon Enigma*, 189.

252　Ibid., 191.

253　Ibid., 194–95.

254　B. W. Richmond's statement, "The Prophet's Death!" *Deseret News*, November 27, 1875.

255　Eliza R. Snow, in *Times and Seasons* 5, no. 22 (December 1, 1844): 735.

256　Buddy Youngreen, *Reflections of Emma, Joseph Smith's Wife* (Orem, UT: Grandin Book Company, 1982), 37.

257　B. W. Richmond's statement, "The Prophet's Death!".

258　Kate B. Carter, *The Story of the Negro Pioneer* (Salt Lake City, UT: Daughters of the Utah Pioneers, 1965), 2.

259　Richard E. Bennett, *We'll Find the Place: The Mormon Exodus, 1846–1848* (Salt Lake City, UT: Deseret Book, 1997), 77.

260　Joel Flake, Jr., "Green Flake: His Life and Legacy," unpublished paper, L. Tom Perry Special Collections, Brigham Young Univeristy, 3.

261　Flake, 5–6.

262　"Letter to Oliver Cowdery, circa 9 April 1836," p. 291, *The Joseph Smith Papers*,://josephsmithpapers.org/paper-summary/letter-to-oliver-cowdery-circa-9-april-1836/3.

263　"Letter to James Arlington Bennet, 17 March 1843," p. 3, *The Joseph Smith Papers*, https://josephsmithpapers.org/paper-summary/letter-to-james-arlington-bennet-17-march-1843/3.

264　Flake, 7–10.

265　Ibid., 13.

266　Bennett, 242–43, Flake, 14.

267　Flake, 16.

268　Ibid., 18.

269　Ibid., 21–22.

270　Carter, *Negro Pioneer*, 6; Flake, 25–26.

271　Ibid., 6.

272　Shanna S. Jones, *William Carter: First Plowman in Utah, 1821–1896, His Ancestors and Descendants* (St. George, UT, Skyline Publishing, 1999), 3-4.

273　Ibid., 6.

274　Ibid.

275　Ibid, 8–9.

276　"Council of Fifty, Minutes, March 1844–January 1846; Volume 2, 1 March–6 May 1845," 17, *The Joseph Smith Papers*, https://www.josephsmithpapers.org/paper-summary/council-of-fifty-minutes-march-1844-january-1846-volume-2-1-march-6-may-1845/20.

277　"Revelation, September 1830–A [D&C 29]," 39, *The Joseph Smith Papers*, https://www.josephsmithpapers.org/paper-summary/revelation-september-1830-a-dc-29/4.

278　Leonard J. Arrington, "Coin and Early Currency in Early Utah," *Utah Historical Quarterly*, January 1952, 56–57.

279　Arrington, "Coin and Currency," 56, 60–61.

280　J. David Harden, "Liberty Caps and Liberty Trees," *Past & Present*, no. 146 (February 1995), 67.

281　Alvin E. Rust, *Mormon and Utah Coin and Currency* (Salt Lake City: Rust Rare Coin Co., Inc., 1984), 38–39.

282　Arrington, "Coin and Currency," 72.

283　Rust, *Mormon and Utah Coin*, 47, 53.

284　Arrington, "Coin and Currency," 64–65.

285　J. Kenneth Davies and Lorin K. Hansen, *Mormon Gold: Mormons in the California Gold Rush*, 2nd ed. (North Salt Lake City, UT: Granite Mountain Publishing Company, 2010), 96.

286　Arrington, "Coin and Currency," 73.

287　Davies and Hansen, *Mormon Gold*, 96–97.

288　Rust, *Mormon and Utah Coin*, 86–91.

289　Ibid.

290　Davies and Hansen, *Mormon Gold*, 97.

291　"Mormon Artifacts on Display at the Smithsonian," *Mormon Newsroom*, https://www.mormonnewsroom.org/article/mormon-artifacts-display-smithsonian

292　Ronald W. Walker and D. Michael Quinn, "Virtuous, Lovely, or of Good Report," *Ensign*, July 1977, 83.

293　Roberta Reese Asahina, *Brigham Young and the Salt Lake Theater, 1862–1877* (Ann Arbor, MI: University Microfilms International, 1980), 37–38.

294　Edward W. Tullidge, *History of Salt Lake City* (Salt Lake City, UT: Star Printing Company, 1886), 737.

295　Asahina, *Brigham Young*, 42–43.

296　Myrtle E. Henderson, *A History of the Theatre in Salt Lake City* (Evanston, IL: n.p., 1934), 28.

297　Walker and Quinn, "Virtuous, Lovely, or of Good Report," 80.

298　Asahina, Brigham Young, 47–48.

299　"Deseret," *Millennial Star* 17, no. 33, August 18, 1855, 525.

300　*Deseret News*, October 1, 1862, in Asahina, Brigham Young, 48.

301　Leonard J. Arrington, Fermorz Y. Fox, and Dean L. May, *Building the City of God: Community and Cooperation Among the Mormons* (Salt Lake

City, UT: Deseret Book, 1976), 111.

302 Ibid., 113.

303 Author's notes from Church History Library Collection, Call No. LDS 98, 122–2, Church History Museum, Salt Lake City, UT.

304 Arrington et al., *Building the City of God*, 111, 114–15, 120.

305 L. Dwight Israelsen, "An Economic Analysis of the United Order," *BYU Studies* 18, no. 4 (1978): 10.

306 Arrington et al., *Building the City of God*, 140.

307 "Uniform articles of incorporation for branches of the United Order, general instructions, and rules," in Arrington et al., *Building the City of God*, 404–5.

308 Israelsen, "Economic Analysis of the United Order," 3.

309 Ibid., 7.

310 Arrington et al., *Building the City of God*, 132–33.

311 Jill Mulvay Derr and Karen Lynn Davidson, comps. and eds., *Eliza R. Snow: The Complete Poetry* (Provo, UT: Brigham Young University Press; Salt Lake City: University of Utah Press, 2009), xvi, xx, xxvi.

312 Ibid., xxiv, xxv.

313 Jill Mulvay Derr, "The Significance of 'O My Father' in the Personal Journey of Eliza R. Snow," *BYU Studies* 36, no. 1 (1996–97): 87.

314 Ibid., 96–98.

315 Ibid., 100.

316 Franklin L. West, *Life of Franklin D. Richards* (Salt Lake City, UT: Deseret News Press, 1924), 175–76.

317 Derr and Davidson, *Eliza R. Snow*, 1026.

318 This certificate was obtained from a private collector. The reason for the divorce of William and Mary Heap is not known because records of Church divorces (cancellations of sealings) are not currently available for research. See Kathryn M. Daynes, *More Wives Than One: Transformation of the Mormon Marriage System* (Urbana: University of Illinois Press, 2001), 142.

319 Edwin Brown Firmage and Richard Collin Mangum, *Zion in the Courts: A Legal History of The Church of Jesus Christ of Latter-day Saints* (Urbana: University of Illinois Press, 1988), 322.

320 Leonard Arrington, *Brigham Young: American Moses* (New York: Alfred A. Knopf, 1985), 318.

321 Ibid., 318–19.

322 "Plural Marriage and Families in Early Utah," *Gospel Topics Essay*, https://www.lds.org/topics/plural-marriage-and-families-in-early-utah.

323 Firmage and Mangum, *Zion in the Courts*, 324–25.

324 Ibid.

325 Daynes, *More Wives Than One*, 148.

326 Ibid., 157.

327 Firmage and Mangum, *Zion in the Courts*, 322.

328 Dallin H. Oaks, "Divorce," April 2007 General Conference, https://www.lds.org/general-conference/2007/04/divorce.

329 Bible Dictionary, The Holy Bible, King James Version, LDS edition, s.v. "Kingdom of heaven or kingdom of God."

330 Richard G. Moore, "The Deseret Alphabet Experiment," *Religious Educator* 7, no. 3 (2006): 63.

331 Bishops' Meetings 1871–79, July 26, 1877, in Leonard J. Arrington, *Brigham Young: American Moses* (New York: Alfred A. Knopf, 1985), 397.

332 "The New Alphabet," *Deseret News*, January 19, 1854.

333 Moore, "Deseret Alphabet Experiment," 69–70.

334 Douglas Allen New, "History of the Deseret Alphabet and Other At-

tempts to Reform English Orthography" (EdD diss., Brigham Young University, 1985), 3–4.

335 Moore, "Deseret Alphabet Experiment," 64.

336 Ibid.

337 Brigham Young to George D. Watt, Winter Quarters, Nebraska, April 16, 1847, in Kate B. Carter, comp., *Our Pioneer Heritage* (Salt Lake City, UT: Daughters of Utah Pioneers, 1969), 12:349.

338 Moore, "Deseret Alphabet Experiment," 63–76. See also William V. Nash, "The Deseret Alphabet" (paper written for University of Illinois Library School, May 1957), 22–23.

339 Moore, "Deseret Alphabet Experiment," 63–76. See also Leslie L. Sudweeks, "The Deseret Alphabet," *Improvement Era*, November 1954, 805.

340 Brigham Young, "Eleventh General Epistle of the Presidency of The Church of Jesus Christ of Latter-day Saints" in James R. Clark, ed., *Messages of the First Presidency*, 6 vols. (Salt Lake City, UT: Bookcraft, 1965–75), 2:130.

341 George A. Smith, "Historian's Office, G. S. L. City," *Journal History of The Church of Jesus Christ of Latter-day Saints*, 7 February 1855, Church Archives, The Church of Jesus Christ of Latter-day Saints, Salt Lake City, UT.

342 Brigham Young in *Journal of Discourses* 12:298.

343 Daniel H. Ludlow, ed., *Encyclopedia of Mormonism* (New York: Macmillan, 1992), s.v. "Deseret Alphabet," 374.

344 Dora D. Flack, "The Deseret Alphabet," *Friend*, July 1985.

345 Flack, "Deseret Alphabet."

346 Ludlow, *Encyclopedia of Mormonism*, 373.

347 D&C 58:27.

348 Joseph Smith History, 1838–1856, volume A-1 [23 December 1805–30 August 1834], p. 465, *The Joseph Smith Papers*, accessed April 8, 2019, https://www.josephsmithpapers.org/paper-summary/history-1838-1856-volume-a-1-23-december-1805-30-august-1834/471.

349 Susan Easton Black, "The naming and blessing of a child is not an ordinance necessary for salvation. Why, then, is it important?" *Ensign*, December 1988, 55.

350 Laurel B. Andrew, *Early Temples of the Mormons* (Albany, State of New York University Press, 1978), 98.

351 Andrew, 97-98.

352 Thomas G. Ford, *A History of Illinois* (Chicago, 1854), 404.

353 *The Complete Discourses of Brigham Young*, ed. Richard S. Van Wagoner (Salt Lake City: Smith-Petit Foundation, 2009), 1505.

354 Richard G. Oman, "Exterior Symbolism of the Salt Lake Temple: Reflecting the Faith that Called the Place into Being," *BYU Studies* 36, no. 4 (1996-97),12.

355 Oman, 12, 21, 32, 48-49.

356 Ibid., 42-48.

357 D. Todd Christofferson, "The Living Bread Which Came Down From Heaven," October 2017 general conference.

358 Oman, 42.

359 David O. McKay, *What E'er Thou Art, Act Well Thy Part: The Missionary Diaries of David O. McKay*, eds. Stan and Patricia Larsen (Salt Lake City, ut : Blue Ribbon Books,1999), 78–79.

360 "Act Well Thy Part," *BYU McKay School of Education Today Magazine*, Winter 2016, 15.

361 David O. McKay, "Pres. McKay Speaks to Pioneer Stake Youth," *Church News*, September 21, 1957, m-4.

362 Quentin L. Cook, "What E'er Thou Art, Act Well They Part: Avoid Wearing Masks That Hide Identity," CES Devotional for Young Adults, March 4, 2012, Brigham Young University–Idaho.

363 "Act Well Thy Part," *Today Magazine*, 15.

364 Ibid.

365 McKay, "Speaks to Pioneer Stake Youth," m-4.

366 Cook, "Avoid Wearing Masks."

367 Peggy Petersen Barton, *Mark E. Petersen: A Biography* (Salt Lake City, UT: Deseret Book, 1985), 126.

368 Susan Easton Black, "Religion C 343 class notes," fall semester 2004, transcription in author's possession.

369 "Act Well Thy Part," *Today Magazine*, 15.

370 Ibid.

371 Russell M. Nelson, "50th Anniversary of the Missionary Training Center, February 24, 2011," and Cook, "Avoid Wearing Masks."

372 Nelson, "50th Anniversary," "Elder Cook Charges Young Adults to Build the Kingdom," Church News, March 4, 2012, https://www.churchofjesuschrist.org/church/news/elder-cook-charges-young-single-adults-to-build-the-kingdom?lang=eng, accessed July 23, 2019.

373 "George Albert Smith Patriarchal Blessing Given by Zebedee Coltrin," 16 January 1884, box 96, fd., 13, George A. Smith Papers, Marriott Library, University of Utah.

374 Francis M. Gibbons, *George Albert Smith: Kind and Caring Christian, Prophet of God* (Salt Lake City, UT: Deseret Book, 1990), 54.

375 Francis M. Gibbons, *Dynamic Disciples, Prophets of God* (Salt Lake City, UT: Deseret Book, 1996), 178–79.

376 George Albert Smith, "Unpublished Journal," 24 January 1909, MS 36, box 67, book 6.

377 Ford McBride M.D., Interview by Mary Jane Woodger, March 26, 2008, transcription in author's possession (hereafter McBride).

378 Glen R. Stubbs, "A Biography of George Albert Smith, 1870 to 1951" (PhD dissertation, Brigham Young University, 1974), 101.

379 George Albert Smith, Journal, 18 and 23 March 1909, book 6, journal 5, George A. Smith Papers.

380 Gibbons, George Albert Smith, 61.

381 George A. Smith to Lucy E. Smith, 13 April 1909, box 27, fd 11, George A. Smith Papers; and Gibbons, 62–63.

382 George Albert Smith to S.L. Paul, July 8, 1909, copy in author's possession.

383 George Albert Smith, Journal, 20–24 August 1909, book 6, journal 5, George A. Smith Papers.

384 George Albert Smith, Journal, 13 and 14 September 1909, box 32, fd 11, George A. Smith Papers.

385 George Albert Smith, "Your Good Name," *The Improvement Era*, March 1947, 139.

386 Lucy W. Smith, as related to Bishop K. J. Fetzer and contained in a letter from Bishop Fetzer to the Smith children, 7 August 1953, box 151, fld. 3, George A. Smith Papers.

387 "History, 1838–1856, volume A-1 [23 December 1805–30 August 1834]," 40, *The Joseph Smith Papers*, https://www.josephsmithpapers.org/paper-summary/history-1838-1856-volume-a-1-23-december-1805-30-august-1834/46

388 Gary Fuller Reese, "Uncle Jesse: The Story of Jesse Knight: Miner, Industrialist, Philanthropist" (master's thesis, Brigham Young University, 1961), 7–8.

389 Reese, "Uncle Jesse," 9–10.

390 Ibid., 14–15.

391 J. Michael Hunter, "Jesse Knight and His Humbug Mine," *Pioneer* 51, no. 2 (2004): 9.

392 Ibid., 10.

393 Ibid., 10–11.

394 See Casey Paul Griffiths, Susan Easton Black, and Mary Jane Woodger, *What You Don't Know About the 100 Most Important Events in Church History* (Salt Lake City, UT: Deseret Book, 2016).

395 Hunter, "Jesse Knight," 11–12.

396 Hunter, "Jesse Knight," 12–13.

397 Jesse William Knight, *The Jesse Knight Family: Jesse Knight, His Forbears and Family* (Salt Lake City, UT: Deseret News Press, 1941), 82.

398 Ibid., 84.

399 Ibid., 85.

400 Ibid., 86.

401 See Malcolm R. Thorp, "James E. Talmage and the Tradition of Victorian Lives of Jesus," *Sunstone*, January 1988, 8–13.

402 Richard Neitzel Holzapfel and Thomas A. Wayment, *James E. Talmage's "Jesus the Christ" Study Guide* (Salt Lake City, UT: Deseret Book, 2014), xviii.

403 James E. Talmage Journal, December 7–8, 1911, James E. Talmage Papers, MSS 229, Box 29, Fd 2b, L. Tom Perry Special Collections, Harold B. Lee Library, Brigham Young University.

404 John R. Talmage, *The Talmage Story* (Salt Lake City, UT: Bookcraft, 1972), 181–84.

405 Ibid.,184.

406 Holzapfel and Wayment, *Study Guide*, xxiv–xxv; see James E. Talmage, *Jesus the Christ* (Salt Lake City, UT: The Church of Jesus Christ of Latter-day Saints, 1915, 1973), 668.

407 Talmage, *Jesus the Christ*, title page, 721, 758, 792.

408 Talmage, *Talmage Story*, 182, 186.

409 "Full Report of Talmage Funeral Given," *Deseret News*, August 5, 1933, 1, qtd. in Holzapfel and Wayment, xiv, xv.

410 Marianne C. Sharp, "Dream for a Relief Society Building," *Relief Society Magazine*, December 1945, 749.

411 Belle S. Spafford, "Plan for Financing a Relief Society Building," *Relief Society Magazine*, December 1947, 797.

412 Spafford, "Relief Society Building," 751.

413 Belle S. Spafford, Marianne C. Sharp, and Velma N. Simonsen, "Financial Plan for the Relief Society Building," 21 October 1947, in Vesta P. Crawford, "A Journal History of the Relief Society Building," Vesta P. Crawford Book Drafts, MSS 1282, box 1, folder 1, L. Tom Perry Special Collections, Harold B. Lee Library, Brigham Young University.

414 Spafford, Sharp, and Simonsen, "Financial Plan."

415 "CPI Inflation Calculator," Bureau of Labor Statistics, United States Department of Labor, https://www.bls.gov/data/inflation_calculator.htm.

416 Sharp, "And What of the Promise?" 727.

417 "Relief Society Building News," Relief Society Magazine, February 1948, 83.

418 Belle S. Spafford, "Joy in Full Measure," Relief Society Magazine, November 1948, 726.

419 Tammy Reque, "Inside the Relief Society Building," *Temple Square Blog*, https://www.templesquare.com/blog/inside-the-relief-society-building/.

420 Julie Dockstader Heaps, "Milestone: Relief Society Building a Symbol of Sisterhood," *Deseret News*, March 25, 2006.

421 Crawford, "A Journal History of the Relief Society Building."

422 Countries that sent gifts for the Relief Society Building included: Argentina, Australia, Austria, Brazil, Canada, China, Czechoslovakia, Denmark, Egypt, England, Finland, France, Germany, Hawaii, Iran, Italy, Japan, Korea, Libya, Mexico, Netherlands, New Zealand, Norway, Palestine, Samoa, South Africa, Sweden, Switzerland, Tahiti, and Tonga.

423   Heaps, "Milestone"; Heidi S. Swinton and LaRene Gaunt, "The Relief Society Building: A Symbol of Service and Sacrifice" *Ensign*, September 2006, 55.

424   Reque, "Relief Society Building."

425   William B. Honey, *Dresden China* (Troy, NY: David Rosenfield, 1946), 5, 7–8.

426   Ulrich Pietsch, *Early Meissen Porcelain* (Jacksonville, FL: Cummer Museum of Art & Gardens, 2011), 15–16; Honey, *Dresden China*, 5, 7–8.

427   "300 Years of Heritage," Meissen 1710, https://www.meissen.com/en/world-meissen-couture/maison-meissen-couture/300-years-heritage.

428   Pietsch, Early Meissen, 17.

429   Marianne C. Sharp, "A Dedicated Home for Relief Society," *Relief Society Magazine*, December 1956, 817.

430   The Church of Jesus Christ of Latter-day Saints, "Chapter Forty: The Saints During World War II," *Church History in the Fulness of Times Student Manual*, 2nd ed. (Salt Lake City, UT: The Church of Jesus Christ of Latter-day Saints, 2003), 530.

431   Robert C. Freeman, "Remembering World War II: Pearl Harbor and Beyond," http://exhibits.lib.byu.edu/wwii/essay.html.

432   Freeman, "Remembering World War II"; Robert C. Freeman and Dennis A. Wright, *Saints at War* (American Fork, UT: Covenant Communities, 2001), 250, 358.

433   L. Tom Perry, "Sacrament of the Lord's Supper," *Ensign*, May 1996, 53.

434   Freeman and Wright, *Saints at War*, 400.

435   Ibid., 250–51, 296–99.

436   Sacrament Trays by Bird Colby and Lavell Miller, made in North Africa during World War II from Army Tank parts, circa 1942—Call No.: LDS 4034–65, Church History Museum.

437   Freeman and Wright, *Saints at War*, 360–61.

438   Ibid., 358.

439   Ibid., 250–51.

440   The Church of Jesus Christ, "Saints During World War II," 532.

441   Freeman and Wright, *Saints at War*, 251.

442   Perry, "Sacrament," 53.

443   D. Todd Christofferson, "The Living Bread Which Came Down from Heaven," *Ensign*, November 2017, 38–39.

444   Matthew O. Richardson, *The Christus Legacy* (Salt Lake City, UT: Deseret Book Company, 2007), 37.

445   Richardson, 13

446   Theodor Opperman, *Thorvaldsen, I Rom og I Kjøbenhawn, 1819–1844* (Copenhagen, Denmark: G.E.C. Gads Forlag, 1930), 42.

447   Rex D. Pinegar, "The Living Prophet," October 1976 general conference.

448   Richardson, *The Christus Legacy*, 24–26.

449   George Cannon Young, Oral History, interviews by Paul L. Anderson, 1973, transcript, 9, The James Moyle Oral History Program, Archives, Historical Department of The Church of Jesus Christ of Latter-day Saints, Salt Lake City, UT. LDS Church Archives.

450   Richardson, *The Christus Legacy*, 27.

451   Ibid., 28.

452   Ibid., 28; George Cannon Young, Oral History, 9.

453   Richardson, *The Christus Legacy*, 38.

454   Philip L. Richards, "Christus," *Ensign*, January 1992, 79.

455   Brent L. Top, "Legacy of the Mormon Pavilion," *Ensign*, October 1989, 27.

456   Top, "Legacy," 27; Richardson, *The Christus Legacy*, 67.

457   Top, "Legacy," 27.

458   Richardson, *The Christus Legacy*, 96.

459   "Christus Enhances Washington Center," *Church News*, July 2, 1988, 11.

460   Dallin H. Oaks, "The Light and Life of the World," October 1987 general conference.

461   Richardson, *The Christus Legacy*, 98.

462   Julie A. Dockstader, "Festive Lights Reflect Love of Christ," *Church News*, December 1, 1990, 7.

463   Bruce R. McConkie, "Christ and the Creation," *Ensign*, June 1982, 15.

464   Chad M. Orton, "Saints in the Secular City: A History of the Los Angeles Stake" (PhD diss., Brigham Young University, 1989), 190–2.

465   "Los Angeles Temple," *Ensign*, May 1977, 120.

466   Sharon Alden, email to Mary Jane Woodger, December 15, 2018, transcription in author's possession.

467   Carole Reid Burr and Roger K. Petersen, *Rose Marie Reid: An Extraordinary Life Story* (American Fork, UT: Covenant Communications, Inc., 1995), 32–33.

468   Burr and Petersen, 35.

469   April Ainsworth, "Introducing Great Designers," *Vintage Vixen* (blog), www.vintagevizen.com/articlesDesigners/vintageRoseMarieReid.asp.

470   Donald Q. Cannon, Richard O. Cowan, and Arnold K. Garr, "Rose Marie Reid." *Encyclopedia of Latter-day Saint History* (Salt Lake City, UT: Deseret Book Company, 2000), 991.

471   Burr and Petersen, *Rose Marie Reid*, 94.

472   Ibid., 97.

473   Alden, email to Mary Jane Woodger.

474   "A Swimsuit That Really Got Around," *Life*, April 16, 1956.

475   Burr and Petersen, *Rose Marie Reid*, 97.

476   Alden, email to Mary Jane Woodger.

477   Burr and Petersen, *Rose Marie Reid*, 97.

478   April Ainsworth, "Introducing Great Designers," *Vintage Vixen* (blog), www.vintagevizen.com/articlesDesigners/vintageRoseMarieReid.asp (accessed January 2, 2019).

479   Burr and. Petersen, *Rose Marie Reid*, 201.

480   See Russell W. Stevenson, *For the Cause of Righteousness: A Global History of Blacks and Mormonism, 1830–2013* (Salt Lake City, UT: Greg Kofford Books, 2014); James B. Allen, "Would-Be Saints: West Africa Before the 1978 Priesthood Revelation," *Journal of Mormon History* 17, no. 1 (1991): 207–47; and "Race the Priesthood," Gospel Topics Essay, https://www.lds.org/topics/race-and-the-priesthood?lang=eng .

481   Allen, "Would-Be Saints," 212.

482   "Race and the Priesthood"

483   Stevenson, *For the Cause of Righteousness*, 74.

484   Ibid., 75.

485   Allen, "Would-Be Saints," 213.

486   Ibid., 214.

487   Ibid., 218.

488   Ibid., 220.

489   Ibid., 223.

490   Harvard S. Heath, ed., First Presidency Meeting, October 11, 1962, in *Confidence Amid Change: The Presidential Diaries of David O. McKay, 1951–1970* (Salt Lake City, UT: Signature Books, 2019), 447–51.

491   Allen, "Would-Be Saints," 230–31; Stevenson, *For the Cause of Righteousness*, 82–84; Heath, *Confidence Amid Change*, 472–73.

492   Heath, *Confidence Amid Change*, 599–600.

493   Allen, "Would -Be Saints," 245; email from Alan Morrell to Casey Paul Griffiths, May 14, 2019, copy in author's possession.

494   Abidjan Ivory Coast Temple, https://www.churchofjesuschrist.org/temples/details/abidjan-ivory-coast-temple?lang=eng.

495   R. Lanier Britsch, "The Latter-day Saint Mission to India: 185–1856," *BYU Studies*, Vol. 12, No. 3, 263-265.

496   Britsch, 265–266.

497   Britsch, 273–278.

498   B.H. Roberts, *A Comprehensive History of The Church of Jesus Christ of Latter-day Saints*, 6 vols. (Salt Lake City: Deseret News Press, 1930), 5:72.

499   Taunalyn Rutherford, "Conceptualizing Global Religions: An Investigation of Mormonism in India," PhD Diss., Claremont Graduate University, 2018, 40–42.

500   Rutherford, "Conceptualizing Global Religions," 49–50.

501   https://newsroom.churchofjesuschrist.org/facts-and-statistics/country/india, accessed June 25, 2019.

502   Russell M. Nelson, "Let Us All Press On," April 2018 general conference.

503   Sarah Jane Weaver, "In India, the story of the India LDS Temple announcement in revealed," *Church News*, April 19, 2018, https://www.deseretnews.com/article/900016345/in-india-the-story-of-the-india-temple-announcement-is-revealed.html, accessed June 25, 2019.

504   https://newsroom.churchofjesuschrist.org/facts-and-statistics/country/india, accessed June 25, 2019.

505   For an overview of these cultural challenges, see Taunalyn Rutherford, "Shifting Focus to Global Mormonism: The LDS Church in India," in *The Worldwide Church: Mormonism as a Global Religion*, ed. Michael A. Goodman and Mauro Properzi (Salt Lake City, Provo: Deseret Book, Religious Studies Center, 2016), 79-91.

506   Rutherford, "Conceptualizing Global Religion," 51–53.

507   Matthew Bowman, *The Mormon People: The Making of an American Faith* (New York: Random House, 2012), 221–22.

508   Shuvi Jha, "The Purpose of the Bindi," The Hindu American Foundation, June 5, 2018, https://www.hafsite.org/blog/the-purpose-of-the-bindi/, accessed June 25, 2019.

509   Trent Toone, "An Answer to Many Prayers: Hong Kong China Temple reaches 20-year Milestone," *Deseret News*, May 26, 2016.

510   John K. Carmack, oral history interview by Mary Jane Woodger, February 21, 2019, Salt Lake City, UT, transcription in author's possession.

511   William S. Bradshaw, interview by R. Lanier Britsch, October 16, 1974, The James Moyle Oral History Program, Church History Library, Salt Lake City, UT, OH 300.

512   Toone, "An Answer to Many Prayers."

513   Monte J. Brough and John K. Carmack, "How the Hong Kong Temple Came to Be," *Ensign*, December 2006.

514   Brough and Carmack, "How the Hong Kong Temple Came to Be," https://www.churchofjesuschrist.org/study/ensign/2006/12/how-the-hong-kong-temple-came-to-be.html?lang=eng#title1, accessed July 25, 2019.

515   Monte Brough, *Life Is a Collection of Stories* (Farmington, UT: self-pub., 2005).

516   Tak Chung Stanley Wan Journal, holograph, *The Heavens Are Higher Than The Earth*, Church History Library, Salt Lake City, UT, M270.1.

517   Sheri L. Dew, *The Biography of President Gordon B. Hinckley: Go Forward with Faith* (Salt Lake City, UT: Deseret Book, 1996), 481.

518   Dew, *The Biography of President Gordon B. Hinckley*, 481

519   R. Lanier Britsch, *From the East: The History of the Latter-day Saints in Asia* (Salt Lake City, UT: Deseret Book, 1998), 296.

520   Brough and Carmack, "How the Hong Kong Temple Came to Be."

521   Lynette Brough, oral history interview by Mary Jane Woodger, March 11, 2019, Farmington, UT, transcription in author's possession.

522   Brough, *Life Is a Collection of Stories*.

523   John K. Carmack, oral history interview by Mary Jane Woodger, 21 February 2019, Salt Lake City, transcription in author's possession.

524   Toone, "An Answer to Many Prayers."

525   Tai Kwok Yuen to Mary Jane Woodger, email, March 12, 2019.

526   Dell Van Orden, "Inspiration Came for Smaller Temples," *Deseret News*, August 1, 1998.

527   Scott Taylor, "Taking a 'Stand': Exhibit Features Noted LDS Pulpits" *Deseret News*, October 2, 2010, A6.

528   Jeffrey R. Holland, "President Thomas S. Monson," *Liahona*, June 2008, 9.

529   Thomas S. Monson, "Yellow Canaries with Gray on Their Wings," *Ensign*, July 1973, 41.

530   Taylor, "Taking a 'Stand,'" A6.

531   Heidi S. Swinton, *To the Rescue: The Biography of Thomas S. Monson* (Salt Lake City, UT: Deseret Book, 2010), 135.

532   Ibid., 135–36.

533   Monson, "Yellow Canaries," 42.

534   Swinton, *To the Rescue*, 142.

535   Holland, "President Thomas S. Monson," 9.

536   Taylor, "Taking a 'Stand,'" A6.

537   Harold B. Lee qtd. in Swinton, *To the Rescue*, 130.

538   Paul R. Cheesman, "An Analysis of the Accounts Relating Joseph Smith's Early Visions" (master's thesis, Brigham Young University, 1965), 126. We are deeply indebted to Matthew Godfrey for the ideas presented in this chapter. See Matthew C. Godfrey, "The Second Sacred Grove: The Influence of Greenville, Indiana, on Joseph Smith's 1832 First Vision Account," *Journal of Mormon History*, 44, no. 4 (October 2018): 5–6.

539   Dean C. Jessee, "The Early Accounts of Joseph Smith's First Vision," *BYU Studies* 9, no. 3 (1969): 3, 12.

540   The full text and original document of the history can be viewed at "History, circa Summer 1832," *The Joseph Smith Papers*, 1, https://www.josephsmithpapers.org/paper-summary/history-circa-summer-1832/1.

541   See "History, 1838–1856, volume A-1 [23 December 1805–30 August 1834]," *The Joseph Smith Papers*, 1, https://www.josephsmithpapers.org/paper-summary/history-1838-1856-volume-a-1-23-december-1805-30-august-1834/1.

542   See "Church History, 1 March 1842," *The Joseph Smith Papers*, 706, https://www.josephsmithpapers.org/paper-summary/church-history-1-march-1842/1, see also Godfrey, "The Second Sacred Grove," 5–6.

543   See "First Vision Accounts," https://www.lds.org/topics/first-vision-accounts?lang=eng.

544   "History, circa Summer 1832," Historical Introduction, *The Joseph Smith Papers*, https://www.josephsmithpapers.org/paper-summary/history-circa-summer-1832/1.

545   "History, circa Summer 1832," *The Joseph Smith Papers*. https://www.josephsmithpapers.org/paper-summary/history-circa-summer-1832/1.

546   There are also indications that the document is the original document. For instance, Joseph and Frederick Williams both made inscription errors more common to original creation, though these could have occurred as part of copying an earlier work. See "History, circa Summer 1832," *The Joseph Smith Papers*. https://www.josephsmithpapers.org/paper-summary/history-circa-summer-1832/1.

547   "History, 1838–1856, volume A-1 [23 December 1805–30 August 1834]," p. 215, *The Joseph Smith Papers*, accessed July 10, 2019, https://www.josephsmithpapers.org/paper-summary/history-1838-1856-volume-a-1-23-december-1805-30-august-1834/221.

548   "History, 1838–1856, volume A-1," *The Joseph Smith Papers*, 214–15, spelling and grammar corrected.

549   "Letter to Emma Smith, 6 June 1832," *The Joseph Smith Papers*, 1, https://www.josephsmithpapers.org/paper-summary/letter-to-emma-smith-6-june-1832/1, spelling and grammar corrected.

550   "History, circa Summer 1832," p. 3, *The Joseph Smith Papers*, accessed July 10, 2019, https://www.josephsmithpapers.org/paper-summary/history-circa-summer-1832/3.

551   "History, circa Summer 1832," p. 3, *The Joseph Smith Papers*, accessed July 10, 2019, https://www.josephsmithpapers.org/paper-summary/history-circa-summer-1832/3.

552   "Vision, 16 February 1832 [D&C 76]," *The Joseph Smith Papers*, 3, https://www.josephsmithpapers.org/paper-summary/vision-16-february-1832-dc-76/3.

553   "History, circa Summer 1832," p. 3, *The Joseph Smith Papers*, accessed July 10, 2019, https://www.josephsmithpapers.org/paper-summary/history-circa-summer-1832/3.

554   See Neal E. Lambert and Richard H. Cracroft, "Literary Form and Historical Understanding: Joseph Smith's First Vision," *Journal of Mormon History* 7 (1980): 33.

555   Henry B. Eyring, Joseph Smith statue unveiling ceremony, Joseph Smith Building, Brigham Young University, October 17, 1997, inscription on plaque at BYU.

556   Joseph Smith, letter to William W. Phelps, January 11, 1833, in Letterbook 1, 19, josephsmithpapers.org. "Revelation, 27–28 December 1832 [D&C 88:1–126]," p. 33, *The Joseph Smith Papers*, accessed July 15, 2019, https://www.josephsmithpapers.org/paper-summary/revelation-27-28-december-1832-dc-881-126/1.

557   "Revelation, 1 June 1833 [D&C 95]," p. 59, *The Joseph Smith Papers*, accessed July 15, 2019, https://www.josephsmithpapers.org/paper-summary/revelation-1-june-1833-dc-95/1.

558   Frederick G. Williams, qtd. in Truman Osborn Angell, *Autobiography 1884*, MS 5688, 14–15, LDS Church Archives, The Church of Jesus Christ of Latter-day Saints, Salt Lake City, UT.

559   Artemus Millet, *Autobiographical Sketches*, n.d., MS 11396, 1, LDS Church Archives, The Church of Jesus Christ of Latter-day Saints, Salt Lake City, UT.

560   Elwin C. Robison, *The First Mormon Temple: The Design, Construction, and Historic Context of the Kirtland Temple* (Provo, UT: Brigham Young University Press, 1997), 79. See also Henry Howe, *Historical Collections of Ohio: Containing a Collection of the Most Interesting Facts, Traditions, Biographical Sketches, Anecdotes, etc., relating to its General and Local History; with Descriptions of Its Counties, Principal Towns and Villages* (Cincinnati, OH: Derby Bradley, 1847), 282; Milllet, *Autobiography*, 6; Harry Black, *Kirtland Temple* (Independence, MO.: Herald House, 1959), 13; C. L. Olson to Earl R. Curry, March 232, 1960, Historical Files, Kirtland Temple Historic Center; Andrew, 37–38.

561   Robison, *The First Mormon Temple*, 56.

562   Linda K. Newell and Valeen T. Avery, "Sweet Counsel and Seas of Tribulation: The Religious Life of Women in Kirtland," *BYU Studies*, 20 (Winter 1980): 155–56.

563   Mark Lyman Staker, Hearken, *O Ye People: The Historical Setting of Joseph Smith's Ohio Revelations* (Salt Lake City, UT: Greg Kofford Books, 2009), 529 .

564   Robison, *The First Mormon Temple*, 56.

565   Joseph Millet, "Millet on C[ape] Breton] Island," *Joseph Millett Reminiscence and Diary*, MS 14870, 93, LDS Church Archives, The Church of Jesus Christ of Latter-day Saints, Salt Lake City, UT.

566   Mark Lyman Staker, Hearken, *O Ye People: The Historical Setting of Joseph Smith's Ohio Revelations* (Salt Lake City, UT: Greg Kofford Books, 2009), 529.

567   Maybelle Anderson, *The Journals of Appleton Milo Harmon, a Participant in the Mormon Exodus from Illinois and the Early Settlement of Utah, 1846–1877* (Glendale, CA: Authur H. Clark, 1946), 158–69.

568   Orson F. Whitney, *Life of Heber C. Kimball: An Apostle, the Father and Founder of the British Mission* (Salt Lake City, UT: Bookcraft, 1945), 80.

569   Lucy Mack Smith, "Lucy Mack Smith, History, 1844–1845," bk. 14, 3, josephsmithpapers.org, "Lucy Mack Smith, History, 1845," p. 227, *The Joseph Smith Papers*, accessed July 15, 2019, https://www.josephsmithpapers.org/paper-summary/lucy-mack-smith-history-1845/235.

570   Edward W. Tullidge, *Women in Mormondom* (1877; reprinted, Salt Lake City, UT: n.p., 1965), 76.

571   "History, 1838–1856, volume A-1 [23 December 1805–30 August 1834]," p. 297, *The Joseph Smith Papers*, accessed July 15, 2019, https://www.josephsmithpapers.org/paper-summary/history-1838-1856-volume-a-1-23-december-1805-30-august-1834/303.

572   Orson F. Whitney, *Life of Heber C. Kimball* (Salt Lake City, UT: Bookcraft, 1945), 88.

573   Lisa Olsen Tait and Brent Rogers, "A House for Our God," in *Revelations in Context: The Stories Behind the Sections of the Doctrine and Covenants*, ed. Matthew McBride and James Goldberg (Salt Lake City, UT: The Church of Jesus Christ of Latter-day Saints, 2008), 169.

574   Orson F. Whitney, *Life of Heber C. Kimball*, 80–82.

575   Eliza R. Snow, *Eliza R. Snow: An Immortal; Selected Writings of Eliza R. Snow* (Salt Lake City, UT: Nicholas Morgan Sr. Foundation, 1957), 54.

576   "Visions, 3 April 1836 [D&C 110]," p. 192, *The Joseph Smith Papers*, accessed July 15, 2019, https://www.josephsmithpapers.org/paper-summary/visions-3-april-1836-dc-110/1

577   Boyd K. Packer, *Holy Temple* (Salt Lake City, UT: Deseret Book, 2014), 129.

578   Correct spellings of Hawn's Mill have often been variable, usually favoring the spelling as H-A-U-N. Historical records from the period of the massacre indicate that Jacob Hawn, the founder of the settlement, spelled his name H-A-W-N, and most recent scholarship reflects this spelling. In accordance with this, all spellings of Hawn in this chapter have been adjusted to the correct spelling; footnotes retain the publication's spelling. See Alexander L. Baugh, "Jacob Hawn and the Hawn's Mill Massacre: Missouri Millright and Oregon Pioneer," *Mormon Historical Studies* 11, no. 1 (Spring 2010): 1–25.

579   Alma R. Blair, "The Haun's Mill Massacre," *BYU Studies* 13, no. 1 (1972): 1.

580   Alexander L. Baugh, "The Haun's Mill Massacre and the Extermination Order of Missouri Governor Lilburn W. Boggs," *Mormon Historical Studies* 10, no. 1 (Spring 2009): 28.

581   See Baugh, "Missouri Millright," 1–25.

582   Baugh, "Missouri Millright," 12–13.

583   "Journal, December 1841–December 1842," page 183, *The Joseph Smith Papers*, http://www.josephsmithpapers.org/paper-summary/journal-december-1841-december-1842/60, spelling and punctuation corrected.

584   Alvin K. Benson, "The Haun's Mill Massacre: Some Examples of Tragedy and Superior Faith," in *Regional Studies in Church History: Missouri, ed. Arnold K. Garr and Clark V. Johnson* (Provo, UT: Department of Church History and Doctrine, 1994), 108–9.

585   Alexander L. Baugh, "Joseph Young's Affidavit of the Massacre at Haun's Mill," *BYU Studies* 38, no. 1 (1999): 192.

586   Benson, "Haun's Mill Massacre," 109.

587   Ibid., 111.

588   Ibid., 112.

589   Alexander L. Baugh, "A Relic of the Mormon Missouri Period: The Haun's Mill Stone at Breckenridge, Missouri," *Mormon Historical Studies* 2, no. 2 (Fall 2001): 211.

590   *Church History in Black and White: George Edward Anderson's Photographic Mission to Latter-day Saint Historical Sites*, 1907 Diary, 1907–8 Photographs, ed. Richard Nietzel Holzapfel, T. Jeffrey Cottle, and Ted D. Stod-

dard (Provo, UT: Religious Studies Center, 1995), 100, https://contentdm.lib.byu.edu/digital/collection/rsc/id/46880.

591   Alex Baugh points out that the marker was inaccurate in two details: seventeen Mormons were killed in the attack and fourteen of them were buried in an empty well. See Baugh, "A Relic," 212.

592   Jamshid Ghaszi Askar, "LDS Church Buys Farmland, Haun's Mill, Far West, Kirtland Property from Community of Christ," *Deseret News*, May 5, 2012, https://www.deseretnews.com/article/865555292/LDS-Church-buys-farmland-Hauns-Mill-Far-West-Kirtland-property-from-Community-of-Christ.html.

593   Jeffrey Mahas, "Remembering the Martyrs," *Revelations in Context*, https://www.lds.org/study/manual/revelations-in-context/remembering-the-martyrdom?lang=eng, accessed December 19, 2018.

594   Ephraim Hatch, *Joseph Smith Portraits: A Search for the Prophet's Likeness* (Provo, UT: Religious Studies Center, 1998), 17.

595   Hatch, 20. Though they share a name, the maker of the death masks should not be confused with George Q. Cannon, a future counselor in the First Presidency, who was only seventeen years old at the time of the martyrdom.

596   Hatch, 20.

597   Curtis G. Weber, "Skull and Crossed Bones?: A Forensic Study of the Remains of Hyrum and Joseph Smith," *Mormon Historical Studies*, Vol. 10, No. 2 (Fall 2009), 6.

598   Hatch, 20–21.

599   Ibid., 22.

600   Ibid., 23-24.

601   Ibid., 22.

602   Weber, 6.

603   See Hatch, *Joseph Smith Portraits: A Search for the Prophet's Likeness*, also, Shannon M. Tracy, *Millions Shall Know Brother Joseph Again* (Salt Lake City: Eborn Books, 2008).

604   "Doctrine and Covenants, 1844," p. 444, *The Joseph Smith Papers*, accessed January 5, 2019, https://www.josephsmithpapers.org/paper-summary/doctrine-and-covenants-1844/446.

605   "History, 1838–1856, volume A-1 [23 December 1805–30 August 1834]," 3, *The Joseph Smith Papers*, https://www.josephsmithpapers.org/paper-summary/history-1838-1856-volume-a-1-23-december-1805-30-august-1834/3.

606   "History, 1838–1856, volume D-1 [1 August 1842–1 July 1843]," 1522, *The Joseph Smith Papers*, https://www.josephsmithpapers.org/paper-summary/history-1838-1856-volume-d-1-1-august-1842-1-july-1843/165.

607   See Michael Hicks, "Minding Business: A Note on 'The Mormon Creed,'" *BYU Studies*, 26, no. 4 (1986): 107.

608   Wasp, June 11, 1842, emphasis in original, qtd. in Hicks, "Minding Business."

609   *Millennial Star* 3, no. 6 (October 1842): 112.

610   *Millennial Star* 4, no. 2 (June 1843): 29.

611   "History, 1838–1856, volume E-1 [1 July 1843–30 April 1844]," p. 1835, *The Joseph Smith Papers*, https://www.josephsmithpapers.org/paper-summary/history-1838-1856-volume-e-1-1-july-1843-30-april-1844/207.

612   "Council of Fifty, Minutes, March 1844–January 1846; Volume 3, 6 May 1845–13 January 1846," [62], *The Joseph Smith Papers*, https://www.josephsmithpapers.org/paper-summary/council-of-fifty-minutes-march-1844-january-1846-volume-3-6-may-1845-13-january-1846/65, punctuation in original.

613   "Signs of the Times," *Deseret News*, February 7, 1852, https://newspapers.lib.utah.edu/details?id=2579190.

614   *The Complete Discourses of Brigham Young*, ed. Richard S. Van Wagoner (Salt Lake City, UT: Smith-Petit Foundation, 2009), 1:615.

615   B. H. Roberts, *The Life of John Taylor* (Salt Lake City, UT: Deseret Book, 1963), 214–15.

616   George Q. Cannon, "Mind Your Own Business," Juvenile Instructor 18, no. 16 (August 15, 1883): 250.

617   "The Mormon Creed," *Deseret Weekly*, March 30, 1889, https://newspapers.lib.utah.edu/details?id=2675058.

618   Joseph F. Smith, *Improvement Era*, March 1903, 388.

619   "Women Are Focus of New Museum Exhibit," *Mormon Newsroom*, May 18, 2007.

620   Gayle M. Chandler, "Belle S. Spafford: Leader of Women" (master's thesis, Brigham Young University, 1983), 23.

621   "Belle S. Spafford Council President," *The Daily Herald*, October 18, 1968, 6, https://www.churchofjesuschrist.org/study/ensign/2006/03/making-a-difference-for-women-belle-s-spafford.html?lang=eng#title1, accessed July 25, 2019.

622   Chandler, "Belle S. Spafford," 22.

623   Janet Peterson and Connie Lewis, "Making a Difference for Women: Belle S. Spafford," *Ensign*, March 2006.

624   "Reaching Every Facet of a Woman's Life: Relief Society—A Conversation with Belle S. Spafford," *Ensign*, June 1974, 15.

625   David J. Whittaker, "The Mark Hofmann Case: A Basic Chronology," *BYU Studies* 29 (Winter 1989): 83.

626   "Joseph Smith's Blessing on Son Discovered, Given to RLDS," *Deseret News*, March 19, 1981, B-1.

627   Dean C. Jessee, ed., *The Personal Writings of Joseph Smith* (Salt Lake City, UT: Deseret Book, 1984), 565–66.

628   Whittaker, "The Mark Hofmann Case: A Basic Chronology," 83.

629   Richard E. Turley Jr., *Victims: The LDS Church and the Mark Hofmann Case* (Urbana and Chicago: University of Illinois Press, 1992), 53.

630   Gordon B. Hinckley, "The Joseph Smith III Document and the Keys of the Kingdom," *Ensign*, May 1981, 22.

631   Whittaker, "The Mark Hofmann Case: A Basic Chronology," 95.

632   Turley, *Victims*, 26, 80.

633   Whittaker, "The Mark Hofmann Case: A Basic Chronology," 99–100.

634   "Revelation Book 1," *The Joseph Smith Papers*, http://www.josephsmithpapers.org/paper-summary/revelation-book-1/1.

635   "Revelations printed in the Evening and the Morning Star, June 1832–June 1833," 1, *The Joseph Smith Papers*, , http://www.josephsmithpapers.org/paper-summary/revelations-printed-in-the-evening-and-the-morning-star-june-1832-june-1833/1.

636   "Revelation, 1 November 1831–B [D&C 1]," 125, *The Joseph Smith Papers*, http://www.josephsmithpapers.org/paper-summary/revelation-1-november-1831-b-dc-1/1.

637   "Revelation, 3 November 1831 [D&C 133]," 116, *The Joseph Smith Papers*, http://www.josephsmithpapers.org/paper-summary/revelation-3-november-1831-dc-133/1.

638   "Revelation, 11 November 1831–A [D&C 69]," 122, *The Joseph Smith Papers*, http://www.josephsmithpapers.org/paper-summary/revelation-11-november-1831-a-dc-69/1.

639   Minute Book 2 "The Conference Minutes and Record Book of Christ's Church of Latter Day Saints," 1838, 1842, 1844. Salt Lake City, UT: Church History Library. Also available at josephsmithpapers.org, cited in "Book of Commandments, 1833," *The Joseph Smith Papers*, http://www.josephsmithpapers.org/paper-summary/book-of-commandments-1833/1, spelling in original.

640   Within Revelation Book 1, see the following: Revelation, ca. June 1829, 23–24; Revelation, ca. early 1830, 30–31; Explanation of scripture, ca. Dec. 1830, 60–61 [D&C 74]; Revelation, 15 May 1831, 85; Revelation, 20 May 1831, 86–87 [D&C 51]; and Revelation, 20 July 1831, 93–94 [D&C 57]. The

seventh revelation in this category is Revelation, June 1829–E [D&C 17]. A partial index to Revelation Book 1 indicates that this revelation was copied on page 25 of the manuscript book, but the page on which it was inscribed is among those now missing. (See Revelation Book 1, 207.) There is no apparent pattern among these seven items to explain why they were not published. "Book of Commandments, 1833," *The Joseph Smith Papers*, http://www.josephsmithpapers.org/paper-summary/book-of-commandments-1833/1.

641   Mary E. Rollins to the Editor, February 12, 1904, *Deseret Evening News* 20 (February 1904): 24, quoted in Peter Crawley, "Joseph Smith and a 'Book of Commandments,'" The Princeton University Library Chronicle 42, no. 1 (Autumn 1980): 24.

642   Statement of John Taylor dictated to Leo Hawkins and George A. Smith, April 15, 1858, original manuscript in the Church History Library, quoted in Crawley, "Joseph Smith," 25. The John Taylor mentioned in this incident should not be confused with later Church president John Taylor, who was not baptized until several years after the Jackson County persecutions.

643   See Richard E. Turley, William W. Slaughter, *How We Got the Doctrine & Covenants* (Salt Lake City, UT: Deseret Book, 2012), 38.

644   Reid N. Moon, "The Ten Most Expensive Mormon Books," January 28, 2016, https://ldsmag.com/the-ten-most-expensive-mormon-books/

645   Richard E. Turley, William W. Slaughter, *How We Got the Doctrine & Covenants*, 35.

646   Moon, "Ten Most Expensive."

647   "Book of Commandments, 1833," 161, *The Joseph Smith Papers*, http://www.josephsmithpapers.org/paper-summary/book-of-commandments-1833/165.

648   History Commission, auditorium inter-office memo, March 5, 1981 (Independence, MO: Community of Christ Library), copy in author's possession.

649   This introduction has accompanied every published version of the translation of the book of Abraham since it first appeared in February 1842. See "Book of Abraham Manuscript and Explanation to Accompany Facsimile 1, circa February 1842 [Abraham 1:1–2:18]," p. [1], *The Joseph Smith Papers*, http://www.josephsmithpapers.org/paper-summary/book-of-abraham-manuscript-and-explanation-to-accompany-facsimile-1-circa-febarury-1842-abraham-11-218/1.

650   "Introduction to the Book of Abraham Manuscripts," http://www.josephsmithpapers.org/intro/introduction-to-book-of-abraham-manuscripts.

651   Joseph Smith Papers, *Documents* (Salt Lake City, UT: Church Historian's Press, 2017), 5:71–72.

652   "Book of Abraham Manuscript, circa July–circa November 1835–A [Abraham 1:4–2:6]," page 1, *The Joseph Smith Papers*, http://www.josephsmithpapers.org/paper-summary/book-of-abraham-manuscript-circa-july-circa-november-1835-a-abraham-14-26/1.

653   JSP, D5:73.

654   "Journal, 1835–1836," page 47, *The Joseph Smith Papers*, http://www.josephsmithpapers.org/paper-summary/journal-1835-1836/48.

655   Richard D. Draper, S. Kent Brown, and Michael D. Rhodes, *The Pearl of Great Price: A Verse by Verse Commentary* (Salt Lake City, UT: Deseret Book, 2005), 237–38.

656   Ibid., 240.

657   Ibid.

658   Ibid., 241.

659   Brian M. Hauglid, *A Textual History of the Book of Abraham* (Provo, UT: Neal A. Maxwell Institute for Religious Scholarship, 2010), 213–14, 222.

660   John Gee, *A Guide to the Joseph Smith Papyri* (Provo, UT: Foundation for Ancient Research and Mormon Studies, 2000), 23.

661   John Gee, "Has Olishem Been Discovered?" *Journal of Book of Mormon and Other Restoration Scriptures* 11, no. 2 (2013): 104–7.

662   Julie M. Smith, "A Note on Chiasmus in Abraham 3:22–23," *Interpreter: A Journal of Mormon Scripture* 8 (2014): 187–90.

663   "Translation and Historicity of the Book of Abraham," https://www.lds.org/topics/translation-and-historicity-of-the-book-of-abraham.

664   Draper, Brown, and Rhodes, *Pearl of Great Price*, 283.

665   "Translation and Historicity of the Book of Abraham," https://www.lds.org/topics/translation-and-historicity-of-the-book-of-abraham.

666   Matthew O. Richardson and Timothy G. Merrill, "Profiles of the Prophets: Spencer W. Kimball," *Religious Educator* 8, no. 2 (2007): 131–41.

667   Edward L. Kimball and Andrew E. Kimball Jr., *Spencer W. Kimball: Twelfth President of The Church of Jesus Christ of Latter-day Saints* (Salt Lake City, UT: Bookcraft, 1977), 261.

668   Ibid., 263.

669   Ibid., 263–64, 273.

670   Ibid., 302.

671   Ibid., 306.

672   Francis M. Gibbons, *Spencer W. Kimball: Resolute Disciple, Prophet of God* (Salt Lake City, UT: Deseret Book, 1995), 209.

673   Gibbons, *Spencer W. Kimball*, 211.

674   Kimball and Kimball, *Spencer W. Kimball*, 311.

675   *Teachings of Presidents of the Church: Spencer W. Kimball* (Salt Lake City, UT: The Church of Jesus Christ of Latter-day Saints, 2006).

676   Kimball and Kimball, Spencer W. Kimball, 305.

677   Ibid. 311.

678   Ibid., 312.

679   Ibid., 390.

680   Ibid., 263, 391, 312.

681   *Teachings: Spencer W. Kimball.*

682   Spencer W. Kimball, "When the World Will Be Converted," *Ensign*, October 1974, 8.

683   N. Eldon Tanner, "Revelation on Priesthood Accepted, Church Officers Sustained," *Ensign*, November 1978, 16–17.

684   Kimball and Kimball, *Spencer W. Kimball*, 273.

685   "Display Honors President Kimball," *LDS Church News*, April 4, 2002, https://www.ldschurchnews.com/archive/2002-04-06/display-honors-president-kimball-21403.

686   Richard O. Cowan, *Temples to Dot the Earth* (Salt Lake City, UT: Bookcraft, 1989), 91.

687   "Spiritual Manifestations in the Manti Temple," *Millennial Star* 50 (August 13, 1888): 521.

688   "Spiritual Manifestations," 521.

689   Cowan, *Temples to Dot the Earth*, 92.

690   "Remarks by President Brigham Young," *Millennial Star* 39 (June 11, 1877): 373.

691   Manti Temple Centennial Committee, *The Manti Temple* (Provo, UT: Community Press, 1988), 7.

692   Cowan, *Temples to Dot the Earth*, 93.

693   Manti Temple Centennial Committee, *The Manti Temple*, 104.

694   Cowan, *Temples to Dot the Earth*, 96–97.

695   "The Dedication of the Manti Temple," *Millennial Star* 50 (June 18, 1888): 403.

696   Ila A. Wright, "Hair Watch Chains and Flowers," *Western Folklore* 18 (1959): 116.

697   Mark L. Staker, "By Their Works Ye Shall Know Them: The World View Expressed in Mormon Folk Art," *BYU Studies* 35, no. 3 (1995): 83–84.

698   Staker, "By Their Works," 84.

699   Ibid., 85.

- Casey Paul Griffiths -

Casey Paul Griffiths is an assistant professor of Church history and doctrine at Brigham Young University. He has published numerous books and articles on Church history, most recently *What You Don't Know About the 100 Most Important Events in Church History*, with Mary Jane Woodger and Susan Easton Black. He is a member of the Mormon History Association, serves on the board of the John Whitmer Historical Association, and is currently serving as president of the BYU Latter-day Saint Educator's Society. He lives in Saratoga Springs with his wife, Elizabeth, and four children.

- *Mary Jane Woodger* -

Mary Jane Woodger, EdD, is a professor of Church history and doctrine at Brigham Young University. Born and raised in American Fork and Salt Lake City, Utah, Mary Jane has always had a great love for teaching. After obtaining a bachelor's degree in home economics education, she taught home economics and American history in Salt Lake City. She then completed her master of education degree at Utah State University, and received from Brigham Young University a doctor of education degree in educational leadership, with a minor in Church history and doctrine.

Since then, Dr. Woodger has written and published more than twenty books, including three books about the life and teachings of David O. McKay, as well as a book on the timely subject of self-esteem. She has also authored numerous articles on doctrinal, historical, and educational subjects. These articles have appeared in various academic journals, as well as the *Journal of Mormon History*, *Mormon Historical Studies*, the *Ensign*, and *The Religious Educator*. Awards Dr. Woodger has received include the Best Article of the Year Award from the Utah Historical Society, the Brigham Young University Faculty Women's Association Teaching Award, The Harvey B. Black and Susan Easton Black Outstanding Publication Award, and the Alice Louise Reynolds Women-in-Scholarship Honor. Dr. Woodger's current research interests include twentieth-century Church history, Latter-day Saint women's history, and Church education.